Police-Related Deaths
in the United States

Policing Perspectives and Challenges in the Twenty-First Century

Series Editor: Jonathon A. Cooper, Indiana University of Pennsylvania

In many respects, policing has evolved over the last two centuries; yet issues that concerned policing in the nineteenth and twentieth centuries continue to be salient to contemporary law enforcement. But how these challenges are manifest to the police today are distinct, as society and politics, too, have evolved. And so understanding the role of police in society, the behavior and organization of law enforcement, the relationship between officers and civilians, and the intersection of theory and praxis remain important to the study of police. To this end, volumes in this series will consider policing perspectives and challenges in the twenty-first century, around the world, and through a variety of disciplinary lenses. Ultimately, this series "takes stock" of policing today, considers how it got here, and projects where it might be going. Policing Perspectives and Challenges in the Twenty-First Century will be of interest and use to a variety of policing scholars, including academics, police executives, and others who study law enforcement.

Titles in the series

Police-Related Deaths in the United States

David Baker

LEXINGTON BOOKS
Lanham • Boulder • New York • London

Published by Lexington Books

An imprint of The Rowman & Littlefield Publishing Group, Inc.
4501 Forbes Boulevard, Suite 200, Lanham, Maryland 20706
www.rowman.com
6 Tinworth Street, London SE11 5AL, United Kingdom

British Library Cataloguing in Publication Information Available

Library of Congress Cataloging-in-Publication Data

Name: Baker, David, 1968–, author.
Title: Police-related deaths in the United States / David Baker.
Description: Lanham : Lexington Books, 2021. | Series: Policing perspectives and chal-
    lenges in the twenty-first century | Includes bibliographical references and index. |
    Summary: "This book examines how police-related deaths occur and why officers are
    rarely held accountable for them. It argues that such deaths are the result of systemic
    and structural issues that are deeply embedded in US society and institutions"—
    Provided by publisher.
Identifiers: LCCN 2021018535 (print) | LCCN 2021018536 (ebook) | ISBN
    9781793611574 (cloth) | ISBN 9781793611581 (ebook)
    9781793611598 (pbk)
Subjects: LCSH: Police misconduct—United States. | Police shootings—United States. |
    Wrongful death—United States. | Police—Complaints against—United States.
Classification: LCC HV8141 .B245 2021 (print) | LCC HV8141 (ebook) | DDC
    363.2/32—dc23
LC record available at https://lccn.loc.gov/2021018535
LC ebook record available at https://lccn.loc.gov/2021018536

Contents

Preface

In the fall of 2015, I was completing a book on police-related deaths in England and Wales. That research was driven by a desire to understand how such deaths are routinely explained by governmental agencies as being unfortunate, but somehow unavoidable. Before I even worked as a university academic, I was always curious about the strange paradox whereby the government is both responsible for providing security for citizens whilst retaining the right to extinguish their lives. I wanted to understand what this told us about policing, justice, equality, the government, and wider society. Around the same time, I was aware of events unfolding in the United States after the killings of Mike Brown and Eric Garner a year before. It seemed clear that the US authorities didn't have any accurate data on police-related deaths, and that the Washington Post and the Guardian Media Group were attempting to compile such data.

The counting of such deaths was vital in terms of establishing the scale of this issue. But counting from the top down, whilst important, could only tell us part of the story about police-related deaths. I knew that from writing the book about this issue in England and Wales. I wanted to examine these deaths from the ground up by talking with the relatives of people who had died. I wanted to try and understand what sort of person their loved one had been, how they had died, and how families had tried to get truth, justice and accountability following their death.

I applied to the Fulbright Commission to be a funded scholar, and was fortunate to be successful. That sparked a process of searching the US for participants who would agree to meet with me, and talk about how their family member had died. Without the help and guidance of a number of community activist organizations, this research project would never have got off the ground. I have written a long list of acknowledgements separate to this foreword to try and reflect this fundamental fact, but really it could have been much longer. I interviewed 58 relatives about 43 deaths, covering 16 states. The interview transcripts represent the foundation stone upon which this book is built. It became clear early on that a lot of people wanted to meet and talk with me about their experiences—largely because few people had ever asked before. In a few cases, I was the only person outside of their family that they'd ever spoken to about the death of their loved one. The vignettes that begin the first seven chapters of the book are drawn from this research project. I have chosen seven people that represent a variety of ages, genders, and ethnicities.

Throughout the research, analysis and publication process I have been driven by a desire to accurately represent what the families of the deceased told me. In addition to interviewing research participants in the US, I spent time talking with community activists, civil rights advocates, journalists, attorneys and university Professors in various locations in the US. This knowledge has been further augmented by several years reading a very wide variety of academic articles, books, policy documents and governmental reports on police-related deaths in the US.

I want to make clear from the outset that this book is not anti-police officers. The vast majority of officers are committed public servants who work in often difficult and potentially dangerous circumstances. I doubt that any officer goes to work with the intention of killing a citizen during their shift. But it happens, and it's very rare that officers are held legally accountable for such actions. Errors can be made by anyone, systems can sometimes go wrong, but the frequency of these deaths indicates the need for critical and detailed investigation into the systems, processes and practices that enable them. As a reader, you'll know that it only takes a minority of co-workers to create problems at work that can undermine everyone's contribution to their work. Most of us, though, don't work in an occupation where this overlaps with us carrying a gun and being mandated to use it as part of our job.

To those who might quite reasonably think this book should also have considered the views of police, justice officials, politicians, or other interested parties, I say that this research project deliberately set out to consider 'other' views. The 'received knowledge' on police-related deaths has long been constructed by groups that enjoyed a monopoly of information production on this issue. It is time some other versions were told. For a long time, very little academic scholarship existed on police-related deaths—that says something about this issue, and about academia. I hope this book will add to the stock of knowledge about this subject and help us understand it better, and hopefully, incrementally, effect change.

Acknowledgments

I owe a debt of gratitude to all of the families who agreed to participate in this project. Without them, there would be no project. I am eternally grateful to them for trusting me to tell their stories. In particular, I would like to thank Dominic Archibald, JoAlice Doggett-Smith, Roxana Harrison, Jay Westwind Wolf Hollingsworth, Melissa Kennedy, Maria Moore, Bernie Rolen, Joseph Santellana, and Rick Williams for their help in telling the stories of their loved ones.

Similarly, the project would never have existed without the support of innumerable community and activist groups in various states in the US. These groups often represented my gateway to research participants—without them, there would be no project. There are too many to mention here, but particular thanks go to SAFE Coalition NC; Every Life Matters; The Justice Committee in New York City; Portland Copwatch; Berkeley Copwatch; Mothers of Murdered Sons (Baltimore); and LDP Peace Institute (Boston). I'd particularly like to thank Robert Dawkins – chair of SAFE Coalition in Charlotte (NC); and Michael Bell Sr in Kenosha, Wisconsin. Robert and Michael were instrumental in enabling me to meet a significant number of research participants in this project.

The project would not have happened without the generous support of the Fulbright Commission who funded this research. I could not have conducted the research without the support of Elon University (NC) who hosted me during my stay and enabled me to have a base from which to conduct the research. I am very grateful to both institutions for having the foresight to support a research project into such a sensitive and contentious subject during an election year.

Thank you to Claire Pillinger for doing such an amazing job in transcribing the powerful and emotional interviews—I will be forever grateful. Dana

Norris for diligently working through the transcripts using Nvivo software to analyse key themes and patterns. Thank you to the following people for helpful and thoughtful feedback on various drafts: Zoe Alker, Veroniki Cherneva, Robert Dawkins, Marta Fidalgo, Fraukje Hackworth, Tucker Kelly, Alice Meakin-Grigor, Dana Norris, Sally Patalong, and Fiona White. Honorable mention for technical support to Scotty.

I would also like to thank Becca Beurer, my editor at Lexington Books for her sage advice and patience with me through this process.

Above all I'd like to thank Jane Hinton who supported me throughout this project, encouraged me to keep going and made sure I stayed safe and well. Without her love I would not have had the strength to see the project through.

List of Abbreviations

ACLU	American Civil Liberties Union
BLM	Black Lives Matter
BWC	Body-Worn Camera
CCR	Center for Constitutional Rights
CDC	Centers for Disease Control and Prevention
CRB	Civilian Review Board
CIT	Crisis Intervention Team
DOJ	Department of Justice
DA	District Attorney
DEA	Drug Enforcement Agency
ED	Excited Delirium
FBI	Federal Bureau of Investigation
IA	Internal Affairs
IACP	International Association of Chiefs of Police
ICE	Immigration and Customs Enforcement
ME	Medical Examiner
NIM	National Institute of Medicine
NIJ	National Institute of Justice
PD	Police Department
PRD	Police-Related Death
PTF	President's Task Force on 21st Century Policing
SWAT	Special Weapons and Tactics

Introduction: Who Counts?

Danielle Willard

'Was so tiny, she weighed one hundred pounds soaking wet' according to her mom, Melissa Kennedy.

She was a White woman aged 21, and lived in West Valley, near Salt Lake City (UT). Melissa says Danielle wasn't a confrontational person, and had 'never met anyone she didn't like.' If anything she was a little too trusting and willing to see the best in people. Danielle was shot dead by two undercover officers from West Valley PD on the afternoon of 2nd November 2012. She was not armed. When Melissa was informed of her daughter's death, she found it impossible to comprehend—how could her daughter represent a threat to anyone?

The official police version of the shooting initially stated that two officers, Detectives Cowley and Salmon were staking out an apartment complex as part of an anti-narcotics exercise. They were in separate cars conducting covert surveillance. They believed Danielle had bought drugs from the building they were watching and that she attempted to conceal the drugs in her mouth as they approached her. When she got into her car, they say they challenged her to stop but that Danielle reversed her vehicle towards Detective Cowley, injuring him and prompting both officers to open fire on her. Six shots were fired, one of which struck Danielle in the back, another of which hit her in the chin and one which terminated her life.

Melissa flew immediately from Washington state, where she lived, to Utah. Upon arriving she began to knock on doors in the apartment complex, asking eyewitnesses questions and compiling evidence about how her daughter was killed. She quickly became aware that there were serious questions to answer about how and why her daughter was shot, but also more generally about the West Valley PD. She spoke with a number of local attorneys who said they were scared of the cops, that they had long been suspected of planting evidence in cars. The more she looked into things, the more she felt the PD 'were going to do some sort of cover up here.'

In the immediate aftermath of the shooting, the scene of death was investigated by a specialist team from the PD. They found no drugs on or near the body of Danielle, but there was a small packet of heroin in the passenger door pocket of her car. Ballistic experts found that the shots from Cowley's gun came from beside Danielle's car rather than the rear as he had reported, meaning the car reversing towards him could not have been the catalyst for him shooting the driver. The investigative team also discovered evidence from previous cases up to a year old in the trunk of the officer's car. The investigation broadened out to consider systemic issues within the narcotics team as a whole and their practices in West Valley PD. This eventually revealed a 'Pandora's box of problems.' The team was disbanded over significant concerns about the conduct of their officers uncovered by the FBI, which found 'rampant and systemic violations' of PD policy, and also law, in the team's practices. Hundreds of cases that were due to be investigated or prosecuted were jettisoned on the basis they were unsafe.

Nine months after the shooting, the District Attorney released initial findings from the investigation stating that the stories of Detectives Cowley and Salmon did not match evidence from the scene. He ruled that the shooting was 'not justified.' Cowley was initially charged with manslaughter, but the case was eventually dropped. Melissa told me he was fired by the West Valley PD—not for shooting Danielle, but on the basis of evidence discovered in the trunk of his car. He successfully appealed that decision on a technicality, and was rehired in 2015, in order that he could claim back pay and benefits before resigning two days later.

Danielle's parents sued the Police Department and settled out of court in February 2015 for $1.425 million. Melissa feels the financial settlement was a 'cop out'—that it represented 'hush money.' Danielle's parents wanted accountability and justice for the wrongdoing that led to their daughter's death. But the city of West Valley didn't see it that way and offered a compensation package instead. That meant not admitting to liability for Danielle's death, and restricting what Melissa could say about the case. The settlement also meant that the case was closed in perpetuity because no further action could be taken, meaning that the officers responsible for her daughter's death have not been held to account for their actions. Melissa told me she would rather have had each officer pay her $1 per month for the rest of their lives 'so that they would have to remember Danielle.'

Melissa openly acknowledges that her views on policing, justice and democracy have changed since her daughter's killing. When she started gathering evidence about the shooting, she admits she was previously unaware of police malpractice and was inclined to be a person who did things in a 'low key' way. That changed as she began to fight for justice for her daughter; she says "as things progressed, I totally understood what 'no justice, no peace' meant." When I asked her what it meant to her, she replied 'it means cops get away with murder.'

Family and friends say Danielle was kind, funny and trusting but had battled on and off with addiction to heroin. She originally went to Utah to join a rehab programme and had chosen to settle there. Melissa thought Utah would be good for Danielle because she loved to take photographs of nature. Her parents had hoped she would return home, and had given her a car for her new life in Utah. But she never came home, she was shot dead in that car.

Melissa was able to get some sort of recognition of the injustices that led to her daughter's death, largely because she intervened early and was tenacious. She went directly to the scene of the killing to organise protests and raise awareness. She was persistent in demanding answers—in her own words 'I got people to know that Danielle Willard—her life mattered.' Many members of Melissa's family are employed in law enforcement, so it was difficult for her to process her experiences in West Valley trying to get justice for her daughter: 'there was a lot of covering up and a lot of trying to hold things back and make it go away.' At the end of every interview I undertook during this research, I asked the participant if they wanted to add anything to their testimony. Melissa concluded with this: 'For me, now, if a cop comes up to me I will be scared. But if you do what you're supposed to do, if you don't do anything wrong then you really should not be scared of a police officer. And these days everybody is, because they know they can get away with it, and I would just really like to see that change.'

COUNTING AND ACCOUNTING FOR KILLING

If we want to change anything, first of all we need to know what we want to change from. In order to know that, we need to know what the current status of the issue is. With police-related deaths, this prompts me to begin this book with a basic question:

Who counts? I mean it in two ways: who counts the people who die, and do the people who die, count? 'No-one' and 'apparently not' are the unfortunate, but simple answers to these questions. You had probably never heard of Danielle Willard, and if it hadn't been for Melissa's tenacity, few others might have heard of her either. This book examines how and why this might be the case. It begins by focusing on the inability of governmental authorities to count such deaths.

In the aftermath of the deaths of Eric Garner and Mike Brown in the summer of 2014, the *Washington Post* and the UK's Guardian Media Group began to examine the official data available on police-related deaths, only to realise it didn't exist. At that time, the *Guardian*'s editor, Katharine Viner, was approached by two of her journalists who suggested that the US version of the paper compiled their own data on a purpose-designed website called 'The Counted.' Viner recalls being nonplussed at the suggestion—surely her journalists had made some mistake? The US authorities must collate this data, mustn't they? By October 2015, the director of the FBI openly admitted that federal authorities did not have an accurate count of the number of citizens who died after police contact, a fact he noted was 'embarrassing.' The Counted website collated these deaths from late 2014 onwards. By the end of 2015, it produced the first accurate annual number of such deaths: 1146. In 2016 the number was 1093 (The Counted 2017). Approximately three citizens per day were killed by police in the US. How can the pre-eminent superpower on the planet not know such elementary information? What does this tell us about its priorities; about criminal justice in the US; about the citizens who die and how governmental authorities and society view them? What does it tell us about democracy and rights in the US? In addition to examining how and why these deaths occur, this book critically examines these wider issues.

It's only natural to speculate that these deaths might not be counted because they aren't considered important enough. The logical corollary of this is to conclude that those who die are unimportant. Such thoughts are profoundly troubling, for they raise the question of whether a country which overtly projects itself as a land of liberty, democracy and equality, is capable of measuring whether it actually is such a place. Is it all a construction—a convenient myth? If there is a lack of data on deaths in the US, what does that say about the value of life in the US? What does it say about the relative value given to data or evidence in US society? Gathering data about an issue is key to being able to understand and measure it. If data isn't being gathered, is it because change isn't considered necessary? Because maintaining the myth is more important than investigating the reality?

STRUCTURES, CONSTRUCTS AND EXCEPTIONALISM IN THE US

Although it may seem straightforward to say that the deaths aren't counted because they're considered unimportant, this overlooks some of the complexity at the heart of why this data doesn't exist. Some of this complexity tells us more about issues relating to democracy, rights and justice in the US than simply about police-related deaths. As a federal system, the US might be better imagined as a relatively loose collection of semi-sovereign states, each able to make their own laws, with relatively autonomous legal systems.

Federal authorities are unable to enforce collection of data on police-related deaths, because they cannot demand it from each state, county or PD. For years, a wide range of academic authors have pointed out the woeful lack of data available on how many citizens die after police contact in the US (Campbell et al. 2017, Cesario et al. 2019, Dunham and Petersen 2017, Johnson et al. 2019, Katz 2015, Zimring 2017, Kleinig 2014, Fyfe 2002). In the aftermath of the revelation that no accurate federal data existed on these deaths, both the FBI and Department of Justice (DOJ) pledged to construct a system that could produce accurate data. That was one of the reasons for the Guardian stopping The Counted website at the end of 2016. But such data still does not exist, and there is still uncertainty about when, how—or even *if*—it might (Finch et al. 2019). Nor does the lack of data apply only to police-related deaths. Gary Younge (2016) notes that the number of suicides per year in the US is also not known with any degree of accuracy. In the aftermath of the war in Iraq, it became clear that whilst the US and their allies had a very accurate count of the number of their own dead, they had no clue about how many Iraqis had died (Hogg 2016). It's difficult to look at these three examples without concluding that life has a relative value, and some lives are more important than others.

Foreigners who have lived and worked in the US for any period of time often note that there is a significant disconnect between the image America projects and what the actual lived experience is for many citizens in the US. Of course, this is true of most countries. As a UK citizen I can acknowledge that. A couple of prominent myths in the UK are that it is a classless and multicultural society. For many people UK society is neither classless nor multicultural, but those myths remain powerful and pervasive nonetheless. The Dutch author, Geert Mak (2014: 112) notes that: 'There is always a gap between the collective fantasies a country lives by and the everyday reality, but [in the US] that gap is very wide indeed.' No other country on this planet has a national 'dream,' but America does, whether or not all of its citizens still buy into that collective dream.

A good deal of literature exists on American 'exceptionalism'—the idea that the country is unique. A commonly cited illustration of this comes from the first governor of Massachusetts, John Winthrop, in 1630: 'We shall be as a city on a hill—the eyes of all people are upon us.' This formulation has been used by numerous presidents in the 20th and 21st centuries irrespective of party affiliation. The idea that the nation is both unique and a beacon of light and hope to the rest of humanity is certainly powerful, but also unusual in terms of how it projects the image of the nation—inwards to its own citizens, and outwards to the rest of the world. Writing about the prevalence of violence in US society, and how it is manifest in police and wider authorities' use of violence, Ta-Nehisi Coates (2015a: 8) states: '[The] banality of violence can never excuse America, because America makes no claim to the banal. America believes itself exceptional, the greatest and noblest nation ever to exist, a lone champion standing between the white city of democracy and the terrorists, despots, barbarians, and other enemies of civilization.' To set a toweringly high standard is one thing; to fail to meet it another; but to not *acknowledge that failure* suggests there are a number of complex factors at play in keeping the dream of the 'city on the hill' alive.

POLICE-RELATED DEATHS IN THE US: CONSTRUCTING REALITY

The Counted compiled two years of data in 2015 and 2016. It recorded 2239 police-related deaths during that period. 95% of those killed were male, and 5% female. 90% of people were killed by gunshots, with the remainder either dying in custody, as a result of TASER usage, or after being struck by a vehicle. The age group most likely to be killed was aged 25–34. The overwhelming majority of the deceased are men killed by gunshot. In absolute terms, of the 2239 dead, 1158 were White, 573 were Black, 378 were Hispanic, 45 were Asian or Pacific Islanders, and 37 were Native American (48 were unknown). In relative terms, when compared to population groups, those most likely to be killed were Black Citizens, followed by Native Americans, Hispanic Citizens, White Citizens, then Asian or Pacific Islanders.

You are more likely to die after contact with police in America if you are a Person of Color. That said, citizens who die in police-related incidents can come from any section of the US population: young, old, Black, White, Hispanic, Native American, male, female, transgender, gay, rich or poor. That was also borne out by my research, as I had a broad demographic of grieving families willing to talk with me. That much will become apparent by the time you finish reading this book, because each chapter begins with a different case study drawn from that broad selection. Danielle Willard doesn't appear to fit the stereotypical profile of someone shot dead by police, and that says something about who we perceive to be stereotypical victims. In relative terms, you're more likely to have lethal force used on you if you're a Person of Color. As an absolute number, more White citizens are shot dead by police than any other group in the US. Whichever category you're from, the outcome of lethal encounters with police officers is the same: death. If you're a police officer, the outcome is almost certain to be that you won't face a court and have to account for your actions (Lara 2017, Zimring 2017, Katz 2015). And if you do go to court, it is highly unlikely that you'll be found liable for your actions (see Jones-Brown and Blount-Hill 2020, Stinson 2017a and 2017b).

The lack of data on these deaths largely enabled them to be written off as individual cases until recently (Baker and Fidalgo 2020, Katz 2015, Fyfe 2002). Sometimes they're considered to be 'tragic errors' where police have made split-second decisions under pressure. More often they're portrayed as being the result of encounters with dangerous people. People who are violent, or criminal, or both. Or are drug-addicted, or mentally unwell, or both. Or are from unstable backgrounds, or dangerous areas, or suffering from some other sort of health issue. Or indeed, any combination of the factors listed above—people are somehow held to be causal in their own demise. The usual construct is that the deceased must have been someone, or done something that somehow contributed to their death (Baker 2019a, Hirschfield and Simon 2010). Such qualities are typically ascribed to the deceased, not the officer involved in the death. Police and governmental authorities are well-versed in getting their version of the story into the media as soon as they can to ensure it becomes the definitive version of events (Hirschfield and Simon 2010, Baker 2016).

We look for factors or 'reasons' that might explain how and why a poor unfortunate met their death. We don't usually rush to ask questions of the officer and their conduct; about their state of mind or their behavior; about their background or training; their mental well-being or whether they are users of opiates or alcohol. That is not the order of things. We trust officers to keep us safe, to protect and serve—that is the construct society buys into. If it results in some tragic errors, on the balance of probabilities, most of society can apparently live with that. If police have to use force to protect us against suspect populations, enough of us would rather that than having to interact with those populations ourselves. There's no smoke without fire, after all, and if officers decide to use lethal force, well, there must have been grounds for it, surely? The natural order of things is that officers maintain order and control crime—that's another construct we invest in. As Zimring (2017: 182) notes, to see an officer in the dock of a criminal court significantly disturbs this order, and to some degree explains why so few officers end up there. These observations should be considered in relation to the lack of data on these deaths—did we really *want* to know how many people die in police-related deaths? The police are a reflection of the society they police. Our strengths and weaknesses, our values and prejudices are all reflected in the police that serve us (Reiner 2010, Balko 2014, Bittner 1975).

These constructs enable easily digestible headlines. But headlines are constructs made up of details. When the deceased is said to be a felon—what were they guilty of? There's a difference between a convicted rapist and someone who hasn't paid a fine. Danielle Willard was possibly in possession of a small bag of heroin, is that a reason to fatally shoot someone? When the deceased is reported to be in the possession of a weapon—what sort of weapon? There's a difference between an assault rifle and a knife. If it was a knife, what sort of a knife? There's a difference between a hunting knife and a bread knife. If the deceased is portrayed as behaving in a dangerous manner with a knife, in what way were they doing so? Dangerously with a bread knife in their own kitchen, for example? Or with a whittling knife with a three-inch blade when the deceased was a wood carver—as will be examined in the following chapter. These are not mere academic distinctions, every one listed above represents aspects of cases I examined during my research. One might argue that police misjudge certain situations, or are confident in their capacity to justifiably use lethal force, or any number of explanations, but the outcome remains the same: death. For the people left behind, the aftermath is irreversible. You may have been nodding along reading this section, acknowledging some typical 'truths' about how these deaths are constructed. You'll also be aware that in 2014, significant events occurred that disrupted the construction of 'business as usual.'

CHALLENGES TO THE CONSTRUCTION OF REALITY

In the summer of 2014, with the deaths of Eric Garner, Mike Brown, and subsequent uprisings in the aftermath of Ferguson, it became increasingly clear that these deaths weren't isolated, individual cases. The prevalence of smart phones and increased use of social media allowed more people to join the dots between these deaths (Vitale 2017, Zimring 2017). It became apparent that many of the deaths conformed to specific patterns of space and place, of the types of citizens who died, and of the encounters that unfolded prior to their deaths. In particular, it was evident that a significant number of these deaths occurred even though the deceased wasn't violent, armed, or necessarily involved in a criminal act. It often seemed that such deaths resulted from low-level encounters that suddenly escalated out of control. The outrage that many people felt coalesced into a desire to ensure that police could be held accountable for using lethal force. The Black Lives Matter (BLM) movement has played a significant role in raising awareness and reframing the way in which policing is perceived in the US. It has been successful in highlighting structural racism and everyday brutality against People of Color (Rickford 2016). Because it's a grassroots organization it has been able to take direct action and make good use of social media to produce and disseminate knowledge (Ray et al. 2017). Its wide-ranging profile—that now goes beyond the US—has ensured that it has been able to keep the focus on police-related deaths in a way that has not previously been seen, and to ensure that more people are aware this issue isn't about individual officers but wider systems and structures of practice.

Long-term campaigners and families of people killed by police dating back decades were sceptical about how realisable the calls for change were. Not because they doubted the character or veracity of those involved in the uprisings and protests that occurred all over the US, but because they knew from bitter experience the entrenched network of overlapping issues that enabled these deaths to be normalised. Widespread protests, the sharing of appalling lethal incidents on social media and an increasing awareness of police-related deaths will not necessarily challenge these deep-seated networks. We fund police to serve and protect us, but somehow that results in three police-related deaths per day. What does this say about how police go about their work, how they're held to account, how they perceive their role, and how society perceives them?

THE ROLE(S) OF POLICE

What do police *do*? This breaks down into two questions: what does society *perceive* the role of police to be, and what is the *actual* role of police? Academic authors and policy makers have conducted extensive research on this issue over the decades, and established that there is a significant difference between the public perception of the police role and its actuality (Reiner 2010, Gaines and Kappeler 2014, Crank 2016, Manning 2010, Bittner 1975, Waddington 1999). Society perceives the role of police to be largely focused on crime; either in terms of preventing crime from occurring, or bringing offenders to justice in the aftermath of crimes being committed. The overwhelming majority of research conducted into policing in the English-speaking world finds that the policing role is not principally related to crime. Certainly, crime is one aspect of their role, but it's not the main aspect. The principal role of police is to maintain order (Reiner 2010, Gaines & Kappeler 2014, Bittner 1975).

Policing as an idea emerged in France in the late 18th century as a way of managing and regulating the growing population of Paris to ensure order and good governance prevailed (Brodeur 2010). Policing was a verb ('to police'), rather than a noun ('the police'). It was not considered to be an organization, but a practice. With the emergence of the first uniformed police in London in 1829 the verb became a noun—the Metropolitan Police. The first police department (PD) in the US was founded in Boston in 1838 (Balko 2014). Whilst police are today considered an essential part of governmental structures at local or regional levels, this has not always been the case, and that tells us something about the role of police in society. Society could apparently police itself (to some degree, at least) without 'the police' as we understand them today. Calls for the defunding or abolition of the police in the aftermath of George Floyd's killing in 2020 are a modern reflection of this essential fact.

The aim of the Metropolitan Police from the outset was to ensure the 'absence of disorder.' This is an important distinction to 'keeping the peace' because it meant they were not being measured by the presence of something, but by the absence of it—quite a different way of conceiving of a public service role, and one which is relevant to understanding some of the present day concerns about policing. Their role was also to prevent the commission of crime, and to apprehend criminals, but these were secondary to their principal role of order maintenance (Reiner 2010, Waddington 1999). With this raison d'être, the Metropolitan Police did not (and still do not) routinely carry guns. Their goal was to police with the consent of the population, not by coercing citizens by the use or threat of force. Consent is key to understanding the relationship between police and society. The police were founded on the principle that they would be a body of citizens living within their communities who possessed extra powers when wearing uniform. This was to allay concerns at the time that this 'new force' in London would possess weapons, use them indiscriminately, or use them on persons they took a dislike to, and be unaccountable as a result (Emsley 2010). Let's park those troubling thoughts there for a moment and jump forward to today.

In the 21st century, police occupy a striking diversity of roles: peace keeping, crime prevention, public reassurance and crime control (Reiner 2010, Gaines and Kappeler 2014), but their principal role remains the same: order maintenance. We expect police to react to any number of complex issues that might occur in society (Crank 2016, Reiner 2010). The diversity of their role is highlighted by an essential paradox—they can be both guarantors and extinguishers of liberty (Baker 2016, Zimring 2017). This raises the issue of what we might call officers to better reflect what they actually do, and the variety of suggestions for this highlights the diversity of their role. Common parlance refers to them as 'crime fighters' and/or 'enforcement officers.' Another phrase commonly used in the US is 'peace officers' (Reiner 2013: 165). The US academic Jon Shane (2013: 69), himself an ex-police officer, considers them better conceived of as 'safety officers,' an issue to which we'll return later in the book.

The great majority of uniformed police work focuses on order maintenance and public reassurance—what might be termed service provision. This is not the sort of policing that is typically portrayed in the media which usually shows officers fighting crime and bringing bad guys to justice (Vitale 2017). This service provision can be seen in traffic work, through 'welfare calls,' in schools, in community policing, and a whole raft of daily tasks routinely undertaken by police in US society (Bittner 1975, Skolnick and Fyfe 1993, Gaines and Kappeler 2014, Crank 2016). As part of this, police also routinely provide assistance to vulnerable citizens in crises: the mentally unwell, the elderly, people dependent on substances, and the homeless being some examples (Vitale 2017). If there is an emergency involving flood, fire, or earthquake, police will attend—and we expect them to. In this sense, crime is not central to their role, but providing an emergency response to citizens is. It seems that the key roles of police are to maintain order and respond to emergencies, however one might define emergencies.

'To protect and serve' tells us this, if we take a moment to consider it. If 'crime' can be located in this statement, it's about protecting citizens from crime—that could be in preventing it, or reassuring citizens in the aftermath of crime occurring. The idea of police as 'crime-fighters' is not very accurate. But it is a relatively modern and commonly held idea, and it might go some way to helping us understand the issue of police-related deaths in the US. It conjures up a variety of scenarios related to challenging citizens, apprehending them, enforcing the law, taking action, and not taking a step back. All of these scenarios can lead to the use of force, and they're all some distance from service provision.

Much of Egon Bittner's work as an academic researching US police practice in the 1960s is still relevant today. He provides us with two key ways of understanding some of the complexities outlined in the discussion above. The title of a seminal paper tells us a lot about the police role: 'Florence Nightingale in pursuit of Willie Hutton.' This refers to an infamous bank robber, Willie Hutton, being chased by a famous nurse, Florence Nightingale. We wouldn't expect nurses to give chase after an armed and dangerous bank robber, but that's exactly what we expect of police. Officers can turn from service providers into apprehenders of criminals in the blink of an eye. Bittner went on to identify police work as being concerned with 'something that is happening, which ought not to be happening and about which someone had better do something now!' In other words, there was literally nothing which could not be conceived of as police work, because police were duty bound to respond to 911 calls irrespective of whether they were about a cat stuck up a tree, an elderly person locked out of their apartment, or bank robbers who've taken people hostage at gunpoint.

All of this contributes to a complex network of issues. We expect police to undertake a very wide variety of roles. Those roles are not always complementary and they may also overlap. Officers have a broad mandate to intervene in a bewildering variety of situations that occur in society. The power to intervene is key. Societal consent enables that power only if officers can be held to account. If they're considered to have intervened for good reason and in a way that is proportionate, for example. Shooting a citizen dead after pulling them over because of an allegedly faulty tail light; using a neck hold to choke a human to death because they were allegedly selling loose cigarettes;

or in the case of Danielle Willard, shooting an unarmed person dead, are an affront to us because they represent evident examples of the disproportionate use of force. If the public view of policing is that it predominantly focuses on bringing bad guys to justice, then the only way people can make sense of their use of lethal force and confer legitimacy on it must be to say that these were bad guys—even if they were 'one hundred pounds soaking wet.'

THE ORGANIZATION OF POLICING IN THE US

The devolved and fragmented system of governance in the US can also be seen in the huge number of PDs operating in the country. The US has in excess of 18,000 PDs for a population of 325M. That equates to roughly 18,000 citizens per PD. In the UK that figure is about 1.5M per PD, in Australia it is 3.1M per PD. Governance, crime and justice in the US is local-ised in nature, meaning it is relatively autonomous. It results in a staggering number of small PDs. Half have fewer than 10 officers, and nearly three quarters have fewer than 25 (President's Task Force 2015). This is significant in two ways: first, small PDs have a limited capacity to function in a way that might be considered consistent with the demands of a complex 21st century society; second, there is a great deal of geographical overlap between forces. In relation to the former issue, it results in a limited number of officers being on duty at any one time, circumscribing their capacity to respond appropri-ately to calls from the public. It also means that there are few supervising officers to oversee junior officers. Smaller forces find it challenging to train officers and keep their skills up to date, because they can't be spared from frontline duties. Consequently, best practice in policing isn't easy to promote at a national, or even state level. It means that the policies of small PDs are often relatively minimal because they don't have time to train officers on how the policies work in reality. Nor is there sufficient time (or senior officers) to oversee adherence to these policies and hold officers to account if they breach those policies.

The geographical overlap of departments means that several are likely to criss-cross each other's turf on a fairly regular basis. Consider any small city that has a university in, or near it. It will have a university PD, a city PD, a county PD and of course state troopers—that will be a bare minimum of four different forces for a city that could have a population of only 20,000. To that, one could also add US Marshalls, the FBI, ICE, DEA and a number of otheragencies with mandated powers to arrest, use force or otherwise act in the manner of a policing agency. Gaines and Kappeler (2014): 8) note that a single city might have a dozen police forces. The implications for this are very significant. Communication is vital in policing—sharing information and acting on it is the bread and butter work of police. Consider the complications involved in four PDs in such close proximity trying to share information at all, let alone in an emergency. Much academic literature on policing tells us that officers aren't keen on sharing information amongst their own force, let alone with other forces (Bittner 1975). The city of Ferguson had a population of 21,000 but 31,000 outstanding arrest warrants at the time of Mike Brown's death (President's Task Force 2015). How can there be more arrest warrants than citizens? Was anyone counting? Did anyone care?

To which the partial answer is: yes, they did, after Mike Brown was shot dead. But only a while after. The effects of his avoidable death were widespread and significant, producing an uprising on the streets of Ferguson and other US cities (Lowery 2017, Vitale 2017). That went on for months and drew a heavily militarized police response. Not only were the police and government in Ferguson in no particular hurry to investigate the shooting of Mike Brown, they weren't going to allow, or pay heed to, citizens' protests in the aftermath of the shooting. Nor were they particularly bothered how any of this looked on national or international news networks, or to the millions watching world-wide via social media. This was replicated in the responses to the uprisings that followed George Floyd's killing in Minneapolis in 2020. If you want examples of how detached police and authorities were from the public, of how they believed they could use force on top of force in attempting to re-establish control, of what their view of policing was, then you'd struggle to get better examples than these.

WARRIORS OR GUARDIANS?

Brodeur (2010: 344) notes that the existence of policing is symbolic in demonstrating normality, whereas using military force: 'symbolises a state of emergency and of exception.' The uprisings at Ferguson and Minneapolis were not isolated examples. Similar events have been replicated across the US to varying degrees and extents for decades, from LA to New Orleans, from Charlotte to Seattle, from Portland to Chicago, from Detroit to New York, from Baltimore to Milwaukee. It's completely normal. So normal, that when it became clear that the widespread protests in Ferguson were not being damped down by police and governmental responses, the federal government knew exactly what to do. Do what it always does: launch a commission of inquiry.

It's difficult to overstate the scale of rioting and unrest in US cities historically. The FBI estimated that in 1968 alone there were in excess of 100 riots in the US (Zinn 2003). In the 1967 uprising in Detroit, 43 people were killed and two active airborne divisions were brought in to restore order. In the LA riots of 1991, 53 citizens died, and again two army divisions were deployed to quell the uprising (Skolnick and Fyfe 1993). Both uprisings were sparked by police violence against Black citizens. Those who believe that the uprisings following the killing of George Floyd in Minneapolis were unprecedented and will lead to changes would be well advised to pause and reflect that America has been here before. One might argue this is another construct—the idea that American citizens can actually effect widespread changes in the systems and structures that underpin how the country operates. Thus far, those systems and structures have remained more or less impervious to demands for change from the citizenry.

In an attempt to understand the root causes of the uprisings noted above, major reviews were commissioned. In the aftermath of Detroit, President Johnson commissioned the Kerner Report; following the 1991 uprising in Los Angeles, President George H. W. Bush announced the Christopher Commission. In 2014, President Obama commissioned a taskforce to examine the state of policing in the US. This acknowledged that the deaths of Mike Brown and Eric Garner which did so much to mobilise public opinion were not isolated or tragic incidents, but were reflective of wider police practice in the US. 1968, 1991, 2014—the symmetry is striking. As Lowery (2017: 17) notes, the 'story didn't start or end on the streets of Ferguson.' This task force set out to establish what policing *could be* in the US. Or perhaps what it *should be*.

The President's Task Force on 21st Century Policing (PTF) settles on a central question: are police warriors or guardians? Warriors who enforce law, using and relying on force to do so; or guardians who provide a service for society? The PTF produced findings and recommendations that come straight out of any academic book written on policing in the last fifty years. None of it is new, or is news to the great majority of police officers in the English-speaking world. Police should seek to work *with* the public in order to be able to police by consensus. This consensus confers legitimacy on police to go about their job of protecting and serving their communities. Police should be reflective *of*, and listen *to* their communities. As their key task is to serve the public, they should be skilled communicators and use their experience to build and maintain relationships in communities. If officers act in ways that cause concern to communities, then citizens should be able to hold officers to account. Officers should use force only as a last resort, and should always seek to de-escalate encounters with citizens where possible (PTF 2015). The PTF essentially set out a vision of what policing should be. As an aspiration, it is certainly laudable. Whether it can be fully or partly realised is another matter entirely, as will be apparent by the end of this book.

CONCLUSION

This book argues that there are a series of constructs that need to be investigated, examined, deconstructed and understood in order to understand how police killing citizens in the US is relatively normal. So normal, it didn't need to be counted. The idea that police serve and protect citizens is a construct. The idea that officers are not above the law and can be held to account is a construct, that much is evident from Danielle's case. Race is a construct. The principle that all citizens are equal is a construct. The American dream is a construct. For some people, in some places, at some times, these constructs are indeed reality—one might even argue for many people, they are reality. But with a population of more than 325 million citizens there is a lot of room for different experiences and interpretations.

Chapters one, two, and three examine how police tend to focus on minority groups such as People of Color and the mentally impaired within society, and how this leads to citizens from those groups being disproportionately more likely to die than citizens from the dominant majority in society. Chapter four considers how various legal and regulatory mechanisms designed to hold police to account for the use of lethal force have had limited success, and how this is affected by a complex variety of socio-legal and socio-political factors. Chapter five looks at how measures to improve police practice are often stymied by the culture and ethos of policing in the US. Chapter six considers the relatives left behind in the aftermath of police-related deaths and how this tide of violence corrodes the essential fabric of US society. Chapter seven concludes by evaluating potential approaches that could address the epidemic of preventable deaths that result from fatal interactions between officers and citizens. It examines not only incremental change, but also completely reimagining the issue of police-related deaths, and the relationship between police and the society they serve. The book argues that to understand police-related deaths in the US, we need to understand the structures and systems that enable police to operate in the way they do.

How and why police are able to use force is central to understanding how and why citizens die after police contact. Without data on these deaths, it was simply not possible to begin to ascertain how and why citizens died, or indeed how many died. The idea that such deaths are individual cases or tragedies is being debunked as a result of us having more accurate data on this issue. The widespread use of social media has thrust these deaths into the spotlight and kept them there, highlighting how many deaths appear to conform to patterns, supporting the idea that the deaths result from structures and systems within policing. That the police role is varied and ambiguous is without doubt, which should lead us to ask: what do police do, how do they do it, and why do they do it that way? If they do see their role as being more warrior than guardian, then how did that happen, and why? Police have a unique power to use force against citizens, so how and why do they use it, and can we hold them to account for its use? These questions will be examined in the following chapter.

Chapter 1

"Comply or Die"

John T. Williams

John T. Williams was a gentle 50-year-old Native American woodcarver who lived in downtown Seattle. He had a number of physical impairments, so walked a little slowly, and with a limp. He was also partially deaf. John was one of the seventh generation of woodcarvers in his family, a member of the Nuu-Chah-Nulth Band, Ditidaht First Nation from Vancouver Island. He had some troubles with alcohol dependency in his time but had been living a stable life for several years in a supported environment in Seattle.

He was shot dead by Ian Birk, a Seattle Police Department (SPD) officer at 4.15pm on 30th August 2010. John had walked across an intersection with a green light in front of Officer Birk's vehicle. He was carrying his wood-carving knife and a piece of cedarwood. The incident was recorded by the dashcam of the officer's vehicle. The officer exits the car with his gun drawn, and yells three times to 'put the knife down.' Less than seven seconds after leaving his car he shot John four times, including two bullets that tore into his back. Rick Williams told me that his brother 'had no chance . . . it was an assassination.'

It is a particular skill of woodcarvers to be able to walk and carve at the same time. The knife John was using had a three-inch blade. This type of knife is entirely legal in Seattle. Rick says it would have been 'sacrilege' for a woodcarver to use their knife as a weapon. In his initial report, Officer Birk described John as 'feisty' and stated that he was in fear for his life as the reason for firing the fatal shots. He said that John had moved towards him bearing a knife with an exposed blade and ignored instructions to drop it.

What we now know, because the dashcam footage is in the public realm, is that John was walking away from the officer, and they had no verbal or physical interaction. It seems highly likely that John didn't hear the officer's instructions, partly due to his impaired hearing, and partly because he was wearing earphones. One of the first officers on the scene is heard to say 'good job Ian' before another officer handcuffs John's lifeless body and apparently shakes it down causing his head to hit the curb. Rick says his dead brother was 'thrown around like a rag doll.' An ambulance finally arrived on the scene approximately one and a half hours after John was fatally shot.

Rick says that his whole family was 'dragged through the mud' in the aftermath of John's death because of a smear campaign conducted by the SPD. That they deliberately targeted him and his sons in the aftermath of the killing, trying to provoke them into a violent reaction so that they could be labelled as 'violent Indians, because they categorise us a race, not the human race.' Rick believes that his people are stereotyped and targeted as a result: 'I'm sad [the police] don't see my brother as a man, because we are Indians, we are a waste of money—a waste of your tax money.'

The dashcam video ensured that police were unable to refute the key facts of the shooting. A series of investigations at both local and national levels ensued. In October 2010 the SPD Firearms Review Board found the shooting was unjustified and that Birk was in violation of seventeen points of SPD policy. At an inquest in 2011 a jury was unable to agree on whether Officer Birk had reason to believe his life was in danger, but the following month the SPD found that the officer did not have probable cause to believe he was at immediate risk from John. He resigned from the police but faced no charges for unlawful killing. Rick's family was awarded a financial settlement of $1.25M—although they wanted the case heard in a criminal court, this route was closed off to them. In order to get some form of justice for his brother, Rick was forced to accept a civil settlement—he told me: 'David, they've got you over a barrel.'

In the aftermath of John's killing, the American Civil Liberties Union (ACLU) wrote to the DOJ, supported by 34 local organizations in Seattle, requesting it launch an investigation into the SPD due to biases in its policing of People of Color and excessive use of force. A federal investigation began in 2011 and the city of Seattle reached an agreement (termed a 'consent decree') with federal investigators in the summer of 2012 to reform the SPD and reshape a number of its policies and practices. The DOJ report (2011: 2) found: 'constitutional violations regarding the use of force that result from structural problems, as well as serious concerns about biased policing.'

It noted SPD officers used force in an unconstitutional manner approximately 20% of the time, and that a minority of officers used force on a disproportionate number of occasions. In the year John was killed, 1% of officers accounted for 18% of all use of force incidents in the city (DOJ 2011: 4). This reinforces the observation by a wide variety of authors that the majority of officers never use their guns, noting that we should probably focus on the ones that do (Vitale 2017, Crank 2016, Gaines and Kappeler 2014). The reforms eventually led to the creation of the Seattle Community

Police Commission in 2013 which pledged to provide citizen oversight of complaints against the SPD. Its founding statement acknowledged the death of John T. Williams as a catalyst in its creation.

Perhaps the most remarkable aspect of this appalling story of avoidable death is Rick's attitude towards solving the issue of police using violence. In his language there is no word for hate, and so he can't say he hates the police. But more than that, he believes the way to deal with a system of violence and oppression is to call for peace and to acknowledge the need for forgiveness. He asks: 'can you be a warrior without violence?'

Rick was the first person I interviewed in my research project. I remember coming out of the interview stunned about how his brother had been killed, but also baffled by a number of things I'd never previously heard of. What was a financial settlement? What was a consent decree? What justification is there for shooting someone in the back? And why would officers handcuff a dead person? By the end of the project, I knew that two-thirds of the families I spoke with had been awarded financial settlements; that consent decrees were fairly common in large city PDs; that one third of the people killed who were examined in my research were shot in the back; and that one quarter of them had been handcuffed after their death. By the end of this book I hope you'll be able to understand how and why these things occur.

'Comply or die' is a phrase widely used by bereaved families and activist groups in the US (see Baker and Fidalgo 2020). John T. Williams was shot dead not because he was being violent or committing an offense, but simply because he didn't comply with an officer's order. He was shot in the back in broad daylight in the middle of Seattle—how does this happen, what does it tell us about policing in the US?

POLICE AND THE USE OF FORCE

Whilst police using force is relatively infrequent in terms of their overall number of contacts with citizens, it's widely acknowledged by key policing scholars that the potential to use force is central to the police role (Reiner 2010, Crank 2016, Gaines and Kappeler 2014, Zimring 2017, Kleinig 2014, Fyfe 1986, Manning 2010). For Bittner (1975), the potential to use force enables police to act legitimately in their role. In order to persuade someone to comply with a request, or to arrest someone, police need to be able to coerce people. They need to be able to say 'do as we say . . . or else.' If you don't comply, or you resist arrest, it will happen whether you like it or not. US police euphemisms for the use of force underline this—'come along,' or 'hurry up'; they both imply 'or else.' And as citizens, we know it. We know that if police approach us, they have an 'or else' option. Just as we know when we call police to ask them to deal with an issue, they have an 'or else' option—that can be a key reason we call the police rather than attempt to intervene ourselves. As was established in the previous chapter—society expects police to react, and we imbue them with powers to do so. For Bittner, the *potential* to use force is the fundamental starting point for understanding police work—without it, police work cannot be done.

Bittner is clear that although police have this potential, they shouldn't necessarily use it. Its overuse could damage their legitimate right to use it, so it should be used sparingly. People usually don't want force to be used on them, they obey because they're aware it's a possibility. Similarly, most officers don't typically want to use force, but they're aware they can if they need to. For these reasons, Bittner (1975: 98) believed that "the most important 'trick' in police work was not to make people obey, but to make it possible for them to obey." Herein lie some key questions in the relationship between police and citizens: In what circumstances should officers use force; once they've decided to use force what sort of force is appropriate; and can we hold police to account for any perceived excessive use of force? In the case of John T. Williams, clearly he didn't have an opportunity to obey because he couldn't hear the command, and also because the officer shot him within ten seconds of leaving his car. Having time to obey is key, as is officers taking time to enable this.

The law in the US is quite clear that force should only be used when officers feel that they have no alternative, a common reason being that they fear for their own safety or that of citizens. Once a decision has been made to use force, it should be necessary and proportionate to the circumstances (Zimring 2017, Katz 2015, Gaines and Kappeler 2014). Whilst these distinctions sound clear on paper, in practice things are more ambiguous. Officers can be called to incidents with very little knowledge of what they're approaching, and be confronted by a confusing and potentially volatile situation once they arrive. The situation might require immediate intervention to stop a crime or serious harm taking place. Officers can thus be put into situations which require them to make split-second decisions with very little contextual information about what is unfolding in front of them (Crank 2016, Fyfe 1986). Bittner states that the potential to use force enables a way for complex situations to be temporarily solved—for example, by breaking up citizens and arresting them in order for further information to be established and a more long-term solution worked out.

Using force has significant symbolic and conceptual problems. Bittner says society knows it needs dragons to fight fire with fire. That much is accepted. But it still leaves us in a society where fire-breathing dragons patrol our streets. If we put it on the table and give it a name, we should really call it violence. We live in a society where violence is part and parcel of our everyday reality. How we decide to live with it says something about how we view ourselves, our communities and the public institutions that serve us. We can't entrust police to solve problems on our behalf without giving them the where-withal to do so. To ask officers to respond to an emergency call where one person is beating another within their shared home, which may contain multiple firearms, without recourse to firearms is clearly an outlandish suggestion. We wouldn't want to go to such a household ourselves, and we wouldn't expect officers to attend without an 'or else' option. This is the reason Bittner (1975: 108) says citizens have 'the belief that he who risks life and limb ought not to be unduly restricted.' It seems we want to give officers the possibility of using force, but tend to become upset when they do so. Is this because we realise that although force is necessary, we also realise it can be misused given the power officers carry with them on every shift? If we know it could be misused, how do we feel about that? And if we believe police shouldn't be 'unduly restricted,' what does that really mean in practice?

THE SPLIT-SECOND SYNDROME

The split-second syndrome is identified by James Fyfe (1986) as a concept that explains how society effectively enables police to use lethal force. Fyfe was an officer, serving for 16 years before becoming an academic and the director of training for the NYPD—he became an authority on the police use of force in the US. In his estimation, PDs knew police work entailed situations such as those set out above. It was therefore vitally important that the training, policies and practice of policing took these situations into account. Officers needed to be aware that they could approach situations where they might have to make quick decisions in complex situations. Consequently, adopting training that encouraged techniques and practices to deal with circumstances that required 'split-second' decisions was vital. This also required an open-minded approach to learning lessons in the aftermath of incidents when better decisions could have been made, to avoid similar errors being made in future encounters. Crucial in all of this was time—if you know you're heading to a situation whereby you might have to make a quick decision that could involve life and death, then the first thing to do is try to buy time to make a better decision—even if it's only an extra few seconds. For Fyfe (1986: 522), police are 'human service workers'—their job is to diagnose problems and use their competence to find solutions to them. It's therefore important that police have good diagnostic skills, and in order to achieve that, as much time as possible should be devoted to making an accurate assessment of 'the problem' in front of them. The first thing to do was to *not use force* unless there was absolutely no alternative. Clearly, in the case of John T. Williams there were plenty of alternative courses of action that Officer Birk might have taken. Fyfe would have said that resisting action in the instant could lead to more informed actions being made which might reduce the likelihood of force being used. Using the 'split-second syndrome' as a way of shaping police practice might enable a style of policing that relied less on force, and more on knowledge, experience and training.

Fyfe believed that although this *should* happen, in reality it didn't. Instead, the 'split-second syndrome' provided a justification for police *to use* lethal force. On the basis that they 'had a split-second' to decide, and in the interests of theirs and other citizens' safety they used lethal force to resolve the encounter. Not only is this a problem in *each* fatal incident, it's a problem because police believe *all* such incidents are one-offs and therefore can't easily be learned from. Such thinking goes that because no two errors are the same, a number of these incidents are likely, and anyway, the person who died probably brought it upon themselves. Is this the cost of police not being 'unduly restricted'? Many people might nod along with this description—and there is, of course, a kernel of truth in it. Transpose it into other settings and it looks less persuasive.

Pilots also work in a stressful environment and have to make split-second decisions. If a plane crashes and passengers die, we don't say 'oh well, they made the wrong decision under pressure—these things happen.' No, we demand that lessons are learned that ensure such crashes and deaths don't happen again. If that didn't happen, it would eventually affect the legitimacy of airlines and ultimately societal belief in the safeness of air travel (see Reason 1997, Doyle 2010, Shane 2013). You might say—hold on, pilots don't have the right to use force. OK—how about surgeons? They are trained to work in life and death environments. They are encouraged to learn lessons and adopt best practice through intense processes of training and reflection to stay up to date with developments in practice. We don't just accept that mistakes are made and people die because they work in a stressful life and death environment. This says something about how we view these respective occupations, and about how we view police and their role in society. If such incidents are perceived as individual incidents that can't necessarily be learned from, then it might explain why these deaths weren't counted in the first place. It might also explain why we tacitly allow police to continue with these practices—because at some level we accept this type of explanation for the deaths of citizens. But a large number of officers never use their weapons, and many that do don't necessarily use them to extinguish the life of citizens.

DISCRETION AND THE USE OF FORCE CONTINUUM

Linked to the issues identified by Fyfe is the principle that the use of force exists on a continuum (Crank 2016, Balko 2014, Manning 2010). Lethal force should be used as a last resort because there is simply no going back from it. Much has been written on what a continuum of force might look like, and many PDs in the US use this concept as part of their training (Dunham and Petersen 2017, Kleinig 2014, Schulhofer et al 2011, Stoughton 2015, Terrill and Paoline 2012). Skolnick and Fyfe (1993) state there are seven gradations on this continuum, beginning with officer presence, which is a version of the 'or else' discussed earlier. The most severe level is lethal force, with the pen-ultimate stage being 'impact techniques'—which includes using tools and/ or physical force. The idea of the continuum underpins the principle of using force in a reasonable and proportionate manner. In this vision of policing, officers begin encounters using a low level of force (by merely being present) before assessing the situation to determine whether an increase in the level of force is required—similar to the 'guardian' style of policing imagined by the President's Task Force (2015).

Lethal force should be the last, not a first resort in officer/citizen encoun-ters. The key is to avoid the need for a 'split-second' decision by taking as much time as possible to make an informed assessment of the situation, something which clearly did not happen when John T. Williams was shot four times, ten seconds after the officer left his vehicle. The split-second syndrome and the use of force continuum both stress the need for officers to use their experience and cognitive skills rather than their feelings and the 'last resort' option (Terrill 2005). There isn't much doubt that the great majority of offi-cers would agree with this in principle, or in practice. Why do some officers not follow the principles of the split-second syndrome and the use of force continuum in practice?

Discretion is considered to be key in understanding how officers decide to use force (Reiner 2010, Gaines and Kappeler 2014, Bittner 1975, Crank 2016, Fyfe 1986, Katz 2015, Manning 2010). This is largely because discre-tion is fundamentally important in understanding how officers go about their work more generally. In principle, police are bound by laws and policies—the former decided by state and federal judiciaries, the latter largely determined by their PD. However, whilst police are notionally servants of the law, Reiner (2010) notes it's more accurate to say that the law is a servant of the police. This is because on the ground, legal principles run up against the reality of police practice. When confronted by situations, police have various courses of action available to them. They can decide if an action contravenes the law—if so, they have to determine which legal statute applies as the action could contravene several statutes. They can therefore decide which law to apply, which in turn will affect which sanctions might apply to the citizen who broke that law. That could lead to a simple fine or a period of incarceration, the latter of which might significantly affect the citizen's life choices (Alexander 2012). Or they could decide to have a quiet word with the citizen, tell them the error of their ways and let them off with a 'don't do that again, next time I won't be so lenient.' Or, of course, the officer could do nothing at all and choose to completely overlook the event—something which could have feasibly occurred in the example of John T. Williams had he walked in front of a different officer's car on what became his final day on earth. That could depend on the severity of the citizen's action, on how busy the officer is, on who the officer is working with that day, on what the current priorities of the PD are, on who the citizen is, on who is watching the incident unfold, or on any number or combination of factors (Reiner 2010, Manning 2010, Gaines and Kappeler 2014, Waddington 1999). That is the nature of officer discretion.

Officers have the discretion to make these decisions—they are legally mandated to do so. Were officers to arrest and charge every citizen considered to have committed a felony, the legal system would quickly collapse due to overload (Waddington 1999). We expect officers to use their experience and training to inform their use of discretion so that it is used appropriately (Reiner 2010, Bittner 1975). Clearly someone riding their bicycle on the sidewalk is less serious than someone riding a motorbike down it, although both riders could seriously injure citizens as a result of their actions. So far, so (relatively) clear. But a good deal of police interactions take place in situations not observed by other officers or overseen by other citizens (Waddington 1999, Skolnick and Fyfe 1993). This has two effects. Firstly, whatever occurs in these situations can often be reduced to 'who is telling the truth, the officer or the citizen?' A key reason for the unjustified shooting verdict in the case of John T. Williams was the incontrovertible evidence of the officer's dashcam. Secondly, justice and enforcement is not only a question of what is done, but also what is seen to be done (Mawby 2002). What happens if no-one other than the two people involved has seen it? It is for this reason that Dworkin (1978) terms discretion the 'hole in the donut of accountability.' In principle, police should be held accountable to laws or to policies, or a combination of both. But they can't be held accountable if we don't know (or can't prove) what happened. Waddington (1999) takes this troubling thought one uncomfortable stage further—not only could we not know what happened, we might not know *if* anything happened at all. So we don't even know *if* discretion was used—that is the nature of discretion in principle and practice. It is for this reason that Waddington believes it may ultimately be impossible to hold officers to account for their actions.

Unsurprisingly, then, discretion has become of very significant interest to policing scholars, legislators and policy makers. Officers reflect the society they serve, and therefore reinforce norms and values within that society. Discretion is subjective because it depends on such a wide variety of factors, which means it can be discriminatory. The principle is that officers should protect and serve all citizens. The practice is that discretion can give them the power to pick and choose who does and does not get targeted, as Stuntz (2011: 4) notes: 'discretion and discrimination travel together.' Bittner's view was that the use of force was disproportionately distributed onto minorities in the US, and clearly Native Americans are one such minority.

NATIVE AMERICAN EXPERIENCES: PAST AND PRESENT

The prevalence of violence in US history largely determines how Native Americans live in 21st century America (Brown 1991). It is no stretch to say the indigenous American population were subject to a process of extermination by White settlers over a period of several hundred years (Mak 2014). Antipathy also extended to peacetime, an example being the 1866 Civil Rights Act. This granted equal rights to everyone born in the US, with the exception of Native Americans (Zinn 2003). You read that right—the original guardians of the United States were the only folk not granted citizenship. Brown (1991) notes that White authority seemed unable to acknowledge its own hypocrisy in talking peace and liberty on the one hand, and on the other systematically destroying both Native American populations and its own solemn treaties to preserve Native lands. All of this bleeds into modern history. In 1973, Native tribes declared the symbolic site of Wounded Knee 'liberated territory' and occupied it, leading to a fierce battle lasting 71 days, during which protestors were fired on repeatedly by police and FBI units (Zinn 2003). The past is not another country, it seems.

The latest census estimate is that Native Americans number 5.2 million in the US (approximately 1.7% of the population). The population is adversely affected by poverty and unemployment (Marcus, J 2016). The Centers for Disease Control (CDC) states Native Americans are negatively affected by health outcomes in relation to drugs, alcohol, and mental illness. In all of these areas Native Americans are affected at a rate similar to, or worse than Black citizens in the US. Their rate of incarceration is proportionally double that of White citizens, with young Native Americans three times more likely to be locked up than young White Americans (Prison Policy Initiative 2020).

This brings us to the disproportionality of police-related deaths, where we encounter a typical problem—we can't be sure what those rates are.

According to The Counted, in 2016 Native Americans were proportionally more likely to be killed by police than any other population group in the US. In 2015 it estimated they were the second most likely to be killed after Black citizens. The CDC data for that year states that both groups were killed at an equivalent rate relative to their population (Marcus, J 2016). In this instance, the problem isn't only data on police-related deaths, but data on who is classified as being Native American due to a historic problem of under-reporting in the census numbers (Prison Policy Initiative 2020, Schroedel and Chin 2020). A striking example of who counts in 21st century America. Schroedel and Chin's (2020: 160) research into the media reporting of Native American police-related deaths found a 'staggering' level of underreporting of these deaths by mainstream media outlets. This reflects the general lack of media interest in Native Americans in the US (Marcus, J 2016) and also the way in which they are subject to negative stereotypical representations (Schroedel and Chin 2020), much as Rick Williams told me. Rick's assertion that his brother was 'assassinated' should lead us to question how and why police use guns in the US, and what that might tell us about police-related deaths.

USING GUNS IN POLICING

In the US, the use of force by police is perhaps an even more significant issue than in the UK, Australia, or Canada. This is because of historical, political and social precedents that mean firearm ownership and usage is far more common in the US than other English-speaking common-law countries. The Colt 45 was called 'The Peacemaker' with good reason: it goes hand in hand with the notion of the law man taming the Wild West—imposing order on chaos, by violence if necessary. Law enforcement in the US is thus inextricably linked with the use of guns. But this isn't the case in Britain, where officers are not routinely armed. This is because the history of policing in Britain is founded on the principle that police should not be armed, largely to ensure they do not routinely use force, or use it in an indiscriminate or unaccountable way. This doesn't stop British police using force, or indeed using it in ways that significant parts of the population find unacceptable and many consider unaccountable, or using it disproportionately on certain sections of the population (Baker and Pillinger 2020, Baker and Norris 2021). Nor do I mention it to assert that British police are in some way 'better' than US police, I'd like to be quite clear about that. I state the differences about being armed here to make clear that the type of policing a society gets reflects the type of society it is. Gun ownership in Britain is minimal compared to the US, and this affects the way each respective society is policed.

Crank (2016: 128) believes that the importance of guns to US police culture, training and practice 'cannot be overstated.' This is backed up by media narratives of police 'showing cops as the last bastion of frontier individualism, armed only with courage, righteousness, and of course, a motherfucker of a gun' (Crank 2016: 131). In this context we should also remember that officers sign up to do this job, and the job is in and of itself one that aims to keep citizens safe. A precondition of this is that citizens remain alive. Somewhere in the complex mix of factors affecting police and citizen interactions, this principle appears to have been somewhat overlooked—as one of the mothers in my research put it: 'If you're scared, why are you a police officer?'

The idea that policing is a dangerous occupation is often cited as a reason for officers using their weapons—it further reinforces the image of them as 'warriors.' It is also stressed in police training with officers shown numerous examples of how they can be attacked, and in some cases killed because they didn't use force early enough in the encounter (Zimring 2017). A number of authors have examined the claim that policing is a uniquely dangerous job and found it to be at best dubious, and at worse disingenuous (Butler 2017, Gross 2016, Crank 2016, Marenin 2016, Gaines and Kappeler 2014). Crank (2016: 156) cites data from 1994 when 76 officers were killed, but notes that this number does not indicate how many were suicides—it being widely acknowledged that the suicide rate amongst officers is relatively high. For example, research by Bishopp and Paquette Boots (2014) found that officers were three times more likely to die by suicide than by felonious murder. Using Bureau of Labor statistics, Marenin (2016) establishes that logging is by far the most dangerous job in the US with 128 people killed per 100,000 employed, compared to policing estimated at 15.8 per 100,000—this is exceeded by construction workers, steel workers, farmers and those working in fishing (Gaines and Kappeler 2014).

Marenin (2016) found that a total of 126 police officers were recorded as dying unnatural deaths in 2014, but that half of them either died in accidents, or due to other health related issues whilst at work. Butler (2017: 53) notes that 97 officers died in the line of duty in 2015, but that we don't know how many citizens were killed by police that year, neatly illustrating the relative level of importance placed on the life of either group and also how this issue is constructed in popular discourse. It might be said that policing being portrayed as a uniquely dangerous occupation is another construct—it's true to say that police might encounter danger in their work, but less accurate to state that they work in a uniquely dangerous job.

That said, there are disturbing signs of deliberate attacks on police in the US. In July 2016, Micah Johnson staged a planned attack on police in Dallas, killing five officers and injuring nine before himself being killed. He had previously served in the army in Afghanistan and was trained in the use of firearms. As a black male he was reportedly outraged about police-related deaths, and his attack was allegedly motivated on that basis. Several participants in my research project commented on this attack, all of whom stressed that whilst the attack was appalling, it was not entirely surprising due to the level of frustration and anger throughout the country. One summed it up: 'If authorities would just take action against rogue law enforcement then people won't seek to be vigilantes.' The FBI (2020) found that in the first nine months of 2019, a total of 37 officers were killed, eight of whom were victims of ambushes.

This atmosphere affects how officers are trained, with danger being repeatedly stressed. The families I interviewed commonly mentioned the '21-foot rule.' This is a training school staple that states if an assailant comes within 21 feet of an officer, and the officer believes them to have aggressive intent, they are justified in using their gun, because at that distance the assailant can be upon them in a split-second (Marcus, N 2016, Gross 2016). 'Aggressive intent' is not the same as being armed, or violent, or being engaged in the commission of a criminal act. This rule also presumes that an officer must stand their ground, rather than give space to someone who might be undergoing a crisis and not necessarily of sound mind. All of this builds an expectation that officers should use their firearm to stay safe, because it's better to be safe than sorry. Even if that apparently means shooting a citizen in the back. Officers are taught that guns are survival tools, if they're going to shoot, they should aim for the middle of a person's mass and shoot more than once (Crank 2016). Training reflects this, with officers receiving 60 hours of training on guns, 51 hours on self-defense, but only 9 hours on mediation/conflict resolution (Reaves 2009). Balko (2014: 275) notes 'These policies have given us an increasingly armed, increasingly isolated, increasingly paranoid, increasingly aggressive police force in America.'

PARAMILITARIZATION AND THE USE OF FORCE

The 1990s represented a turning point in the way police began to conceive of, and use force in the US. The political ramping up of the 'War on Drugs' led to an increase in the number of Special Weapons and Tactics (SWAT) teams in the US (Balko 2014, Alexander 2012). There has long been a tendency for American police to reflect aspects of a quasi-military force in terms of rank, hierarchy, parades and the use of weapons (Crank 2016, Kraska 2007). The crossover between military and police in the US should not therefore surprise us. It gives a clear indication of how policing in the US is considered to be both different from other types of policing in English-speaking countries, and reflective of the society it polices. In Britain, it is relatively unusual for ex-military personnel to become police officers after completing military service. Police are viewed as being first and foremost concerned with order maintenance. Therefore social skills such as communication and negotiation are considered to be key to their role, much as noted in Maurice Punch's (1979) description of British police as 'the secret social service.' This is considered to be quite a different skill set to that of military personnel who principally approach issues by considering how order can be enforced.

On the one hand Punch's (1979) conception doesn't seem too far from Fyfe's (1986) description of US police as human service workers, other than in time, rather than place—and it's notable that Fyfe was writing before the 1990s. In the US, ex-military personnel are seen as possessing key policing skills—enforcing (rather than maintaining) order, understanding tactics and practice around the use of weapons, and being able to follow orders and maintain discipline. Then again, military units have frequently been used to enforce order in the US in ways that are unthinkable in Britain, Australia or Canada. This most commonly occurs through the use of the National Guard in states of emergency, but has also seen active military units deployed in the aftermath of major uprisings, as discussed in the previous chapter. Balko (2014) traces this lineage to a paper written by George Patton in 1932 entitled 'Federal Troops in Domestic Disturbances' in which, amongst other things, he advocates firing machine guns into crowds of strikers if necessary. In the city of brotherly love, Mayor Rizzo notoriously proclaimed in 1979 that he'd armed the Philadelphia PD so well 'we could invade Cuba and win' (Skolnick and Fyfe 1993: 139). If all this seems like ancient history, bear in mind Rizzo's statue was torn down during the uprising that followed George Floyd's killing in 2020. Bear in mind also President Trump's exhortation to use the army and national guard to 'dominate' those uprisings, and that the then Secretary of Defense (Mark Esper) instructed the National Guard to control the 'urban battlespace.' Nor is this confined to one political party—police paramilitarism is truly bipartisan. Consider the then NYC mayor Michael Bloomberg's febrile statement in 2011: 'I have my own army in the NYPD—the seventh largest army in the world' (Balko 2014: 333).

The connection, then, between policing and military functions in the US is long established (see, for example Skolnick and Fyfe 1993, Vitale 2017, Balko 2014). SWAT teams emerged and proliferated in this fertile soil. The War on Drugs provided a catalyst for the growth of SWAT units. PDs were encouraged by provision of federal grants to acquire military equipment in order to aggressively pursue this 'war' on American soil (Alexander 2012, Schrader 2019). It became incumbent upon PDs to have personnel capable of using this equipment. This led to military trainers becoming more commonly involved in police training, and to personnel moving from jobs in the military to law enforcement. All of this led to a more significant overlap between police and the military, which further affected how police went about their daily jobs in the US (Conti 2011, Malmin 2013). It affected their training, their outlook and their culture (Baker and Fidalgo 2020). This is commonly stated as driving an 'us versus them' agenda, whereby citizens began to be seen increasingly as 'the enemy' to be subdued or controlled (Stoughton 2015). The Center for Constitutional Rights (2012: 3) noted that: 'Entire New York City neighbourhoods exist under conditions that residents compare to a military occupation.' Balko's (2014: 241) research cites a SWAT officer stating: 'There's us and there's the enemy.' A remarkably similar sentiment to a New Orleans PD officer cited by Greene (2015: 22) in the aftermath of Hurricane Katrina: 'It was us against them. It was war.' Clearly, we have moved some distance from the consensual and legitimate model of policing outlined in the previous chapter and envisaged by the President's Task Force (2015).

PERPETUAL WAR AT HOME AND OVERSEAS

The War on Terror in the aftermath of 9/11 added further impetus to the use and prevalence of SWAT teams. With two 'wars' being fought on domestic soil the number of SWAT teams expanded and the scope of their operations broadened. Small towns with low crime rates acquired SWAT units (Kappeler and Kraska 2015). An arms race broke out between PDs as to what equipment could be acquired—at the more extreme edge of the spectrum bazookas, tanks, and armoured cars were snapped up (Balko 2014). At the more mundane end of the spectrum, SWAT teams commonly acquired flash grenades, machine guns, and sniper rifles (Hall and Coyne 2013).

The police and military becoming more closely intertwined has been examined from the other end of the equation by Bacevich (2005) and Schrader (2019). The former argues that the American military being perpetually engaged in warfare overseas has affected the way America conceives of order, law and democracy at home. He quotes James Madison: 'No nation could preserve its freedom in the midst of continual warfare' (Bacevich 2005: 7). Much has been written about how communities across the US increasingly feel that police behave like an occupying force. Put this together with continual uprisings, states of emergency, and scenes from the media that appear to show American cities resembling battlefields (see, for example McCormick 2015), and Madison's statement strikes quite an unsettling tone. Lyle Rubin—an ex-marine lieutenant who served in Afghanistan writes about how he and his comrades viewed the US citizens who lived adjacent to their domestic training camps as analogous to the Afghans who lived outside their forward operations camps—seeing them as other, as suspect. In his analysis, the US is the biggest global seller of arms, the most energetic nation state on the planet in pursuing military action, and has a domestic prison population of 2.3 million, leading him to conclude that these elements are all part of the same web of violence that characterises power in the US (see also Coates 2015a). He soberly declaims: 'The war is the society and the society is the war' (Rubin 2018). Violence abroad begets violence at home.

The overt valorization of military personnel and veterans is something that often startles visitors to the US, because they see it as essentially a valorization of force, which is, of course, another word for violence. This symbolic power has seeped into the groundwater of US society and politics, much as Madison warned, and changed perspectives of rights, democracy and liberty. The idea of being perpetually alert to threats, and of being on a permanent war footing affects our outlook of what society is. We become keener at identifying enemies and threats, and less likely to seek consensus and legitimacy. Who needs consensus when one has an M16? Hardware, technology, and counterinsurgency tactics have all bled into the thinking and language about how law enforcers go about their work. Crank (2016: 113–118) notes that the 'crime as war metaphor' plays well with many officers, an increasing number of whom tend to see suspects or criminals as enemies.

Schrader (2019) examines how US involvement in overseas missions directly affected domestic policing. Police now routinely use 'non-lethal' force to manage perceived threats as a result of direct policy transfer from conflicts such as Vietnam. The use of CS gas ('tear gas') is a powerful example of this. It was used by the US military extensively in Vietnam for the first time, coinciding with the Detroit uprising of 1967. The Kerner Commission of 1968 into those events advised that firearms not be used in future disturbances due to the significant and unnecessary loss of life, and recommended the use of agents such as CS gas. Then, responding to anti-war protestors, President Ford banned the use of CS gas by the US military in 1975; this was codified when the US signed the global Chemical Warfare Convention in 1997 (Schrader 2019). Whilst the US military have been forbidden from using it for 45 years, police have enthusiastically embraced its use. Hence the keenness to also use pepper spray, flash grenades and smoke bombs—all acquired from military arsenals.

All of these tools are 'non-lethal'—which sounds reassuring until one considers two issues. Firstly, it hasn't reduced the amount of lethal force used by police, so these are additional tools in their armory, meaning that the use of force has likely broadened and intensified. Secondly, 'non-lethal' does not mean 'not harmful.' Such weapons are intended to cause maximum discomfort and upset, and they are used typically on crowds of protestors that often contain vulnerable people: the elderly, young people, people with respiratory issues, and pregnant women. The whole point of firing tear gas is that it affects a broad swath of people as quickly and as painfully as possible. It's not only that US cities come to look like war zones, they're policed as though they're war zones. Or more accurately, they're policed using weapons forbidden to the American military in war zones. Small wonder that one of the demands of protestors in the aftermath of George Floyd's killing was that police should be banned from using CS gas. All of the above demonstrates how conflict and violence have become normalized. The maintainers of order have become order wreckers in the name of enforcing control and security in their own homeland.

CULTURE AND PRACTICE IN POLICING

The preceding sections have established some key issues about how police use weapons in the US. The possibility of using force is fundamental to their role in being able to quickly establish order in fraught situations: force is their 'or else.' In such situations, police may have a split-second to make a decision about whether to use force, and about how much force should be used. The overuse or indiscriminate use of force is a perpetual concern for policing organizations world-wide, because it threatens the legitimacy of officers to police in a consensual fashion (Katz 2015, Dunham and Petersen 2017, Vitale 2017, Sherman 2018, Baker 2016). Zimring (2017) believes this has become the principal issue affecting police/community relations in the US. For this reason, law and policy makers have sought to increasingly restrain the use of force in order to try and ensure PDs remain legitimate and accountable (Terrill and Paoline 2017 and 2012, President's Task Force 2015). However, as we've seen in this chapter, discretion provides a mandate for officers to use force, and in some cases, lethal force. Concerns about legitimacy, accountability, consensus, community relations, the law applying equally to everyone, and policies restraining police in their everyday work meet at one juncture: discretion.

How and why do officers act in the way they do? Even in the face of societal concerns; even when confronted by data; even when social media is awash with images that society finds disturbing; even when apparently obvious lessons aren't learned that could prevent future deaths? The occupational culture of policing is considered to go some way to explaining this state of affairs. Culture is seen to exert a powerful influence on how officers work in practice. Academic authors have long focused on culture as being central to understanding how and why police use force (Bittner 1975, Reiner 2010, Crank 2016, Manning 2010).

Police occupational culture has been established by a variety of academic scholars as being variously driven by a sense of mission, solidarity, cynicism, and machoism (Reiner 2010, Vitale 2017, Crank 2016, Butler 2017). Using weapons is a unique power entrusted to officers, and officers consider themselves to be unique in their role. John Van Maanen (1978) found that officers believed society consisted of discrete groups of citizens. The group officers found most contemptible was the 'asshole.' Assholes were citizens who didn't follow officers instructions. Assholes challenged officers' authority in public, answered them back, asked awkward questions—assholes *didn't comply.* Assholes didn't pay enough attention to (or didn't appear to care about) officers' capacity for 'or else.' For this reason, Van Maanen (1978) said that officers believed assholes got everything they deserved—because they were assholes.

Such a portrayal of policing culture evidently depicts an 'us and them' mentality. It doesn't square easily with an agency whose mission is to 'protect and serve' society. Similarly, it doesn't sit comfortably with key concepts such as legitimacy and consensus in policing. Police culture has been affected by training, paramilitarization and a sense of fearfulness that has begun to stress officer safety over and above that of citizens (Balko 2014). A common phrase amongst officers is now 'better be judged by a jury of twelve, than carried by six.' In other words—do not hesitate to use lethal force in encounters, as not using it might result in your death, and a jury is highly unlikely to find you guilty for using it. The sense of solidarity in policing also means that officers tacitly approve of force being used, even if they don't agree with it, and even if they don't use it themselves. Schaeffer and Tewksbury's (2018: 44) research into police cultural narratives about how officers validate and valorize the use of force is instructive. They give an example of four detectives in a canteen discussing the shooting of Tamir Rice, emphatically laying the blame on everyone apart from the police, and saying they were sick of 'protestors and liberal media making ignorant comments on shit they don't know about.' The authors conclude their observations by noting that when officers tell each other stories about critical incidents they must: 'Emphasize the singular right [of officers] to use force and violence, and require support of such action regardless of the means, methods or outcomes' (Schaeffer and Tewksbury 2018: 50).

John T. Williams was shot in the back despite not committing an offense, or being violent, but apparently because he didn't comply with an officer's request. My research revealed that one third of the deaths I examined occurred as a result of people being shot in the back. A number of researchers have noted that a key factor in officers using force is non-compliance, rather than citizens being armed, or violent, or criminal, or dangerous (McCormick 2015, Kleinig 2014, Stoughton 2015, Marcus, N 2016). Just as Van Maanen (1978) noted, not following what officers believe to be a legitimate request might be enough to make officers use force to ensure compliance. This might explain why many police-related deaths appear to begin with relatively low-level incidents that then escalate into the lethal use of force. We have moved some distance here from the guardian style of policing envisaged by the President's Task Force (2015). Who are these people police believe to be 'assholes'? Are these the people who don't fit into 'normal' categories and who might consequently deserve special treatment from those who enforce symbolic authority on behalf of the dominant societal majority?

Chapter 2

Suspect Populations
Nathaniel H. Pickett II

Nathaniel H. "Nate" Pickett II was diagnosed with a mental impairment at the age of 19, after enrolling in college . He was a Black man, aged 29, living quietly and independently in Barstow, a small city of about 22,000 people in California. Nate was Dominic Archibald's only child, she told me: 'he wasn't a kid, although he is *my* kid. He was just a person who had a disability and was quietly trying to live his life.' On the evening of November 19th, 2015 he had been out to buy snacks from a local store and was walking home. Deputy Kyle Woods of the San Bernardino County Sheriff's department was patrolling in his cruiser, accompanied by a civilian participating in a ride-along and saw Nate near the El Rancho Motel. Within moments Deputy Woods had shot Nate dead, even though he was unarmed, non-violent and not committing a criminal act.

Initial media coverage reported that Woods stopped Nate because he was acting suspiciously. The Deputy claimed that Nate jumped over a fence. He then followed Nate on to the Motel premises and asked him his name, at which point Nate became belligerent, and struck him. In this version of events, the officer tried to handcuff Nate and became involved in a prolonged scuffle during which the two men wrestled on the ground. It was reported that Nate struck Deputy Woods repeatedly in the face, and failed to comply with the officer's requests. Dominic told me that the DA's report into the incident stated Nate had tried to grab the officer's gun and that Woods felt he was engaged in a 'life or death struggle.' This was his justification for shooting Nate twice, resulting in his death.

None of that information is true—we know that because it has been proven in a court of law. When I met Dominic, she showed me the same video that the jury saw in this case. She left the room while I viewed it because it was too painful for her to watch. As the area is extensively covered by CCTV, the entire incident was captured in real time. There is also an audio recording of the exchange between Nate and Deputy Woods. In it, one can clearly hear Nate speaking respectfully to the Deputy and answering all of his questions. Deputy Woods is, for some reason, unable to vocalise Nate's name correctly when communicating via his radio, and tells Nate he'll have to 'take him in,' as nobody with that name is registered in the area. At this point, Woods reached out to grab Nate, who then turned to run, but tripped and fell. He was then shot twice, at close range, in the chest. At no point was there an altercation between the two men. The video shows Woods and the civilian ride-along kicking and punching Nate on the ground as if fighting with him. Dominic told me that after Nate's body was removed by the Coroner's truck, the Fire Department hosed down the area, presumably to ensure any evidence was scrubbed.

In the aftermath of the incident, news reports stated that Deputy Woods was taken for medical treatment due to multiple injuries, including broken bones. If that were the case, it was not due to anything that occurred during the fatal incident that led to Nate's death. The DA's report into Nate's death took two years to be produced, and concluded that it was a 'justified shooting,' meaning that the case would not be heard in a criminal court. Dominic had no choice but to pursue justice for her son in a civil court. During depositions, Deputy Woods knew he could not use his original version of events, because it had been disproven by video evidence. He simply reconfigured his story to say that he'd stopped Nate because Nate had looked at him repeatedly whilst crossing the street in front of his car.

In March 2018, a jury determined that Deputy Woods had unreasonably detained Nate, unreasonably delayed medical aid, and was negligent in the use of deadly force. It found that both the officer and the civilian ride-along had struck Nate's body with their fists and boots. It further ascertained that at no point during the incident did Nate strike anyone. The jury awarded $33.5M in damages to Nate's family. The PD immediately voiced its dissatisfaction at this outcome, and vowed to contest the decision—a decision which, at the time of writing, still stands. Dominic told me that Deputy Woods was never so much as put on administrative leave at any point during this process. He carried on working as normal, and in early 2018 was apparently involved in the shooting of another citizen whilst on patrol. Dominic was informed that Woods was then moved to the firing range to instruct recruits on how to use their weapons, and thereafter stationed at a courthouse.

Nate's mom told me that the whole case would have been covered up and forgotten if it wasn't for her tenacity and persistence in seeking justice for her son. That at every stage she was obstructed and deflected by any and every representative in the law enforcement and justice community in San Bernardino County. She believes the officer should stand trial in a criminal court for homicide, and that he poses a risk to other citizens while he remains a Deputy Sheriff. As far as she is concerned, her family has not had justice for Nate's killing. She states that the financial award is a 'down payment on justice.'

Dominic was appalled that an officer had acted with such instinctive brutality towards her son; that the local police and County Sheriffs had concocted a story they evidently knew to be untrue; that the officer did not face trial in a criminal court; and that he was still working as a Deputy Sheriff. Dominic served her country as an Army officer, completing two tours of combat operations and was assigned to the Pentagon on 9/11. She knew about working in dangerous and stressful environments; about carrying a weapon; and about being responsible for it. She lamented that, 'we have more rules of engagement in a combat zone than law enforcement has on the streets of the United States.' It was inconceivable to her that Deputy Woods could have been fearful for his life, or that the county authorities could produce such a detailed and false report into this incident—one which fell apart under independent examination. She expected that officers on patrol would be trained to serve and protect citizens. She expected that if officers knowingly lied, and wilfully killed, then the justice system would investigate them and hold them to account.

Even when a court of law has determined that police have acted in an unlawful way, and used lethal force without good reason, it seems that police cannot accept this. The justice system did everything it could to avoid hearing this case in a criminal court, and continued to employ the officer and deploy him on patrol duties—resulting in another citizen being shot by him. The police and justice system did not hesitate to construct and disseminate a story that portrayed Nate as a dangerous, non-compliant, unpredictable Black man violently failing to comply with an officer's reasonable request.

THE VALUE OF LIFE

Eric Garner's alleged misdemeanor was selling loose cigarettes on Staten Island. He died after an NYPD officer throttled him with a chokehold, despite the maneuver being banned by his employer more than 20 years previously, and despite Mr Garner repeatedly gasping 'I can't breathe.' Several other officers were involved in 'restraining' Mr Garner, and at least six more stood and watched. George Floyd was killed by an officer kneeling on his neck for eight minutes and forty-six seconds, whilst also pleading 'I can't breathe.' Eight minutes and forty-six seconds—put a timer on now and sit and wait for it to reach that mark—that's how long Officer Chauvin kneeled on another human's neck. That's how long the officers looking on with their hands in their pockets heard George's desperate pleas for his mother, and for his life to be spared.

What was perhaps most notable in the Rodney King beating in 1991 was that multiple officers on the scene stood by and watched while other officers administered a brutal beating to a Black man cowering defenseless on the floor (Skolnick and Fyfe 1993). And remember that Nate H. Pickett II was shot dead after walking home with snacks from his local store one calm, quiet evening. All Black men; none being violent; none of them had a weapon; none of them committing serious criminal acts; all of them subject to extra-legal force. These are not aberrations; they are not just the result of problem officers; they are part of the structures and systems of policing and criminal justice in America. When multiple officers watch but don't inter-vene, one wonders what they think the principal purpose of their job is. What does this tell us about life for Black citizens in America?

The best evidence we have tells us Black citizens are disproportionately more likely to be killed than any other societal group in America. Ta-Nehisi Coates (2015a: 103 italics as per original) voices this with emphatic concise-ness: 'In America, it is traditional to destroy the Black body—*it is heritage.*' This chapter examines how historical, political, legal, economic and cultural factors enable this to be the case, and why it continues to occur. The myth of post-racial America is deconstructed by surveying statistical data that illustrate the lived experiences of Black Americans. The social construction of Black citizens as often being dangerous, unpredictable and ultimately creators of disorder is examined in attempting to understand how such stereotypes prevail in 21st century America. Once these issues have been examined, the chapter goes on to assess how all of this affects Black citizens' interactions with the criminal justice system, and in particular, the police. It examines why these issues appear to be so intractable, and how the factors that enable them to persist go far beyond purely the police and criminal jus-tice system and into the core of US society.

STRUCTURAL INEQUALITIES: DECONSTRUCTING THE MYTH OF POST-RACIAL AMERICA

In order to put these deaths into the context of lived experiences in the US, it's necessary to examine statistics providing an overview of health and well-being for Black citizens in America. Poverty is the obvious starting point—not least because, as Vitale (2017: 53) notes: 'modern policing is largely a war on the poor.' In 2019, the median household wealth for White citizens in the US was $76,057 compared to Black household wealth at $45,438 (US Census Bureau 2020). One quarter of Black families have fewer than $5 in savings

(Butler 2017: 141). You read that right. The last US census found that 25.8% of Black Americans lived in poverty compared to 11.6% of White Americans (US Census Bureau 2013), and it's estimated that one in three Black children live in poverty (Mak 2014: 451). Unemployment rates for Black citizens are nearly double that of their White counterparts (US Bureau of Labor 2019).

Segregation in the housing market serves to exacerbate some of these problems, particularly access to education (The Century Foundation 2019a). For example, homes situated in Black communities are valued at 23% less than those of comparable quality located in largely White communities (Perry et al. 2018). At the other end of the housing spectrum, Black citizens account for 40% of the homeless population in the US despite representing only 13% of the overall population (PEW 2019). Where you live also significantly affects the state of your health. In their article 'Being Black is Bad for Your Health,' Risa Lavizzo-Mourey and David Williams (2016) point out that if Black citizens had the same mortality rate as White citizens, then 100,000 fewer Black citizens would die every year. Levels of obesity, diabetes, hypertension and heart disease for Black communities exceed those experienced by other societal groups in the US. The overlap between income and healthcare also plays a part in disadvantaging Black citizens' access to healthcare, because with a lower median income, a larger proportion of it is spent on healthcare than in White Households. Black citizens are also significantly less likely to have healthcare insurance than White citizens (The Century Foundation 2019b).

In education, the segregation that determines where you live often combines with low incomes and means that Black children are more likely to go to schools that have less qualified and experienced teachers, fewer resources, and less access to rigorous courses that will provide preparation for college enrolment than their White counterparts (Center for Law and Social Policy 2015). Tolliver et al. (2016) state that Black citizens are ranked on the low end of every indicator measuring human well-being in the US. The Covid-19 pandemic will further entrench these inequalities in income, housing, healthcare and education. When police yell through their bull-horns at protesters to 'go back to your communities,' they essentially mean—go back to where many of you live in poverty, with poor access to education and healthcare and will likely die early (Younge 2020).

Examples of how racial segregation affects Black citizens have long been documented by authorities in the US. 'The Negro in Harlem'—a report written in the aftermath of a 1935 uprising stated it occurred due to 'injustices of discrimination in employment, the aggressions of the police, and racial segregation' (Lowery 2017: 31–32). These statistical facts combine to paint a clear picture of how Black America is disadvantaged, disenfranchised and oppressed. 'Post-racial America' does not exist in any sense that can be concretely measured. All of this affects how the police and criminal justice system interact with Black citizens but also the outcomes they can expect as a result of these interactions. Skolnick and Fyfe's (1993: xi) book 'Above the Law' written in the aftermath of the Rodney King beating begins by unequivocally stating that 'America is, culturally speaking, two countries.' The way the justice system 'sees' you largely depends on which country you live in.

DISPROPORTIONALITY IN THE CRIMINAL JUSTICE SYSTEM

We simply would not recognise the term 'White on White crime.' When we talk about 'race and crime' we automatically assume which race is being discussed (see Russell 2000, Epp et al. 2014). Michelle Alexander (2012: 198) suggests saying 'we need to do something about White crime' to a room full of people and watch the laughter that ensues. This is the entrenched nature of the discourse of race and crime in the US. The word 'thug' or 'urban' aren't typically used in relation to White people in America. Put those words together: race and crime; urban and thug, and you have a potent cocktail of phrases that evoke powerful images and representations. People of Color in the US have long been constructed as being dangerous, unpredictable, and potentially criminal predators (Butler 2017, Alexander 2012, Nelson 2000). Whilst Black citizens make up 13% of the population of the US they represent 36% of the prison population (Lamont Hill 2016: 123). Butler (2017: 45) notes that one in three Black men born in 2001 will serve time, whilst Alexander (2012: 7) states that three out of four young Black men in Washington DC can expect to spend time behind bars. Butler (2017: 70) characterizes the whole system of evident racist injustice as being 'at once obvious and hard to prove in a court of law.' One aftereffect of the Ferguson uprising was a twitter feed 'criming while White' in which various well-intentioned (if perhaps misguided) White people gave examples of where they'd acted in an obviously criminal or disorderly way in front of law enforcement officers but not been arrested. Jackson (2016: 317) relates one such tweet by a White teenage girl: 'Underage and completely drunk, knocked on the window of a cop car and demanded they drive me home. They did.' This would be unthinkable if it were a Black teenager.

A commonality in the shootings of Nate H. Pickett II, John T. Williams and Danielle Willard was that they were examples of street justice. Rick Williams used the word 'assassinated.' Those killed did not have a functional weapon, were not in the commission of a criminal act, were not arrested, did not get booked, did not go to court, and did not go before a judge to have their case heard. These issues point directly to another important construct: due process in the legal system, largely considered to be a myth by key authors writing about criminal justice in the US (see Alexander 2012, Butler 2017, Vitale 2017). Street justice as a function of policing is noted in Miller's (1976) comparative historical analysis of the NYPD and the Metropolitan Police, noting that from its inception, NYPD officers were more likely to deliver street justice than police in London. Black citizens are disproportionately represented in police-related deaths because police tend to identify them as innately dangerous, suspicious, criminal, or any combination thereof (Holmes and Smith 2012).

THE PAST IS NOT ANOTHER COUNTRY

One step to criminalizing a group of people is to dehumanize them. Clearly enslaving people, trading in their human flesh and exploiting their labor for centuries is at the root of the welter of statistics cited above. It's difficult to think of something more dehumanizing than enslaving people, chaining them, beating, whipping and killing them because they are ultimately your 'property.' The historical roots of social order profoundly affect the US today. The legacy of plantation slavery and subsequent mutation into Jim Crow practices led to the ghettoization and segregation that still characterizes modern-day urban living (Alexander 2012). A very substantial body of academic literature points to the myth of a race-blind America and the continued existence of structural racism (see, for example Brown et al. 2003, Weitzer 2017, Moore et al. 2016, Hall et al. 2016, Tolliver et al. 2016, Yancy and Jones 2013, Nelson 2000). As Gary Younge (2016: 89) notes: 'How could [this] not be? It's only been fifty years since [America] ascended from an essentially apartheid state.' The idea that historical baggage accumulated over 350 years could be jettisoned so swiftly illustrates the extent to which this myth is a convenient construct. The focus on the police-related deaths of Black American males, such as George Floyd, Mike Brown and Eric Garner underlines the way in which this myth is being increasingly contested (see, for example Lowery 2017, Vitale 2017, Butler 2017).

Michelle Alexander (2012) sketches the way that the post-civil rights era was able to perpetuate the previous system of Jim Crow. A significant number of uprisings during the mid-1960s led to a widespread perception that law and order had broken down in the US, particularly in urban areas. That uprisings often broke out in the aftermath of police killings of Black American males has also been widely identified (see, for example Butler 2017, Vitale 2017, Skolnick and Fyfe 1993) and resonates with events in Ferguson in 2014 and Minneapolis in 2020. A Gallup poll in 1968 established that 80% of those surveyed felt that law and order had broken down, and a majority felt this was due to 'negroes who start riots' (Alexander 2012: 46). She goes onto join the dots in how this narrative was constructed—post 1968, urban areas experienced 'White flight' and became more commonly associated with People Of Color, and also crime. Thus was the apparently immutable link between area, race and criminality fixed. 'Cracking down on crime' became code for police disproportionately focusing on Black Americans (Alexander 2012: 43).

There is a clear lineage in US public discourse post-WW2 illustrating the continued dehumanization of Black citizens in America. The 1965 Moynihan report represented the 'Black family' as being part of a 'subculture' and a 'tangle of pathology' (Alexander 2012: 45). American political discourse frames poverty as being about family, race and culture rather than inequality, power and exploitation (Skolnick and Fyfe 1993: 104), so it's perhaps unsurprising that the Moynihan report tapped into this whilst at the same time perpetuating grossly misleading racial stereotypes. The psychiatrist Frederick Goodwin stated in a report by the Department of Health and Human Services during the George H. W. Bush presidency that the inner city was a 'jungle' where 'hyperaggressive . . . and hypersexual monkeys' existed without civilizing social structures (Lamont-Hill 2016: 141). Possibly the high priest in all of this was Charles Murray with his strident views on the underclass and supposed genetic weakness of 'other races.' Supposed racial differences are social constructs which were codified by legal segregation. This erected a dividing wall to justify such a construction. For James Baldwin, the social construction of race is a White invention that enables this division to be justified. The desire to ascribe biological and genetic differences is tenacious and deep rooted as a result of that historical legacy. Not only does this dehumanize Black citizens, it also pathologizes them and leads directly to the enforcement of the 'code' of police disproportionately focusing on People of Color. It has real and pernicious effects for Black citizens living in 21st century America.

It was in this febrile atmosphere that broken windows and zero-tolerance policing were born in the 1970s (Kelling and Wilson 1982). Briefly stated, this proposed that cracking down on minor misdemeanors in urban areas would also reduce the incidence of more serious offenses. Officers clamping down on urinating in public and panhandling would purportedly reduce burglary and violent crime. The War on Drugs was also getting into gear at this time and both zero-tolerance policing and funding to aggressively pursue, arrest, charge and imprison any miscreants meant that US law enforcement went on the offensive against urban populations with a clear mandate about what order should be enforced in cities (Alexander 2012, Vitale 2017, Balko 2014). This combination of factors led to two outcomes, the first of which is that officers know what group in society to target; the other is that they know where to look for that group.

Skolnick's (1967) examination of police culture identified the concept of the 'symbolic assailant.' On this reading, police use 'perceptual shorthand' allied to instincts and experience to identify suspicious persons. Given the constructs outlined earlier, it's not difficult to imagine that a group of people who fit the classic description of 'the other' are constructed as criminals and then focused on by police who know exactly where to look for them. Here's the rub—police are typically *looking* for problems rather than *responding* to emergency calls from citizens—another commonality in the killings of Nate H. Pickett II, John T. Williams and Danielle Willard. And when they look for problems, unsurprisingly, they find them.

CONSTRUCTING CRIME AND CRIMINALS

When we remember that policing focuses more on order than crime, this construct starts to unravel. One only has to return to the arrest warrants in Ferguson, a city with a 67% Black population that was overwhelmingly represented in minor arrest statistics, making up 97% of arrests for 'failure to comply'; 92% for 'resisting arrest'; and 89% 'failure to obey' (see Butler 2017: 47). Klinger et al. (2015) examined survey data on police shootings in nearby St Louis and found that they only occurred in 40% of the city precincts—there were no shots fired in the other parts of the city. In a city where 50% of the population is Black, 93% of people shot at by police were Black. Nix et al. (2017) found from the available data that Black Americans were twice as likely to be unarmed and then shot and killed than White Americans. The historical precedent of police enforcing order on slaves in the American south is difficult to overlook here, as is the link to lynching (Tolliver et al. 2016). In my research, several Black mothers in the southern states drew a direct line from their sons being fatally shot in the back to their ancestors' experiences in plantation slavery.

The dehumanization of Black citizens can be seen in the derogatory use of language. As Coates (2015a: 60) observes, 'hate gives identity.' A number of writers on police culture have commented on officers' use of language to distance themselves from the human reality they regularly encounter—irrespective of their Color. The use of bodily metaphors is similarly enlightening. Aside from Van Maanen's (1978) infamous 'assholes' comment, he also found that officers viewed a specific group of citizens as 'shitheads,' 'jerkoffs,' and 'bums'; Young (1991) notes the uses of terms such as 'vermin,' 'scum,' 'dross,' 'bitches,' and 'sows'; leading Crank (2016: 118) to observe that police tend to view citizens who commit offenses as 'less than human.' It's not much of a step to make a connection with officers in the Ferguson PD exchanging texts that compared President Obama to a 'chimpanzee' (Lamont-Hill 2016: 23), or LAPD patrol officers sharing messages such as 'sounds like monkey slapping time' (Christopher Commission 1991: 74), and commonly recording incidents as 'no human involved' (Butler 2017: 28).

The US has, though, always been keen to use Black citizens in its military, which has served to further emphasize the fact they were not equal to their White comrades. Zinn (2003) notes that during the 1898 wars in the Philippines, Black troops commonly questioned why they were oppressing People Of Color in another country when they themselves were oppressed as People Of Color on their return to the US. The Black activist Robert F. Williams railed against the fact that German Prisoners of War were allowed to eat in canteens that were off limits to the Black GIs that had captured them (Tyson 1999). During the Vietnam war, Black soldiers first heard about the 1967 Detroit uprising and subsequent military suppression via Hanoi Hannah, leading one Black GI from Detroit to reflect: 'Our own military is killing our own people. We might as well have been Viet Cong' (North 2018). During the cold war, it was common for communist regimes to call out the US for hypocrisy when it demanded more focus on human rights and democracy in the world while patently tolerating—if not openly promoting—segregation, injustice, inequality and violence in its own backyard. The uprising in Minneapolis in 2020 in the aftermath of George Floyd's killing and subsequent global media coverage returned this issue to prominence and was catnip to authoritarian leaders around the world. China's Ministry of Foreign Affairs called on the US to 'safeguard and guarantee the legal rights of ethnic minorities,' whilst the Russian Foreign Ministry announced that this was 'far from the first in a series of lawless conduct and unjustified violence from US law enforcement.' The myth of the post-racial society is another construct that disintegrates upon contact with reality.

PERCEPTIONS OF ORDER

Academic literature on policing consistently stresses the prevalence with which police focus on marginalised groups and minorities within society (Reiner 2010, Bittner 1975, Butler 2017, Vitale 2017, Crank 2016). If a key aspect of the police role is to reinforce the rule of the 'dominant majority' (Reiner 2010) then it won't focus too much on the majority, but instead on minorities. Clearly, the Black population in the US represents a marginalised group. Robert Reiner (2010) terms this group 'police property.' Police knew they were there to enforce the view of the dominant majority, not least because they were (or aspired to be) from the dominant majority themselves, and needed to be seen to be enforcing order. Reiner calls this 'symbolic authority'—and can be directly linked to the practices outlined in this chapter: letting marginalised groups know who is boss, reinforcing the message that they *are* police property. Police exist to enforce and preserve existing structures and order, not to challenge them, whether or not they reinforce inequalities, unfairness, injustice or immoralities (Butler 2017, Vitale 2017, Lamont Hill 2016). There appears to be a direct line from being the literal human property of slave owners to being police property in 21st century America.

The relationship society has with police (and vice-versa) is characterized by two apparent paradoxes. The first—as we saw in chapter one—is that while society believes the police to be principally concerned with crime fighting, they're actually focused on order maintenance. The second is that the less contact communities have with police, the more they tend to think positively about them. People who often have contact with police tend to think less positively about them, based on their actual experiences. The commonality with both paradoxes is perception and reality. Societal perceptions about what the police do and how effective they are depends on where one sits within the social order (Reiner 2010, Weitzer 2017).

In 2017, Gallup asked citizens if they had 'quite a lot,' or 'a great deal of confidence in the police.' 61% of White citizens agreed with these statements, compared to 30% of Black citizens. In a survey questioning racial groups what the major issues in the US were, Black respondents put racism first and police brutality second, but White respondents didn't have either of these in their top five responses (Weitzer 2017). A sobering reflection of perceptions and realities in one of the richest countries on our planet in the 21st century. If one believes the police are largely effective at doing their job, and the nature of that job is maintaining order in society then an obvious question is—is this about the maintenance of order, or the enforcement of order? Maintenance suggests seeking the consent of those policed, of doing so by communicating and negotiating with citizens, and of trying to keep interventions to a minimum. Enforcement seems to be more focused on intervening when there is a perceived need to do so, which raises the significant issue of *whose* behaviour is being perceived. As was previously established , the introduction of the Metropolitan Police in London was intended to maintain order in a very large (even by today's standards) city. Their perception of what sort of order was to be promoted tells us a good deal about modern day policing.

Bear in mind there were no police before this, so any new organization would not only be duty bound to keep the peace, but perhaps more importantly, they would need to be *seen* to be doing so. If that wasn't the case, what would be the point of this 'new police'? And who would be doing the 'seeing'? It would be the dominant majority of society—fine upstanding folk in possession of decent morals and hard-working principles. Small business owners, office workers, merchants—good law-abiding people. Consider: who is not in this group? People of Color, the working class, anyone who isn't heterosexual, the unemployed, the mentally unwell, the homeless, people dependent on alcohol or substances, and sex-workers to name but a few. For 1829, read 2021—these are the groups that police still disproportionately focus on—the suspect populations. During the trial into Nate's death, one of Deputy Woods' fellow officers volunteered this opinion about the area where Nate lived: 'Typically, the type of people [that] walk around that area are bums . . . and prostitutes.'

It's often said that police commonly come into contact with marginalised groups, but it might be more accurate to state that officers exist to police the margins of the dominant majority in society. Kelling and Wilson's seminal article on broken windows policing is revealing in this regard. They state that the maintenance of order is more about perception than reality. Here is the policing mandate writ large, to prevent: 'the fear of being bothered by disorderly people. Not violent people, nor, necessarily, criminals, but disreputable or obstreperous or unpredictable people: panhandlers, drunks, addicts, rowdy teenagers, prostitutes, loiterers, the mentally disturbed' (Kelling and Wilson 1982: 32).

From their inception, police have focused on intervening in social problems. This means they've always been on the lookout for social problems, and consequently *defining* what social problems are. Because police have such a broad mandate, they're aware they can intervene in more or less any situation they think they ought to. The power of discretion further reinforces this, because they have the legitimate right to intervene or not intervene as they deem fit based on a variety of contingencies. The right to use force is a further tool in their armory enabling them to intervene in social problems. Not only do they have the power to define social problems, and decide whether or not to intervene, they also have the power to use force to resolve issues should they escalate, and then claim they had a right to do so in the name of maintaining/enforcing order. All of these aspects were apparent in the fatal shooting of Nate. This is the classic link between order and force—one can quickly become the other, and it is at the discretion of the officer on the scene. Consider all of these points in relation to the practice of stopping citizens and it becomes clear how situations can escalate to a point where lethal force might be used on someone who should never have been stopped in the first place.

This connects with Kahn et al's (2017) findings that officers are more likely to use force early in encounters with People of Color, and Fryer's (2016) findings that officers are more likely to physically handle or draw a baton or gun on Black citizens than on White citizens. Clearing street corners and managing public spaces is at the heart of symbolic and actual policing in US cities. Making sure the punks and stumble-bums don't affect the lives of the god-fearing majority is everyday order maintenance. The roots of broken windows policing can be traced to it, and the 'zero-tolerance' approach adopted by patrol officers as a result—which is to say, 'intolerant.' Unsurprisingly, this is reflected in police training which encourages a tendency to perceive citizens as 'other' (see Hall et al. 2016). When we say zero-tolerant policing, what we really mean is a zero-tolerant society, and a zero-tolerant polity, because police reflect society and our political will.

If there were any doubt about this, consider a key early law in England and Wales: the 1824 Vagrancy Act that enabled the 'new police' to define who should and should not be present in public areas. When this law was introduced strident voices opposed it on the basis of it being a 'catch-all' Act—one that police could use for whatever purpose they liked (Waddington 1999). That's exactly what happened, with it eventually becoming appropriated as the 'sus' law—meaning that if an officer suspected a citizen of anything, they had the right to stop and search them. The spirit of the sus law is still at the heart of police stop and search practice in the UK that results in Black people being disproportionately far more likely than White people to be stopped and searched by officers (Gov.UK 2020).

LIVING WHILST BLACK

This strategy was replicated in the US in the aftermath of the civil war when former Confederate states adopted vagrancy laws, requiring people to prove they had work. If they were unable to do so, they were imprisoned and used as convict labor on plantations (Alexander 2012: 21). It can be traced to the 'dragnet' approach identified by so many authors (for example, Butler 2017, Vitale 2017, Lamont Hill 2016, Balko 2014, Alexander 2012) that has seen People Of Color disproportionately targeted by police. Again, there is a tsunami of data to illustrate this. Stop and frisk is a good example—another direct transplant of policing practice across the Atlantic. The NYPD were found to have conducted 53% of stop and frisks on Black communities despite those citizens comprising 23% of the city's population (CCR 2012). The official justification for the vast majority of these stops was because of 'furtive movements'—in other words, the 'sus' law is alive and kicking in 21st century America. Arrests were made in only 6% of all stop and frisks—and half of these were eventually not booked. People of Color were no more likely to be arrested than White citizens despite being significantly more likely to be stopped in the first place (CCR 2012). So approximately 680,000 citizens were publicly targeted and humiliated for no outcome—other than outcomes of fear and distrust of the NYPD. That's just one city in a single year.

Butler (2017) notes that stop and frisk is a vital tactic in reinforcing who is in control and who is subordinate, and crucially it leaves no marks. It does, though, have a significant impact on how people act in their everyday lives, through what Alexander (2012: 136) calls 'ritual dominance.' The CCR (2012) review noted that the practice of stop and frisk created a climate of fear among People of Color, where mistreatment at the hands of police came to be expected. Authors (see, for example Weitzer 2017, Younge 2016, Lowery 2017, Coates 2015a) commonly refer to the 'talk' that Black parents give their children about how to act when police approach them, aggressively question them, or order them to 'assume the position.' I interviewed some research participants in a New York community centre which was covered in hand-drawn posters by *school children* talking about how to deal with police interactions and what their legal rights were. As Butler (2017: 112) notes: "In another context, we might describe these behavior modifications by saying 'the terrorists have won.'"

The term 'driving while Black' has been used by various authors (Epp et al 2014) to highlight the disproportionate number of traffic stops on People Of Color. This being another manifestation of stop and frisk practices. A study of drivers through the New Jersey Turnpike found that although only 15% were Black, they accounted for 42% of traffic stops and 72% of all arrests (Lange et al. 2005). All of this leads Baratunde Thurston to observe that a more accurate term to sum up all of these experiences is 'living while Black.' The ubiquity of the combinations of life experiences in this chapter can be summed up by a judge's statement to a DOJ investigation into policing in New Orleans: 'If you are a Black teenager and grew up [here], I guarantee you have had a bad experience with the police' (Greene 2015: xii). Think about that for a moment—*guarantee*—then consider what society's reaction would be if it was a *guaranteed* experience for a White teenager. It would be considered utterly unacceptable, wouldn't it? If zero tolerance policing was practiced in predominantly White neighborhoods there would likely be vocal protests proclaiming a 'police state' (Lamont Hill 2016: 46). It's common to meet officers who are critical of this type of policing and know that structural changes are required to deal with issues such as homelessness, poverty, poor housing and mental ill-health. But as we've established, much of society doesn't know what police actually do in their everyday work. As part of my job teaching university students about policing, I often teach in collaboration with police officers. A while ago, in a classroom debate, a student asked an officer who they mostly dealt with on a daily basis. He answered 'victims'; the student replied 'you mean victims of crime?' No, said the officer, 'I mean victims of life.'

The hypocrisy at the heart of the myth of post-racial America can recently be seen in the way the narrative of the 'War on Drugs' has been challenged by the opioid crisis in the 21st century. The 'War on Drugs' could just as easily be termed a War on People of Color, given its focus on crack users (predominantly People of Color) over cocaine users (White people) (Alexander 2012, Vitale 2017). There has been no War on Drugs on those affected by the opioid epidemic, largely because they are predominantly White. Consequently, they are portrayed as sufferers and victims rather than criminals; and so the approach taken predominantly focuses on welfare and healthcare responses rather than police and correctional enforcement, as was the case with People of Color during the height of the War on Drugs phase. The difference in reaction can also be seen in law enforcement responses to public protests. In Minneapolis in May 2020, peaceful protestors—many of whom where Black—were met by hundreds of officers aggressively using tear gas, flash grenades and smoke bombs. Weeks before, scores of heavily armed White libertarians protesting the terms of the Covid-19 lockdown descended on the statehouse in the nearby state capitol of Michigan with some of them attempting to force entry to the chamber of the state legislature. They were met with a low-key police response that sought to de-escalate the situation. That this was effectively replicated in the storming of the Capitol in DC in January, 2021 only serves to reinforce this point. One wonders what sort of police response the protestors at Ferguson would have met had scores of them exercised their constitutional right to turn up armed with assault rifles, and how the media might have portrayed this.

RECONNECTING POLICE AND COMMUNITIES?

Mirroring the discussion on police as guardians rather than warriors is the call for police to embrace community policing as a way of better understanding, reflecting and representing the citizens they are employed to serve and protect. This is a standard institutional response when uprisings and protests won't readily disperse; and when tensions between police and communities are perpetually simmering and in danger of reaching a boiling point. It seems to be an entirely reasonable suggestion, because the foundation of policing is that officers are essentially citizens with additional powers who live within their communities and are able to maintain safety and order largely because they understand the concerns of those communities. There are, though, still concerns over the dominant majority within communities, as observed in McLaughlin's (1994) research into community policing in Manchester. One of his findings was that minorities still tended to be disproportionately focused on, partly because that was what the more vocal parts of the community wanted from police. In the US this can be seen in recent research undertaken by Gascón and Roussell (2019) into community policing in Los Angeles. They found that it led to police having further reach into communities and focus being even more targeted on People Of Color—it effectively consolidated aspects of police power over communities. Police prioritized which voices within the community were heard, and unsurprisingly they tended to be voices that accorded with police priorities. The upshot of this is that police-community relations suffer—the opposite of the intended outcome. Vitale (2017) asserts a view which appears to be gaining traction at the time of writing, notably to remove police from communities and instead invest in communities to address structural inequalities and encourage them to find ways of policing themselves.

During my research with Black Americans who'd lost loved ones, it was common for them to refer to the legacy of slavery and intergenerational trauma—indeed, several made reference to 'post-traumatic slave disorder.' A very common refrain was: 'if you've got a problem and you call the police, you've got two problems.' It was typical for Black participants in particular to reject the idea that they should engage in activities to enhance police-community relations. One mother, whose 19-year-old son was fatally shot in the back was emphatic: 'I am not going to let my grandson build a relationship with someone that was supposed to protect his dad and killed him. I am going to honor my son's name through his son and he won't ever be rubbed on the head and patted like a dog at the cook out that we have for the police officers in the community to get together. Because thirty minutes later the community are going to be mourning another child that got killed by a police officer, just watch and see.' Reiner (2010) believed that a by-product of police demonstrating 'symbolic authority' was that it would be periodically met with 'symbolic resistance,' and this is increasingly apparent in the US. Centuries of oppression and subjugation aren't going to be overcome by cookouts and softball games. Particularly when citizens continue to be killed at the rate of three per day and Black citizens are disproportionately represented in that epidemic of avoidable death. Nate's mom believes there will be no trust in the community until law enforcement are held accountable for their actions.

There are also fundamental problems with the principles of community policing failing to accord with what counts for 'modern policing' in the US. This is typically driven by a means/ends formula that molds and measures policing. A significant by-product of broken windows policing is the measurement of quantitative data that assesses the performance of police. Compstat is the apotheosis of this approach and worked hand in glove with the broken windows approach of policing driven by the NYPD in the 1990s (Eterno and Silverman 2010). Compstat is a computer mapping program that charts where crime and disorder occurs and identifies those areas as 'hot spots.' Officers are then directed to heavily police those areas, typically leading them to find more incidents of disorder, further feeding and reinforcing the Compstat data that sent them there in the first place (Gilsinan 2012). It is universally used and revered by PDs and politicians alike, who assert that this approach is working to target crime and disorder in a 'scientific' way (Willis and Mastrofski 2012, Eterno and Silverman 2010).

This approach is now known by a variety of terms—'evidence based policing' or 'problem oriented policing' are most commonly used (Willis and Mastrofski 2012). A better term for it would probably be 'measurement based policing' because the reliance on a statistical model results in reducing policing practice to data, when the overwhelming majority of the literature and knowledge on policing tell us it's anything but this. A good deal of literature suggests that police have a tendency to game any system they're measured by—what cops call 'piss collars' (Skolnick and Fyfe 1993: 127, see also Gilsinan 2012). If you're down on your quota towards the end of the month, you know where to go and who to look for to make up the numbers. Community based policing should theoretically be based on interactions and relationships; made up of a myriad of miniature social events. These are things that can't necessarily be measured, indeed shouldn't necessarily be measured. We return here to a key paradox—reality and perception: policing is largely about perception, and unsurprisingly perception cannot be measured in a straightforward way.

Skolnick and Fyfe (1993: 125) say this results in measuring how often police do something rather than whether they do their job properly or not. They equate it with measuring surgeons by how many operations they did rather than how many patients were cured. Peel's original assessment on the 'new police' was that they were to be measured by the *absence* of disorder and crime, not their *action* in dealing with them. This creates a further dilemma. A good officer practicing proactive community policing may barely be registering on Compstat, potentially leading to analysts at headquarters speculating about whether an officer should continue to be posted in that location. Another common call is to increase racial diversity in policing. The belief being that if the demographic of officers better reflects the demographic of the community, then policing will be more consensual, more legitimate, more accountable and officers less likely to use force. It's worth noting that the officer who killed Nate H. Pickett II was of mixed-heritage, and there is a significant amount of literature that casts doubt on this undoubtedly noble aspiration (see, for example Jones-Brown and Blount-Hill 2020, Vitale 2017, Greene 2015).

IMPLICIT BIAS TRAINING

The increasing societal awareness that post-racial America is indeed a myth has led to soul searching over the disproportionate policing of People of Color.

We can see the effects of this in the focus on community policing, but also in the increasing prominence of implicit bias training in this debate. Whilst the concept of implicit bias has existed for decades, it has only recently become of interest to policing scholars and professionals (James 2018). It states that humans have a propensity to unconsciously categorize subjects as types in order to function in society, and this leads us to build up a repository of unconscious stereotypes that affect our behavior without us being cognizant of them. As Fridell and Lim (2016: 38) note: 'this process does not require animus; it requires only knowledge of the stereotype.' The hypothesis posits that police disproportionately use force on Black citizens because they unconsciously identify them as being more associated with crime, or being a greater threat than other population groups (Fridell and Lim 2016).

A substantial amount of research has been undertaken to test this hypothesis under lab conditions with mixed results. However, there are no conclusive findings that demonstrate implicit bias results in disproportionate police responses to Black citizens. In a review of the available literature Fridell (2017) observed that researchers appeared to manipulate their findings to fit their preferred narrative—somewhat ironic in research focused on bias. James (2018) is not alone in suggesting that it's possible that implicit bias also applies to geographical areas, and not purely to population groups. There are also a number of studies that produce counterintuitive findings of counter-bias, whereby officers deliberately override any bias they might have due to a desire to avoid disciplinary action, or being labelled racist (Fridell and Lim 2016).

In terms of the training available to address implicit bias, Fridell and Lim (2016) note that role play in cutting edge 3D simulators would be the best method of educating individual officers about their unconscious prejudices, although one is bound to wonder how many of the 18,000 PDs in the US have access to such training facilities. James (2018) also acknowledges the possibility that officers might 'game the system' by deliberately trying to appear unbiased while being assessed. In short, research is inconclusive about the usefulness of implicit bias in explaining the disproportionate police use of force on Black Americans, and also about whether training might reduce it. It seems implicit bias training is another example of a possible 'remedy' that was initially welcomed as a possible solution but was found to be less clear-cut than it first appeared. That said, if something can be used in training that makes officers more aware of why they act in certain ways in specific situations then it should probably be embraced rather than rejected. It is likely that this could be another piece in the jigsaw of making improvements to officer/citizen interactions and encouraging officers to be more reflective about their craft, rather than a way of 'solving' the problem of officers disproportionately focusing on People of Color.

Centuries of exploitation and oppression are not going to be swept away by a Black citizen becoming president. Anything that has existed for so long is deeply embedded in social, legal, political and cultural structures and systems, knowingly or otherwise. It is beyond doubt that Black citizens in the United States are disadvantaged compared to White citizens on any index of well-being or quality of life. In addition to this, they are disproportionately focused on by the criminal justice system and, as Alexander (2012) notes, this serves to perpetuate oppression via other means. One of the by-products of the social construction of race is that 'Black people' are constructed as being 'one thing,' or 'a community' when this is patently absurd. Again, we wouldn't talk about the 'White community.' Forty-eight million humans are clearly not a monoculture. This is one reason for the increasing focus on intersectionality as a way of examining different varieties of experience that go beyond race, as will be examined in the following chapter.

Chapter 3

They Musta Done Somethin'

Kayla Moore

Kayla Moore was a gentle, friendly person who loved to chat with friends and family. She was a 41-year-old Black trans woman who lived with a friend in downtown Berkeley in the San Francisco bay area and had a home caregiver at times. Kayla weighed 347 pounds and had a diagnosis of paranoid schizophrenia. Her sister, Maria, told me sometimes Kayla would display symptoms such as to talking to people that others couldn't see. At times like this it was usual for Kayla to be voluntarily admitted to hospital and have her medication rebalanced. On 12th February 2013 her caregiver felt Kayla was a little 'off.' During the evening her housemate also concluded Kayla was unwell and called the police. Officers arrived just before midnight, and within forty minutes of their arrival Kayla died after being physically restrained by multiple officers whilst face-down on a mattress in her own home.

Officer Gwendolyn Brown, one of the first responding officers, knew Kayla. She had made previous wellness checks when there had been low-level concerns reported by Kayla's family or friends. But Maria told me this visit was of a different nature from the outset. Upon arrival the police were met by her roommate who had called them. The two officers promptly arrested him, apparently on an outstanding warrant and initially confined him to the police vehicle, only to then release him from the vehicle in order to unlock the door of the apartment before returning him to their 'custody.' In this way, the officers were apparently able to gain entry to the apartment covertly, and confronted Kayla, taking her by surprise.

Maria told me that the original plan of the officers arriving at the scene had been to transport Kayla to Alta Bates Hospital in Berkeley so she could receive support and treatment. On two previous occasions this process had been enabled with trained clinicians, who were able to support Kayla into voluntarily receiving medical help at hospital. Upon arriving at the apartment however, this plan changed, as the police sought information regarding any outstanding warrants on Kayla. One surfaced for a Xavier (Kayla's birth name) Moore. Before they approached the apartment, one of the officers acknowledged that the age of the person on the warrant did not match Kayla's age. When they discussed the warrant with her, they reported that she became resistant and combative. The officers attempted to handcuff her, but in the scuffle that ensued, Kayla ended up face-down on a mattress with them restraining her. They called for backup, with eight officers eventually attending the scene. Thirty-five minutes after their arrival the officers reported that Kayla had stopped breathing. Heart compressions were initiated by officers, but not resuscitation.

The officers had not received specialist training in dealing with people undergoing mental health crises. The warrant was apparently a case of mistaken identity, and it is still unclear why officers pursued this approach when they claimed it was not their original intention. Kayla's weight should have been taken into account before she was restrained and observations of her vital signs should have been undertaken throughout the period of restraint, but were not. Maria believes that resuscitation was not attempted because of prejudice about Kayla's gender identity. She told me that officers were disrespectful to Kayla as she lay (dead) in her apartment, joking about whether she was a man or woman, referring to her as 'it,' and exposing her genitals. The police reports were filed using masculine pronouns. All of these actions indicate a fundamental lack of understanding and respect for people whose gender identity is complex.

The facts around Kayla's death were very slow to emerge and be shared with her family. They were informed by police of her passing that night, but were never able to pay their respects in a chapel of rest due to police and coroner obstruction. Initially the family thought Kayla had died of natural causes. Given some of the inconsistencies in the police version of the story, and also because Kayla's caregiver was present for a significant period of the incident, they sought further answers from police. The initial report by police apparently described Kayla as becoming psychotic and attacking the officers upon their arrival, a story refuted by the caregiver. Kayla's family then found out by chance that there was to be a Police Review Commission meeting at which her case was to be discussed. At that meeting, attended by media and city officials, the family repeatedly asked entirely reasonable questions about how Kayla came to die after contact with the police in her own home. The meeting was video recorded and clearly shows the BPD chief ordering the removal of Maria's partner, Carl, apparently for asking too many inconvenient questions, or 'being disruptive,' as the police saw it. Maria told me that one of the officers involved in Carl's removal was Gwendolyn Brown, one of Kayla's assailants. During the incident, Kayla's dad was also manhandled by several officers who had been at the scene of his daughter's death. For Maria, that was 'the ultimate disrespect.'

Only when Maria got Berkeley Cop Watch involved did more information come to light, despite repeated requests for reports from the police and coroner. Cop Watch conducted their own enquiries at the apartment block where Kayla lived, talking to witnesses—echoing how key evidence was gathered by the mothers of Nate H. Pickett II and Danielle Willard. The DA apparently declined to investigate Kayla's death because it was not a police shooting, so the investigation was undertaken by the Berkeley Police Review Commission (PRC). The composition of the PRC is partly civilian and part law enforcement officers. Maria told me that the PRC failed to conclude the investigation within twelve months, which meant the deadline passed for any officers to be charged. Eventually, Kayla's family were able to bring a court case in August 2016, but that was dismissed by the judge. Two further attempts to bring the case to court were unsuccessful.

Maria wishes police would show respect for all people whatever their gender identity. She believes that a mental health crisis should be treated as such whatever time of day. It seems that if you are going to have a mental health crisis in Berkeley, then you can only get an appropriate response during office hours, as the Mobile Crisis Team only works then. Maria believes that a mental health crisis is not a criminal act, and police should be trained to understand deescalation and how to talk to those in crisis. Why aren't these basic issues the case, given the frequency with which police encounter people who are mentally unwell?

INTERSECTIONALITY

So far, the book has examined four deaths. In simple terms one woman, one trans woman, and two men. Two citizens were Black, one was Native American, the other was White. But we know humans don't live in simple categories, in binaries of male/female and White/Black. Two of the four had mental impairments; two had issues with substance dependency; three were shot dead, one died as a result of restraint. Did you know any of their names before reading this book? Once one begins to list the names of people who have died, it becomes clear as Lamont Hill (2016), Zimring (2017) and Vitale (2017) note, that these were not extraordinary incidents. A list is used by Janelle Monae in her influential song 'Hell You Talmbout.' Each and every name, and each and every list is a story of avoidable killings and largely unaccountable law enforcers. They represent indictments of the inability of the US justice system to learn lessons that prevent future deaths. Each death is the result of a specific interaction between police and citizens, but together they accumulate into a story of systemic and structural power relationships that eventually end in an ultimate power relationship—an officer is alive, a citizen is dead.

Janelle Monae's song sparked an alternative version by Vita Elizabeth Cleveland: 'Hell Y'all Ain't Talmbout'—the simple but powerful point of which is: when we name certain names, we don't name others, and that says something about how we perceive the identities of people who die after police contact. Whilst Cleveland principally highlights homicides of Black Transgender citizens, the point remains that the construction of the deceased in police-related deaths tends to fit within certain categories. We don't immediately think of trans citizens being killed by police, but they are. When we ask 'who counts' we need to consider how society constructs these deaths. The 'Say Her Name' campaign began as an attempt to highlight how Black women are also killed by police, but typically receive less attention than Black men—as a way of moving the focus and discussion beyond Mike Brown and Eric Garner, and it has had some success in doing this.

We could apply the same principles to Native American or Hispanic citizens of either genders, or of White women—and so on, the list (once again) goes on. When I was working in the US I was twice approached by UK-based news organizations who knew about the research I was doing. Both journalists asked me: 'if you were going to run a story on this issue, what would you do?' My answer was that I'd either focus on Native American populations, or on Black females or transgender groups. They were intrigued, and asked me to explain why that was. The short answer to that is those populations are also subject to disproportionate focus from police, but receive very little media focus. In both cases, those journalists said they'd talk with their editorial team and get back to me: they did, and they both informed me that they'd decided to keep the focus on Black males who died in police-related deaths. The way we build the narrative determines who gets highlighted and who gets left out. In no way am I downplaying the very serious and systemic, structural injustices that lead to Black men being killed by police in the US. But there are more pieces in this jigsaw. As has been established thus far, police disproportionately focus on minorities, and we should therefore not lose sight of the complex picture of minorities and intersectionality. If we want to see how the entire puzzle of police-related deaths (PRDs) fits together, we need to look more carefully at all of the pieces involved.

POLICING HEALTHCARE

Wesley Lowery (2017: 190) notes that one of the 'stunning findings' from the *Washington Post* data on police-related deaths was that one in three of the deceased had mental health issues. Mulvey and White's (2014) study in Arizona found that people who were mentally unwell were four times more likely to be shot by police than citizens who were not. These findings mirror academic research into this issue in other countries—similar findings apply in the UK, Australia and Canada (see, respectively Baker 2016, Australian Institute of Criminology 2013, Razack 2015). Similarly, people who are mentally unwell commonly come into contact with police the world over, and make up a substantial proportion of day to day police work. In 2016, the NYPD (2017) responded to 157,000 calls directly relating to mental health issues—that's 430 per day. It's evident that people who are mentally unwell are part of the core business of policing (Thompson and Kahn 2016, President's Task Force 2015). Why do we think it appropriate for police to be key first responders for healthcare issues, and in many cases healthcare crises? We wouldn't expect police to turn up for citizens experiencing a heart attack or stroke, so why do we expect it when people are mentally unwell and what can this tell us about how we view both policing and mental health?

The origins of police being first responders to mental healthcare crises lie in two connected issues, both of which occurred in the 1960s and 70s (Baker and Pillinger 2019, Rossler and Terrill 2017). The first was a concerted push to deinstitutionalize mental healthcare provision and to provide more care for people who experience mental health issues in the community to reduce stigma and also enhance their civil rights (Ruiz and Miller 2004, Whitaker 2002). The second was cuts to funding for mental healthcare in the US, meaning that there were simultaneously more citizens who were mentally impaired in mainstream society whilst there was reduced provision to care for their needs (Teplin and Pruett 1992). In the absence of a healthcare response, police have become a de facto emergency response for mental healthcare crises. They have become 'street corner psychiatrists' (Teplin and Pruett 1992). A principle purpose of policing is to be reactive—as has already been established, the police role is extremely broad. Members of the public will call 911 to report anything they perceive to be odd, unusual or alarming, and the behavior of some citizens who are mentally unwell can be any combination of these.

Most people in society would not expect police to be providers of healthcare on a regular basis, and particularly not crisis healthcare. I say 'healthcare' because writing 'mental healthcare' reconstructs how we view this issue. Society tends to frame physical healthcare differently to mental healthcare, and this is probably at the heart of why police are a de facto mental healthcare service (Baker and Pillinger 2019). We've already established that policing focuses on vulnerable populations in society, and that the dominant majority in society either tolerates this, or actively embraces it. Mental health has typically been seen as a taboo subject by the dominant societal majority, and this might be one reason police have ended up being a default response to mental healthcare crises.

POLICE PRACTICE AND TRAINING

In the aftermath of deinstitutionalization, it became clear that police needed to find alternate ways of approaching calls related to mental health issues, due to the variety of complex issues that citizens might exhibit. Shouting commands, demanding compliance or asking citizens to be reasonable won't necessarily work if the citizen is mentally impaired (see, for example Morabito et al. 2012, Kerr et al. 2010). Whilst police have a good deal of discretion, how they use it is largely based on their experience of previous encounters. If an officer doesn't have previous experience, they may use their gun to shoot someone who appears to be threatening, only to discover that such behavior resulted from their illness (Rossler and Terrill 2017). For these reasons, the first attempts at alternative responses from police used officers with experience of dealing with mentally impaired citizens to informally train other officers (Bittner 1967, Teplin and Pruett 1992). This effectively fixed a pattern that persists today—police have tried to adapt their approach to citizens who are mentally unwell, but in a nonsystematic and piecemeal way with the best available resources they have to hand. Which is another way of saying that some PDs made significant changes that tried to focus on the wellbeing of people who are mentally unwell, and others did almost nothing at all. This leads to what Wood et al. (2011) term a 'zip-code lottery' of police responses to mental healthcare crises—as was apparent in Kayla's death.

From the 1990s onward there were more concerted attempts to deliver training to officers on mental ill health that could provide basic information about what sort of symptoms and behaviors they should be aware of and how to manage them as a result. Key here is identification, which goes back to Fyfe's split-second syndrome. Officers taking time to assess the situation unfolding in front of them is vital, but first they need to be able to make an accurate assessment based on knowledge and training in the absence of experience (see Hails and Borum 2003, Morabito 2007). Evidence tells us that officers are disproportionately more likely to use force on citizens who are mentally impaired than on citizens who are not. This occurs largely because officers fail to recognise issues and use force as a first resort to rapidly 'solve' the encounter (see Borum et al. 1998, Morabito et al. 2012). It also occurs because citizens who are mentally unwell can often resist officers, or fail to comply with their orders because they're in crisis. This can lead to officers using force for reasons of perceived noncompliance (Mulvey and White 2014). Therefore, the overwhelming focus of training on how to better manage situations involving citizens who are mentally unwell typically emphasises the importance of deescalation strategies from the outset.

Training officers in working with citizens with mental health issues is fraught with the same types of contingencies we've previously encountered in this book. Principal among these is the organizationally fragmented structure of policing in the US. The vast majority of PDs have fewer than 25 officers, leading to significant issues in training, keeping up to date with best practice and also the formulation of policies (Baker and Pillinger 2019). Unsurprising, then, that research tells us police training on citizens with mental health issues is highly variable depending on place, and the available resources of the PD (Wood et al. 2011). It is also dependent on the content of the training. Most readers might imagine training on mental health issues would be delivered by experts in mental healthcare, and probably involve role-play or interaction of some sort. Evidence tells us, however, that a good deal of this training is classroom based and delivered as rote learning by police trainers (Hails and Borum 2003). Even with training, there is evidence that officers feel poorly equipped to deal with calls related to people who are mentally unwell (Watson and Fulambarker 2012, Wells and Schafer 2006). Of further concern is how this approach effectively criminalizes people who experience healthcare crises, and how an interaction with law enforcement officers might exacerbate their condition and lead to further harm, potentially of a lethal nature. Nor should we underestimate the capacity of force being used to lead to delayed and ongoing trauma, particularly to younger people undergoing mental health crises in the aftermath of encounters with police (Meade et al. 2017).

CRISIS INTERVENTION TEAMS

By the late 1980s it was clear that other types of interventions were required—that better training was of only limited utility. In 1988 Memphis PD implemented the 'Memphis model' as a way of better responding to people who were mentally unwell; this is the basis of what is now known by the generic term 'Crisis Intervention Teams' (CITs). The essence of this model is that officers volunteer for selection and receive specific training on citizens with mental impairment. That team becomes the principal PD response for any call relating to mental health issues (Thompson and Borum 2006). The purpose of CITs is to divert citizens who are mentally unwell from the criminal justice system towards care-based solutions. It's worth noting that at the time this model was introduced, it was viewed by the global policing community as a hugely innovative development, underlining the fact that US police are perhaps not the monolithic force-based organization they're sometimes portrayed as being. It is considered to be a model of best practice and its principles have been adopted by a large number of police organiza-tions world-wide (Watson and Fulambarker 2012, Watson et al. 2014). The President's Task Force (2015) asserted that all officers should be trained in CIT practice, whilst the International Association of Chiefs of Police (IACP) stated that 20% of officers should be trained in this programme (Thomas and Watson 2017). This is all very laudable, but it does lead to questions about the effectiveness of this scheme in providing a service to citizens who are mentally unwell given that it is still a 'police response' model to what is very much a healthcare issue.

Research into this model has not produced clear-cut evidence to sug-gest that it is effective (Watson and Fulambarker 2012). That said, there is evidence to suggest it improves officer knowledge and diagnostic capacity when responding to people who are mentally unwell; that it reduces the use of force and arrest; and minimizes the risk of injury to officers and citizens (Wells and Schafer 2006, Morabito et al. 2012, Watson et al. 2014). There is, though, uncertainty over what CIT means in practice as it has been used as a catch-all term, as can be seen from the pronouncements of the PTF and IACP. The Memphis model is generally adapted to the specific resources and needs of each PD rather than being adopted as a 'best practice model' (Hails and Borum 2003). Moreover, a significant number of PDs don't have agree-ments with local healthcare providers to enable effective diversion (Wells and Schafer 2006). Evidently, if the model is to work effectively as a diver-sion from the criminal justice system, it needs to be able to divert people somewhere.

These developments put into context the current drive towards defunding PDs and redistributing funds to other service providers, in this case mental health service providers. It also underlines calls at the time of writing to use social workers in tandem with officers on response calls as a way of provid-ing a care-based rather than a force-based service. CITs are not a panacea for dealing with mental health crises—they still represent a law enforcement response to healthcare issues. From my research, bereaved relatives were sup-portive of the model, largely on the basis that some improvement in provision was better than none, and it did seem to improve perceptions of policing. The arbitrary nature of CIT provision can be seen in Kayla's death—when she was visited by the Berkeley Mobile Crisis Team on a welfare check there was a cordial interaction between her and the officers. But the PD only provides this cover for part of the day, and the next response was from patrol officers with fatal consequences—same place, same day, just a different time. In another city the CIT cover might have been 24 hours, in yet another there might have been no cover at all.

Clearly there is both thinking and action evident in police responses to peo-ple who are mentally unwell; there are progressive initiatives; and—broadly stated—a desire to provide a more thoughtful response to citizens who are mentally impaired. However, at the same time, as we've seen earlier in the book, this is occurring during a period where policing is considered to have become increasingly paramilitarized. We can see similarities here with the discussion in the previous chapter about how community policing is promoted at the same time as policing which is perceived to be increasingly aggressive and invasive. The essential paradox of police as force or service, warriors or guardians manifests itself in many different ways, and the way in which mental ill health intersects with other issues—particularly in relation to minority groups—perhaps emphasises the paradox even further.

POLICING VULNERABILITIES

A powerful combination of factors comes into play here with regards to how people with mental ill health are represented. A group of people who are manifestly unwell, but without exhibiting obvious physical symptoms; who might also have substance dependency issues; who might also be People of Color; and who might also be of nonbinary gender. It would be difficult to construct a societal grouping that could be more 'other' than the dominant majority. When one of the officers referred to Kayla Moore as 'it'—was it in reference to her Color, her gender, her mental impairment, or all three? The way in which people who die after contact with police are constructed often determines whether the public has sympathy with them (see Hirschfield and Simon 2010). And this largely depends on how much the public can identify with them, for which read: how much it *wants* to identify with them.

Intersectionality can loom large in such cases—firstly, it can amplify the racial aspect of police-related deaths. If Black citizens are disproportionately more likely to be killed than White citizens, and people with mental ill health are more likely to die than those who aren't mentally unwell, then clearly someone who is Black and mentally impaired is even more disadvantaged. Second, intersectionality is often manifest as an overlap between health and substance dependencies—there is a strong link between mental ill health and dependence on alcohol, licit or illicit drugs, or both (Pollack and Humphreys 2020). Third, there is a strong link between those issues and homelessness (see, for example Wood et al. 2011). All of these issues reflect two significant findings noted already in this book. First, police are more likely to focus on marginalised groups in society—and if you have a series of overlapping vulnerabilities, then you're even more likely to be focused on. Second, that police are more likely to use their discretion to use force on you, largely for those same reasons. The dominant majority do not want to be troubled by the mentally unwell or homeless when going about their daily business.

Spitzer (1975) refers to the requirements for officers to police 'social junk' and 'social dynamite.' The former is considered to be the bottom of the pile in society—the misfits and 'never-to-fits.' They will always be there, and they'll always need to be managed, so we need someone to take care of the 'junk.'

CONSTRUCTING THE DECEASED

Police culture acknowledges this: the dirty work, the stuff society doesn't want (or care) to take care of (Marenin 2016, Young 1991, Spitzer 1975). A lexicon exists to describe officers' views on what this work is and how it reflects society's disinterest in its own 'junk' and 'dynamite.' At the root of this is a tacit understanding that police are therefore granted a good deal of latitude in dealing with such groups, largely because of societal disapproval or disinterest in them. The labelling of citizens who die after police contact as drug addicted, homeless, drunk, mentally unwell, or felons provides society with a quick headline that they're police property anyway, and therefore police can pretty much do what they think best with them (see Young 1991). As the use of bodily metaphors in the previous chapter illustrated, police culture has an inbuilt system of morality (see Crank 2016). In this sense, 'junk' represents the 'dregs of society' (Young 1991: 157). Echoing Rick William's comments in chapter one about his folk being perceived as a 'waste of tax money'; Sherene Razack (2015: 9) notes that in Canada: 'Indigenous people who die in custody are the detritus of modern society.'

Spitzer's (1975) 'dynamite' refers to unstable groups, those who might explode without warning and should therefore be dealt with accordingly. The criminal justice system perpetuates these constructions, with investigations into police-related deaths tending to emphasize the atavistic behaviour of the deceased, rather than the actions or omissions of officers in relation to the citizen's death (Razack 2015, Baker 2016). The mentally unwell particularly fit this description. In these narratives, the intervention of police is seen as being caused by the actions or behavior of the deceased. The intervention can further be deemed necessary by a member of the public calling 911 and reporting such behavior—consider this discussion in relation to Kayla's death. In combination, these factors are seen as necessitating police intervention and thus enable a narrative to be constructed that portrays their intervention as rational, proportionate and considered (Baker 2019a).

The construction of the deceased as someone who conveniently fits one, or any combination of these categories is a precondition to constructing a narrative that neatly explains their death (Hirschfield and Simon 2010, Razack 2015, Baker 2016 and 2019a). Police are keen to portray lethal encounters as unfortunate, but unavoidable, because society and/or officers had to be protected from that person. In order for that necessity to be justified, police are able to sketch a wide range of characters and behaviors onto their canvas in order to paint a picture based on the context in which the death occurred. In the case of social junk, it might be needing to bring order to chaos, or bring hygiene where there is filth. In the case of social dynamite, it might be to create safety from danger, or to use harm in order to prevent further harm. Whatever is the case, it is first necessary to portray the deceased as the *creator of the problem*. For if there were no problem, police would not have needed to intervene.

From this starting point, police are able to fix the frame of the encounter firmly on the victim as being a necessary recipient of their contact. This could be because they're portrayed as being dangerous, violent, unpredictable or resistant, or any combination of these factors. In order to apply shorthand, they can then fix appropriate labels that dovetail with those portrayals: Black males with 'superhuman strength'; the 'drunk Indian'; the addicted; the mentally impaired; the homeless; the nonhetero. Here is society's junk and dynamite, police property, waiting to be dealt with because 'they musta done somethin.' If these citizens can also be portrayed as criminals or armed—it doesn't matter if that's a 'criminal offense' for selling loose cigarettes, or 'armed' with a 3-inch whittling knife, then that will enhance the power of the headline. Police know the value of establishing the first version of the lethal encounter as quickly as possible in the media to ensure as many labels stick as possible. Even if they don't all stick, they create doubt and uncertainty about the causes of death. Police the world over are acutely conscious of how their role is perceived and are well versed in managing how that perception is constructed to ensure maximum legitimacy (Manning 2010, Mawby 2002).

LEGITIMATION STRATEGIES

Police also know that they will never enjoy the legitimacy of the vast majority of the population. Their goal is to ensure they have enough of the population onside, enough of the time, in enough of the cases. Writing more broadly about policing and legitimacy, Terpstra and Trommel (2009) use a concept called 'pragmatic legitimacy' which can help us understand this. It's the idea that a sizable enough majority of the public grants police legitimacy on the basis that on the balance of probabilities, the police do enough to warrant it, and ultimately, it doesn't affect them personally. This is how the dominant majority in society largely get left in peace while minorities receive the focus of police attention. Whilst periodic scandals erupt, they're not frequent enough to disturb the equilibrium. Although groups within the dominant majority might be discomfited by the events they see on their screens, it still tends not to personally affect them. Broadly speaking, this is what Fyfe (1986) argues enables the split-second syndrome to be so persuasive.

A further strategy that appears to be used is a sort of symbolic appeasement that acknowledges the ferocity of protesting and anger—a sop to throw to the angry masses that has been used by powerful elites since time began, to placate the masses for long enough to feel that something has been done to recognise their discontent. Then time passes, and things carry on as before with the essential structures and systems unchanged. In this portrayal, an officer can be hung out to dry as a scapegoat—an aberration, a bad apple—so long as it ensures the system that produced that supposed aberration is preserved. It would not necessarily be a surprise if the officer who killed George Floyd were to be convicted and sent to prison. Whilst this would provide a degree of accountability and justice, it by no means indicates that the systems and structures that produced this violence are being addressed. But it does mean that the protests and anger subside somewhat, whilst something, somewhere else in the news cycle, will distract society's attention once again.

If we consider some of the points made so far in the book, we have a catalogue of questions about Kayla Moore's death. Why were police called to her home and not healthcare professionals? Once they were called, why did they decide to enforce a warrant despite the fact that's not what they were called to do? How can it be that an agency, supposedly characterized by intelligence and data makes such basic mistakes in interpreting which person the warrant was intended for? Why did they decide to escalate what became a tense situation? Why did they then decide to call for backup? An obvious question James Fyfe would have asked is: what would have happened if those officers had done nothing at all? Kayla Moore would still be alive. No one would have been harmed, and no criminals would be at large.

If the dominant majority start picking those questions apart, then significant aspects of how they view wider society might start to unravel, so it's easier to consider Kayla as neatly fitting the definition of 'police property.' In this sense, pragmatic legitimacy means pragmatic for the person from the dominant majority. Yes, that death was unfortunate, a 'tragedy,' but that sort of thing doesn't happen to me or people like me. Therefore, in my own best interests, I'm going to put it away in a locked mental compartment and think about something less troubling. That is the nature of this issue: not enough people ask enough questions often enough, and the police know this. They know that managing the narrative of lethal events is key to ensuring pragmatic legitimacy. There have been enough cases where video footage has disappeared and questions go unanswered to tell us that it's not just about the narrative that police promote, but about the one they intentionally withhold.

Another manifestation of this is that physical or mental conditions are often used as a way of justifying actions in retrospect. This occurs by presenting such conditions as being causal in the citizen's death. A common example of this in the UK is to state that the deceased had an underlying heart condition and that this was partly causal in their demise. When that coincides with four officers restraining you for six minutes while you're pinned face-down with a combined weight of 750 pounds on top of you, then the causality seems much less plausible—as was the case in the death of Sean Rigg in London in 2008 (Baker 2016). Sherene Razack's (2015) book 'Dying From Improvement' about the deaths of indigenous citizens after contact with police in Canada examines the case of Paul Alphonse. She notes that at his inquest, his alcohol dependency and pneumonia were discussed at length, whereas the large purple boot print in his chest put there by an officer that resulted in five broken ribs received scant attention.

In the US, LAPD Chief Daryl Gates claimed that Black men were more susceptible to dying from choke holds due to genetic problems with their arteries (Butler 2017: 3). In the UK and US for many years it was authoritatively asserted that Black men were more likely to die in custodial situations due to sickle-cell anaemia, claims which have since been disproved (Dyson and Boswell 2006). Such claims are reductionist explanations that underline the social construction of race by pointing to supposed biological differences between social groups. All of these issues provide legitimation strategies and conveniently distract societal attention from the structural and systemic issues that might have led to the death. We look first to the deceased and who they are, what they did, and how they could have avoided this tragic situation, rather than examining who the officers were, what they did, and how they could have avoided this tragic situation. This is no mere idle speculation. Plenty of research tells us officers are disproportionately more likely than other professions to overuse prescription opiates, indulge in risky behaviour, abuse alcohol, and work whilst knowingly mentally impaired (see Bishop and Paquette Boots 2014, Crank 2016). This unerring focus on the deceased, and their underlying health issues leads us to the constructed condition par excellence—excited delirium (ED).

EXCITED DELIRIUM

This condition is seen to principally affect a specific group of people. Typically citizens of Color, who are often mentally impaired, and/or affected by either alcohol or opiate drugs, or both. An almost perfect storm of intersectionality waiting to break: police property exemplified, waiting to be dealt with and taken care of. Individuals said to be exhibiting signs of ED can present paranoid symptoms, be extremely agitated, strip off their clothes for no apparent reason, have increased endurance, lowered pain thresholds, and an increased propensity to sudden violence (see for example Wetli 2006, Samuel et al. 2009). Given this description, one can imagine how officers responding to such an individual could be anxious and alarmed about what they might encounter upon their arrival to a 911 call (Baker 2018).

Brodeur (2010: 286) calls ED a 'convenient illness' because citizens afflicted with it tend to die after contact with police, but otherwise it typically seems to be a nonfatal condition. Deaths in these cases only occur when police have used force. Brodeur's point is made with tragic, bone dry irony. Strangely, citizens with ED who don't have force used on them tend to remain alive. There is good reason for his scepticism. The medical community profoundly disagrees about whether ED actually exists. It is not recognised by the American Medical Association or the World Health Organization (Wozniak, 2016, Samuel *et al.* 2009). It is, however, recognised by the American National Association of Medical Examiners and the American College of Emergency Physicians (Hall *et al.* 2013, Storey, 2012, Vilke et al. 2012). This disagreement extends to other parts of the world—in Australia it goes unrecognised. In the UK it was used as a death classification in some police-related deaths (Baker 2016 and 2018). However, it was not recognised by the Department of Health as a medical condition, and a major review into deaths in custody forbade its use as an official cause of death due to its uncertain aetiology (Angiolini 2017).

This view is reflected in some of the Canadian literature on ED (see for example Brodeur 2010, Razack 2015, Anaïs 2014). The latter states that ED is a 'made up' condition that conveniently muddies the waters in police deaths and distracts attention from other causes of death by playing the ace card in death investigation: medico-scientific evidence. This is seen to possess a veracity that other types of evidence might not (Wozniak 2016). Storey (2012) and Anaïs (2014) note that the condition has similarities with Sudden Infant Death Syndrome—once used as a causal factor in deaths of babies but now viewed with scepticism by medical and legal professionals. On the other hand, similar terms existed before ED: 'acute behavioural disorder' (ABD) and 'extreme behavioural disorder' (EBD) were both used in death certification in the UK (Baker 2016). I've recently heard the term 'cocaine induced paranoia' being used in inquests into police-related deaths in England, which sounds remarkably similar to the now banned ED. It seems that the words we use might change, but the urge to pin labels and ascribe conditions persists.

The evident doubt over whether ED exists as a medico-scientific condition that can be used as a causal factor in deaths after police contact might be less relevant than acknowledging that something like a 'constellation of symptoms' exists that police should be cognizant of when approaching people who are exhibiting certain types of behavior (Baker 2018). The great majority of literature on ED notes that people exhibiting it represent a 'medical emergency' and should be approached using processes involving deescalation and clinical knowledge (Storey 2012, Hall et al. 2013, Vilke et al. 2012). In this sense, if police were able to use this knowledge as a diagnostic tool, they might be better placed to follow CIT principles to find medical solutions to what is, after all, a healthcare crisis. If ED could be used as term to better educate police about how to deal with citizens experiencing crises rather than as a way of explaining a citizen's cause of death after contact with the police, then the label might be less problematic.

ATTEMPTS TO RESTORE TRUST IN
MARGINALISED COMMUNITIES

As has been established, police are not a monolithic entity, any more than the 'Black community' is, for example. To some degree they have to respond to concerns about their performance in order to maintain their legitimacy. In addition to this there are—and have been—visionary police chiefs and PDs that approach issues in different ways based on alternate principles (see, for example Balko 2014, Crank 2016). This led to groundbreaking initiatives such as CITs. These weren't imposed from above, the Memphis PD took the initiative to introduce CITs based on a perceived need garnered from experience in practice. In the previous chapter, community policing and implicit bias training were examined as ways of policing organizations attempting to respond to and improve their poor relationships with communities of Color.

We may be sceptical about why these programs were introduced, and wary of proclaiming them as successes. We may also believe that these programs are window dressing, a façade that improves perceptions of policing while enabling the practical reality of policing to proceed largely unchanged. But that does not invalidate the fact that police demonstrably attempt to respond to community concerns. Further chapters will examine the use of body-worn cameras (BWCs) and Citizen Review Boards (CRBs) as ways of attempting to enhance transparency and accountability in police-related deaths. For now, we turn to procedural justice as a way of trying to understand how police have responded to concerns that their disproportionate focus on marginalised groups in society leads to a breakdown in relationships with those groups.

Procedural justice emerged as a key principle in the 21st century in attempts to restore legitimacy in policing and rebuild societal trust, both of which are perceived to have been damaged, or broken down, particularly with marginalised groups in society (Gau et al. 2012). It focuses largely on how society perceives police do their job, essentially whether justice *is seen to be done*. The mechanics of procedural justice revolve around the perceived fairness of procedures used by police (Tyler and Huo 2002). It comprises four key tenets of police behavior towards citizens. Officers are expected to demonstrate: dignity and respect; trustworthy motives; neutrality; and participation. When police are perceived to treat citizens with respect; demonstrate trustworthiness by showing care and concern for the wellbeing and quality of life of citizens or society in general; are unbiased in their decision-making; and allow citizens a voice in decision-making processes, then they are more likely to be seen as acting in a procedurally just manner (Schulhofer et al. 2011). As such, procedural justice is viewed as being fundamental in shaping societal perceptions of police legitimacy (Jackson et al. 2012).

Research typically demonstrates that a procedurally just approach to policing is more important in shaping public perceptions of the police than instrumental concerns such as police performance and outcomes (Murphy et al. 2017). This is partly because police don't always have control over the outcomes of their encounters with citizens, but they do remain—in principle, at least—in control of maintaining fair treatment of those they interact with (Tyler 2004). In this sense, a citizen who has had an encounter with officers might not be happy with the outcome of it, but despite that might still feel they were treated fairly and with dignity.

Given all of this, procedural justice is closely linked to feelings of identity, inclusion, trust and feelings of self-worth. It can confirm a citizen's status, reaffirm a sense of community identity and encourage allegiance to authority (Sargeant et al. 2014). The converse of this is that if the treatment citizens receive from police is perceived to be disrespectful, that can produce negative consequences for an individual's self-worth but also for their belief in the rule of law (Jackson et al. 2012). Ultimately, police treatment of citizens in a procedurally just manner encompasses many benefits such as enhancing trust, cooperation and compliance—but does not come without limitations. A major issue relating to the concept of procedural justice is subjectivity surrounding judgements about the fairness of police procedures and treatment towards individuals. What police believe to be fair may not be subjectively perceived that way by others (Dai et al. 2011). Moreover, citizen interpretations of their experiences with the police can be subject to the influence of previously held attitudes (Piquero et al. 2004, Worden and McLean 2017). Procedural justice is not a short-term 'fix.'

All of this translated into policy in the aftermath of the Ferguson uprising. The President's Task Force (2015) unequivocally asserted that the principles of procedural justice should be adopted by PDs, largely on the basis of the discussion above. Interestingly, it also promoted these principles because it believed officers would be more positive and engaged working in PDs where there were clear principles and policies underpinning their work. Theory, principles and policies are not practice, they aspire to influence practice. Undoubtedly there are PDs embracing and pursuing these ideals, and officers within PDs also doing so, despite not being overtly told to. But it would be misguided to believe this program has been wholeheartedly embraced by police organizations in the US. Not just because of the scale of police kill- ings; not just because of the militarized responses to protests and uprisings in the aftermath of such killings; but also because of continuing routine activities like stop and frisk that serve to underline the dominant/subservient nature of police/citizen relationships for so many marginalised communities in America.

Similar to the previous chapter then, we find that on the one hand police are asked to pursue an aspirational program focused on winning hearts and minds, whilst on the other hand simultaneously being told to pursue two 'wars' on domestic soil and exhorted to use overwhelming displays of force on unarmed protesters. The outcomes of decades of police practice aren't eas- ily forgotten. When one considers the tens of thousands of dead, the hundreds of thousands who have been on the receiving end of police violence, and the millions affected by stop and frisk practices, one is bound to ask what the longer-term effects of these practices are on citizens and society—something which is examined in more detail in chapter six. But the real question is: why do the police get all of these jobs, by default—why are they charged with dealing with the 'social junk' and 'social dynamite'? As a society, why do we think this is the right thing to do—to expect police to be experts in social welfare, mental health, homelessness, drug addiction, counselling, and all the rest? Is it because we really don't care enough to provide alternative services, or are so apathetic we don't care as long as it's not us or ours? For Alex Vitale (2017: 27) it is fundamentally a political problem because elected officials have converted social problems into police problems, partly driven by policies such as broken windows.

Radley Balko (2014) views it in a similar light when considering the increasingly paramilitarized nature of policing. That politicians and policy makers drove the War on Drugs rhetoric and enabled funding and protocols for police that encouraged them to become more aggressive and also more militarized. I don't necessarily disagree with either of those authors, but I would take one step back from politicians and consider the people who elect them: us. Police are a reflection of the political will, or apathy in society. As has been established in the first four chapters, they reflect the views, norms and values of the dominant majority in society. As first responders, they are duty bound to react to 911 calls. We all know plenty of examples where police have been called to Citizens of Color out walking their dog, going for a run, watching birds in a public park, or simply sitting with friends in a café. The initiators of those contacts are the people that call 911. I am not excusing the police from their actions on all occasions, but if they hadn't been called by concerned members of the public there would have been no contact, and consequently no opportunity for escalation. At that point, it's the Citizen of Color who has to account for themselves, not the concerned citizen who called 911 on someone acting in an entirely peaceable and legal way. The narrative that underpins 'they musta done somethin' sells, because enough of society wants to believe that is what happened. But there are increasingly occasions where this isn't the case in police-related deaths, and attempts are made to hold police to account for their actions. The following two chapters consider the processes that aim to facilitate this, and evaluate their effectiveness.

Chapter 4

Move On, Nothing to See Here

Daniel Ficker

Daniel Ficker had two children aged five and seven with his fiancé of nine years. He was a White male aged 27 and lived in Parma (OH). His mom—Bernie Rolen—described him as a very loving, family person who worked hard to provide for his family. He'd worked in the same job for nine years and was outgoing: 'the type of person who'd do anything for anybody.' On the evening of 3rd July 2011, he returned home with his fiancé to find Officer Matthew Craska and an off-duty officer (David Mindek) waiting for him in a police cruiser. Both were outside their area of jurisdiction. Neither were officers in the City of Parma PD, but from nearby Cleveland—they therefore had no legal power of arrest, and no search warrant. Daniel and his family had been at a party thrown by Mindek's wife, which they left at about 6pm. Bernie told me that Mindek's wife believed some of her jewellery had been stolen, and suspected Daniel as the thief. Mindek accused Daniel of stealing the jewellery, Daniel denied it, and Craska attempted to detain Daniel and force him into the cruiser. He resisted the detention and Craska began to physically beat Daniel, who shouted for neighbors to call local police to intervene—without success. Craska and Daniel grappled in the front garden and in the ensuing struggle Craska initially fired a TASER at Daniel before fatally shooting him, using his service weapon. Daniel was pronounced dead on Independence Day, 2011.

In the aftermath of the shooting, Bernie was informed of the incident by her daughter whose friend had witnessed some of what had happened. She rushed to the hospital but wasn't allowed to see Daniel. At that stage police told her that Daniel was going to make it, but didn't tell her that an officer had shot her son. Daniel passed away in hospital hours later; emergency surgery couldn't save his life. Bernie initially trusted the investigating officers who reassured her they'd do everything they could to get to the bottom of how her son had been fatally shot. One of them said they'd investigate it as though it was 'my own son.' Those feelings began to change after she consulted with her family. In retrospect she realizes she made a good decision early on in engaging a lawyer to pursue justice for her son. Whilst her instincts were to trust the police, she increasingly began to think that they might be a 'band of blue brothers' who stuck together and protected each other.

Bernie genuinely believed Craska would be arrested, tried and sent to prison for what he'd done. After months without hearing anything about the investigation, she decided to take direct action, but didn't know how to go about it. She contacted an advocacy group called Black on Black in Cleveland who gave her practical advice on the 'do's and don'ts' of protesting, and also turned up to lend a hand for the initial demonstrations. After a month of protesting, both officers were taken before a grand jury—Craska's case was no billed, but Mindek was charged with dereliction of duty for failing to help Craska subdue Daniel. That case was dismissed when it went to court some months later.

It emerged that the two officers involved were put on administrative leave during the investigation into Daniel's death. Once the investigation was complete, the shooting was deemed to be 'justified,' and the officers returned to work. Bernie told me: 'What boggles my mind is that everybody knows they were wrong and yet they are free.' Bernie says that a lot of her awakening came from talking to Black citizens about their experiences with police and other organizations, that she was previously: 'oblivious to all this stuff, because I mean racism is alive and well, I see it now, or I notice it now, I should say.' She started to attend protests organised for Black citizens who died in police-related incidents and noticed that she was sometimes the only White person at the protest.

For her, the fight for justice is the same whoever you are if your loved one has been killed by police. She tried everything she could to get justice after the legal process failed, but there was no explanation offered by the PD or apology for what had been done, and the individuals involved were still working as officers. She told me that the chief of police refused to meet with her, as did the mayor. Nobody responded to her letters or emails demanding answers about what had happened and why Craska and Mindek were still employed as police officers. Eventually, at a public meeting she was able to grab a microphone and shame the police chief and mayor in front of TV cameras, and from that point on things began to move.

A second internal investigation was begun over three years after Daniel's death, and recommended that both officers be fired because of the litany of errors they made. Before that could happen, both officers apparently took retirement on the grounds of disabilities. There was to be no prosecution and no disciplinary action for either officer. Still searching for answers, Bernie took her concerns to the DOJ and in part this led to a consent decree being implemented on Cleveland PD in May 2015, but the DOJ are not able to open individual cases into police-related deaths.

In the aftermath of Daniel's killing, Bernie sometimes saw Officer Mindek on patrol—she worked near his beat area, and twice happened to be eating in the same restaurant as him. She found out that Craska was a military veteran of the Iraq war, and wonders whether this had some bearing on his actions and fitness to be a police officer. The subsequent police investigation into the jewellery Daniel was alleged to have stolen found no evidential trace of him in the room where it was stored, or on the box in which it lay. After nearly six years of fighting for justice, in January 2017 Daniel's family were granted a financial settlement of $2.25 million in a civil suit which would provide for his children's future. The PD tried to appeal the suit on three occasions before it was eventually concluded. Bernie told me that the civil suit wasn't about the money: 'It has never been about the money. I just want someone to say they were wrong, and they are guilty. I want them to pay the penalty for being guilty. I don't know that a civil suit is saying they are wrong and they are guilty—I mean how are they getting hurt from a civil suit?' Daniel was unarmed and at home when he was confronted by two officers working outside their jurisdiction, they had no warrant to search the house or arrest him, and one of them was off-duty. He was shot dead in his own garden and the two officers walked away without consequences. For Daniel's family, Independence Day will forever have a different meaning, it marks a time when their belief in truth, justice and accountability in the US altered.

Having spent the opening four chapters establishing how citizens come to meet their death in police-related incidents, this chapter turns to what happens in the aftermath of these deaths. Police are not mandated to kill citizens without consequence. The chapter examines how such deaths are investigated, and the mechanisms that come into play to uncover truths about the death. It also evaluates the usefulness of these mechanisms in holding police to account for the use of lethal force.

SETTING THE SCENE

When citizens are killed by other citizens, we expect police to arrive and attempt to bring the killer to justice. The homicide scene will be sealed off in order to preserve as much evidence as possible for use in the case. Specialist teams of forensic experts and homicide detectives will descend and determine a course of action to bring the killer to justice. Officers will be despatched to tell the deceased's next of kin the devastating news. They will be told that officers will use the full power of the law to bring the killer of their loved one to justice. Support will be offered to them by way of counselling services or other specialized services within the criminal justice system. Once the suspected killer has been apprehended, they will be taken into custody pending trial. We've all seen police procedurals, we know well enough how this works.

This does not occur when an officer has used lethal force on a citizen. The scene will not be secured. Specialist teams will not arrive. Usually, the next of kin will not be told face to face that a member of their family is dead, and if they are, they won't necessarily be told how they died. A common feature in my research was that relatives tended to be informed by third parties of the death. There will usually be no prosecution. There are no support services. Relatives will often be prevented from seeing their loved one's body until the coroner or medical examiner (ME) discharges it, and this may take weeks. The officer will go back to their station, they will change their clothes and go home. There has been a killing, and we know who the perpetrator is. But that doesn't mean there are immediate consequences, nor does it mean there will be. From the very start, then, these cases are treated differently to other cases of avoidable death. As one father in my research put it: 'Normally, when your loved one is killed you have the police helping you solve it, we had the police working against us because it was the police that did this.'

The number of prosecutions of officers in PRDs is minimal. Between 2005 and 2017, 82 officers were charged as a result of using lethal force and 29 were convicted, usually for a lesser charge such as involuntary manslaughter (Stinson 2017a and 2017b). It's already been established that police-related deaths number just over 1000 per year, so that time period most likely accounts for the deaths of at least 13000 citizens. That means a prosecution rate of 0.006% and a conviction rate of 0.002%. We can't be sure how accurate either of those datasets are, but it's our best guess at this point in time given the absence of accurate federal data on these issues. Undoubtedly, the public perception is that officers are prosecuted infrequently in police-related deaths (see Zimring 2017, Dunham and Petersen 2017, Katz 2015). This lack of transparency and basic information is a constant when one examines issues of justice and accountability in these cases, as this chapter will further demonstrate.

TRANSPARENCY AND ACCOUNTABILITY

Transparency fosters trust and legitimacy in governmental organizations as it enables the public to see 'through the windows of an institution' (den Boer 1998: 105). Such openness endorses dialogue between authorities and the citizens they serve and acts as a tool for organizational accountability (Coglianese 2009, Contradie and Choenni 2014). Transparency is widely recognized as being a defining characteristic of institutional strength and healthy democratic governance (Albalate 2013, Bertot et al. 2010). It is a significant indicator in fostering the belief that police are operating in a manner that is fair, just and legitimate (Bradford, Jackson and Stanko 2009, Jackson and Bradford 2010). These principles link to those of procedural justice examined in the previous chapter. Bovens (2007) notes that the concept of accountability portrays an image of transparency which in turn conveys a perception of trustworthiness in institutions. Even in 2009, 80% of Americans wanted an increase in transparency and accountability in policing (Coglianese 2009). Unsurprisingly, then, in the aftermath of the Ferguson uprising, the President's Task Force (2015: 11) exhorted police leaders to 'establish a culture of transparency and accountability.' The simple fact that this needed to be overtly stated tells us something about how American policing has been perceived by the public for some considerable time, supporting Manning's (2010: 8) view that: '[Transparency] is a miraculous buzzword when applied to an organization whose root and foundation are secrecy, misdirection, dissembling and lying in the interest of order maintenance.'

Crank (2016: 286) notes that US police have: 'A historically abysmal record of accountability.' The wider context to this statement can be demonstrated by the remarkable number of scandals that have engulfed US policing within the last fifty years. In New York, major commissions were conducted into the NYPD in 1972 (Knapp) and 1993 (Mollen) that uncovered systemic corruption, the widespread use of indiscriminate violence and outright criminal activities (Punch 2009). In Los Angeles, the same story. The Christopher (1991) and Rampart (2000) commissions examined the LAPD's practices and found widespread racism and discriminatory practices, excessive use of force and, again, outright criminal activities. The Rampart investigation uncovered a: 'police corruption scandal of historic proportions, involving allegations not just of widespread perjury and corruption, but of routine evidence-planting, and incidents of attempted murder and the beating of suspects' (Rampart Independent Review Panel 2000: 1). All four commissions were instigated because of widespread concerns over police powers and activities in those cities. In both cases, the second commission was undertaken within 20 years of the first yet produced remarkably similar findings to its predecessor. One would struggle to find better examples to illustrate systemic malfeasance in two of the three largest PDs in the country. As far back as 1931, a commission set up to investigate corruption and endemic violence in the Chicago PD concluded that the entire force be disbanded and a new organization begun from scratch from a different headquarters (Skolnick and Fyfe 1993). Calls for changes in policing culture and practice have been persistent, vocal and have a long history in the US. We should not necessarily expect the shock waves that unfolded in the aftermath of the George Floyd killing to produce either widespread, rapid or significant change in American policing, as will be demonstrated in this and the following chapter.

Connected to these scandals is the frequency with which rioting and uprisings occur in the US. Policing scholars would contend that in, and of themselves, these represent repeated failures of policing—events where they have lost control and had to revert to military type hardware and tactics to restore order. The great majority of uprisings occur after police-related deaths and are often ignited by news that the officer is either not going to be indicted, or that the prosecution into their case has failed (Jones-Brown and Blount Hill 2020, Skolnick and Fyfe 1993, Russell 2000). Consequently, accountability and justice are seen to be absent and act as catalysts to the societal eruptions that follow. Whilst the societal perception is often that justice, transparency and accountability is lacking in these cases, the official line states that there are full investigations into these deaths—so why is there such a disparity between these two points of view?

DEATH INVESTIGATION 'SYSTEMS'

An oft-overlooked aspect of investigations into PRDs is the overly partial and apparently arbitrary system of death certification in the US. Consistent with many of the issues examined in this book, medico-legal death investigation is hugely inconsistent across the nation, with the National Institute of Medicine (NIM) openly stating that there is no 'system' of death investigation in the US (NIM 2003: 3). The role is either performed by Coroners or MEs, dependent on which county the death occurs in. The majority of counties use Coroners; these are typically elected officials with no medical qualifications, and often no requirement to possess any professional qualification (Jentzen 2009). Added to this, they're considered to be significantly underfunded and lacking the technical facilities required to conduct proper autopsies (NIM 2003). They are also widely perceived to lack independence, and there have been cases where the same individual is both coroner and sheriff in some counties.

All of this adds up to a tendency for the Coroner to cleave to the police version of how deaths occur, often by emphasising certain aspects of the deceased's health, or aspects of their toxicology report. Hence media reports tend to mention that cannabis was in their bloodstream, or that they had an underlying heart condition—as though those were causal reasons explaining their demise rather than being shot to death. After the death of George Floyd, for example, the initial autopsy report referenced underlying health conditions of hypertension and coronary artery disease, in addition to intoxicants in his bloodstream—comments made under the 'cloak of authoritative scientific rhetoric' (Crawford-Roberts et al. 2020). The previous chapter established how the deceased's character and behavior were constructed to create the impression that they had in some way caused their death, and the process of medico-legal death certification appears to further complement that narrative.

There has been long-standing concern about the effect this 'system' of death investigation has on the accuracy of mortality data in the US in general, but also specifically in relation to PRDs. Recent research estimates that slightly more than half of these deaths are classified incorrectly (Feldman et al. 2017). None of this sounds like best practice in the world's most advanced economy. It isn't ground-breaking to suggest that a failure to accurately count deaths is connected to a failure to accurately classify them. Nor is it a stretch to state that being unable to properly classify deaths more generally creates significant concerns related to public health and learning lessons that might prevent future deaths (Jentzen 2009). Do we *really* want to know? Is there, perhaps, something exceptionally American about the right to extinguish life rather than preserve it? The way in which police and local prosecutors investigate these deaths suggests that we have to seriously consider this question.

INVESTIGATIONS AND JUSTIFICATIONS

A lack of independent medical and police investigation characterizes PRDs. The great majority of cases are investigated by the same PD that employed the officer who fired the shots. That leads to the vast majority of these killings being officially recorded as 'justified,' something reflected in the findings of my research (see also Lowery 2017). For a shooting to be justified, one might imagine that there would be some sort of measurement criteria for the investigation process. One that assessed the evidence, used witness statements, and sought to gather all available video evidence from the scene. One might imagine that once this process was complete, the investigation would attempt to assess whether the use of lethal force was proportionate, necessary and appropriate to the context—for example, that the officer reasonably feared for their own life or the lives of others. Such instances might include the victim being aggressive, being armed, threatening the officer or others, or committing a criminal offense. We might imagine any of the issues laid out above, but the reality is we just don't know because of the opacity of the investigatory processes which Lowery (2017: 53) says operate under 'a unique cloak of darkness.' Public perception tends to be that transparency is lacking in these cases. The principles of procedural justice are notably absent in these types of investigations, underlining the view that principles don't equate to practice when it comes to law enforcement and the criminal justice system (Baker and Norris 2020).

Investigations into PRDs are notionally two stage affairs. The first is conducted by the PD and assesses if the officer involved committed a crime (Katz 2015). A report is produced and passed to a local prosecutor (usually the DA) to ascertain whether a crime has been committed and whether charges should be filed against the officer—this is the second stage of the process (Lara 2017). This system of internalized criminal investigation and evidence evaluation has been widely criticized for its inherent bias (Zimring 2017, Otu 2006). The investigations are commonly considered to be cut and paste affairs that rely on 'boilerplate' descriptions of events (Chemerinsky 2001: 316; see also Katz 2015, Jiao 2020). Family members in my research who'd heard audio recordings of interviews with the officers stated that interrogators often asked closed and leading questions, signaling to the officer 'what he is supposed to say in order to get off the hook.'

The DA and police have a symbiotic working relationship—they rely on each other to successfully prosecute cases on a daily basis—that is the operational nature of the criminal justice system. In a police-related death, if the DA indicts an officer, that could jeopardise this working relationship (Letitia 2014). One family member remarked to me that: 'The DA and the police are joined at the hip. The DA reviews the police investigation that they did on themselves and he has a 100% record finding that whatever the cops found was justified.' Unsurprisingly, then, prosecutors are perceived to be overly partial when assessing these cases (Jones-Brown and Blount Hill 2020, Green and Roiphe 2017). The lack of data, the lack of independent medical and police investigation, the conflict of interest between the PD and the DA, the lack of information given to families and the wider public, and the apparent secrecy cloaking all of these processes is a toxic mix that adds up to a widely held perception that there is little possibility of justice and accountability emerging from these processes (Katz 2015). An overriding concern is that police-related deaths are examples of summary justice, redolent of the bad old days in America when the sheriff acted as judge, jury and executioner (Gross 2016). It's difficult to read Daniel's story without concluding this, I think.

This system creates what Jacobi (2000: 781) terms a 'cycle of impunity,' effectively empowering officers to use lethal force, safe in the knowledge they're unlikely to face consequences for it. Research supports this view. Within a two-year period, 441 cases of police misconduct were identified in Chicago, but no officer was formally convicted for violating the law (Adeshina 2014). Greene's (2015: xii) research in New Orleans revealed that when the PD reviewed all discharges of weapons over a six-year period: '[They] did not find that a single officer shooting so much as violated departmental policy.' Investigations, yes. Meaningful outcomes, not necessarily. The fact that PDs and DAs do little to address such perceptions only serves to further reinforce them. If procedural justice is a way to build consensus and legitimacy with communities, then ignoring those concerns and operating in secret whilst consistently producing the same outcomes isn't going to do anything to assuage them.

The President's Task Force (2015: 2) states unequivocally that there should be: 'External and independent investigations of officer-involved shooting and other use of force situations and in-custody deaths.' As established in chapter one, the PTF largely sets out an academic text book approach to policing, which in principle is sound, but in reality does not reflect policing practice in the US. Moreover, it cannot directly affect practice due to the heterogeneous organization of PDs. It can assert what best practice might look like, so it does have *some* degree of influence. But on the ground, evidently this is not happening in any meaningful or widespread way—as was blindingly apparent in the aftermath of Daniel's killing. Consequently, practical change has been sought via a number of other channels that bypass the internal systems of investigation outlined above. Whilst police accountability has recently become a hot topic, there is a long history of American communities finding ways to hold their PD to account. This has produced a bricolage of accountability measures that mirror the heterogenous nature of policing in the US. (I use the term *bricolage* because it is defined as a construction made from whatever is to hand, and can also be conceived of as a process of structured improvizations. In no way could the mechanisms of accountability and regulation surveyed in this book be considered as a 'system.') If police reflect the society they serve, then regulators also appear to reflect the police they oversee.

CRIMINAL PROSECUTIONS

Whilst there is a very low rate of prosecution and conviction in these cases, it's worth noting that prosecutions do at least occur in the US. In the UK, often held up as a paragon of probity, accountability and consensual policing (see, for example Zimring 2017), the last known successful case of criminal prosecution in a police-related death was in 1971. Cases that *are* prosecuted in the US split into two categories. One occurs when the DA makes a direct decision to indict the officer. The other, when they present the case to a grand jury via a pretrial hearing, and the jury decides whether to indict the officer. The failure of prosecutors to persuade grand juries to indict officers is seen by a number of authors as another example of accountability being a façade in these cases (Gross 2016). If the DA fails to persuade a jury in pretrial to proceed with a case, they are effectively able to say publicly that they did their job but the jury declined to indict, conveniently shifting any blame away from themselves. Critics point to the way in which these cases are framed, with legal experts stating that juries would likely be amenable to indict were enough evidence presented for them to consider (Taylor Ross 2016). The implication being that DAs deliberately present minimal evidence, setting the case up to fail and leaving the jury with no choice but to decline the prosecution (Fairfax 2017).

As these cases are heard ex parte (effectively in secret) the family of the deceased and their legal team are unable to view the evidence beforehand or hear it being presented, and are consequently unable to protest the way in which the case is framed. The families I interviewed who went through this process largely felt it was a sham—a façade that provided a simulacrum of legitimacy for the justice system. If the case does go to trial, another impediment to successful prosecution is jury bias (see, for example Jones-Brown and Blount Hill 2020, Roiphe 2017). The failure to convict any officers in the Rodney King beating despite clear video footage is a good example of this and is reinforced by Vitale's (2017) observations about repeated examples of racial bias in juries.

These issues aside, there is also the law itself, which over time has increasingly taken the side of law enforcement in terms of interpretation and application, what McDonald Henning (2016: 274) terms 'the evolving tolerance of police mistakes.' One example of this is the doctrine of qualified immunity which affects how officers' actions are interpreted. Previously, it had been held that officers should know the laws under which they operate and adhere to that constitutional framework. It is now effectively interpreted as what officers might be reasonably expected to know. Meaning that if an officer conducts a traffic stop on unconstitutional grounds, they will not necessarily be held to account for it unless it can be proved they did not believe the stop to be unconstitutional (McDonald Henning 2016, Gross 2016). You read that right. This further encourages and enables the use of officer discretion and sends a clear signal that courts require a very high standard of proof to indict and convict officers. Another aspect of this is the standard officer tactic of the 'fear defense'—that despite whatever evidence to the contrary, the officer genuinely feared for their life (Baker and Fidalgo 2020). Skolnick and Fyfe (1993: 196) believe criminal cases are set up to fail from the get go because juries aren't criminal justice professionals and are easily 'hoodwinked,' which may be one of the reasons some cases go to court—to fail.

Marc Morial, the ex-mayor of New Orleans believed that to successfully convict police officers one required evidence *beyond all doubt*, it wasn't enough to have evidence beyond reasonable doubt (Greene 2015: 107). Fairfax (2017) examined 180 police-related deaths in Georgia between 2010 and 2015, all of whom were either unarmed or shot in the back. Prosecutors took 48 of those cases to a grand jury; only one was indicted, and the subsequent charge of manslaughter was dismissed by the judge. Houston PD shot dead 121 citizens between 2008 and 2012 resulting in zero indictments (Taylor Ross 2016). In New York, the NYPD terminated the lives of 179 humans in the ten years to 2015 resulting in only three indictments. I include these examples, because in the absence of accurate national data on these issues, this is what researchers are reduced to. I leave it to you, the reader, to conclude what this might say about policing, citizens, rights, values, democracy, law, transparency, politics and governance in the United States.

CIVIL SOLUTIONS

As has been established, the vast majority of PRDs are considered to be 'justified shootings.' Once this determination has been made, the door effectively closes on pursuing a criminal case. This leaves families with very limited options in terms of trying to pursue justice and accountability for their loved one. Their attorneys usually direct them towards civil claims. These effectively provide compensation, and a recognition that what occurred was on some level preventable. But settlements mean there is no admission of liability or wrongdoing, and also seal the case in perpetuity once they're signed. In a very real sense, the price of a human's life is calculated, if not their value. Not only is that price calculated, it is routinely budgeted for. Chicago paid out half a billion dollars to complainants against their PD over a ten-year period to 2015 (Coates 2015b). In the aftermath of Freddie Gray's death in Baltimore his family were paid $6.4M, what one resident called 'riot insurance' (Lamont Hill 2016: 84). In 2018, New York paid out $228M in settlements for cases of police malfeasance; in the same year, Chicago paid out $113M (Baker 2019b). Quite apart from anything else, police extinguishing the lives of citizens is a costly business.

The use of settlements also has a long history—presumably demonstrating their effectiveness in sweeping malpractice and lethal force under the carpet. Skolnick and Fyfe (1993: 194) state that between 1988 and 1991 a total of $65M was paid out by Los Angeles county to settle claims purely against excessive use of police force. Gaines and Kappeler (2014) note that 50% of police misconduct cases are settled out of court. Two thirds of families in my research project received settlement payments. All of those families would have preferred to see the officer who shot their loved one dead in court and answering questions in public, rather than receive a payment in private and be muzzled, as we saw in Daniel's case. But structural impediments stymied those desires for justice.

Settlements can effectively be seen as a way of governmental authorities enabling police misconduct by funding it, as neither the PD nor the officers pay (Rushin 2017a). They can also be viewed as an extension of the wider criminal justice system's fiscally driven processes that subvert due process in favor of financial calculations (Vitale 2017, Lamont Hill 2016, Alexander 2012). The costs of brutality are also ameliorated—financial settlements are typically cheaper than jury awards in these cases (Gaines and Kappeler 2014). It's notable that of the five financial awards considered so far in this book, the jury award for the killing of Nate H. Pickett II was far in excess of the other four out of court settlements combined. We could take this further and consider the lack of federal data on these payments, and what that says about justice, legality and rights. The twin constructs of due process and all citizens being equal before the law also crumble in the face of reality. Zimring (2017: 137) sums up this grim state of affairs: 'There is a major disconnection between the substantial impacts of killing by police in American urban life and its importance in dollars and cents of public budgets.' Reading these examples one is bound to ask: procedural justice?

LOCAL GOVERNMENTAL INTERVENTIONS

In the absence of legal redress leading to changes in police policies and practices, various states and cities have begun to enact their own legislation aimed at regulating policing. Wisconsin passed a law requiring any PRD to be investigated by an independent agency, Seattle and Sacramento have passed legislation to enable their PDs to more effectively discipline officers. Some states have independent investigative units. For example, the Office of Civil Rights and Public Trust in Delaware can investigate PRDs (Lara 2017).

State Attorneys General (AG) can notionally overrule a local prosecutor's decision and press ahead with criminal charges, albeit it is rare in police-related deaths (Lara 2017). States have also intervened by appointing what are effectively special prosecutors to be used specifically in these cases, as has occurred in Connecticut and Pennsylvania (Marcus, N. 2016). In the aftermath of Eric Garner's death, Governor Cuomo mandated the AG to oversee the investigation and potential prosecution of PRDs. Although Lara (2017) notes this was more likely an exercise designed to improve public perception and create a façade of legitimacy rather than be more effective in bringing officers to justice.

The most common method of providing independent oversight of police is through Civilian Review Boards (CRBs). The principle underpinning these boards is that police actions should be subject to review by citizens who are independent of the law enforcement community. This typically means that complaints made by citizens are examined by CRBs, although some boards possess powers to review policy or systemic practices. CRBs have existed for some time, initially being proposed in LA in 1928 (Rushin 2017b). It took until 1948 for the first to become operational in Washington DC and thereafter they became more common from the 1960s onwards in response to increased concerns over police brutality and rights abuses (Alpert et al. 2016). During this period there was notable push back by police unions, but CRBs were also often rejected by voters (Skolnick and Fyfe 1993), underlining the point made in the previous chapter about the lack of social will to promote change. On the one hand, it might be expected that unions would be against such oversight, but experience from Britain suggests quite the contrary. Reiner (1991) notes that senior police officers and unions welcomed such oversight, largely because they believed it would be less effective (and therefore more lenient on officers) than internal oversight bodies, but would make police appear to be more legitimate to society. A thoroughly depressing reflection of both country's police forces.

By 2015, there were estimated to be 152 boards in operation in the US (De Angelis et al. 2016a). Although this may seem to be a relatively low number given the number of PDs, Walker (2006) notes that the great majority of larger PDs have these oversight boards, meaning that a significant portion of the population resides in areas overseen by CRBs. The heterogenous nature of policing provision is not only mirrored by police regulation in general, but also specifically in relation to CRBs with a variety of models and practices employed across the US. The composition of boards vary in terms of how the members of the board are recruited, whether or not they are paid, and how many members make up the board (De Angelis et al. 2016b).

Criticisms of CRBs are numerous. Firstly, despite covering the larger PDs, there are in excess of 17,500 PDs that aren't subject to such oversight (Alpert et al. 2016). Second, their members are typically not experienced in investigative work, or police matters, so they lack both the technical knowledge and critical skills to oversee or investigate experienced law enforcement officers (Prenzler 2016b). Connected to this is a lack of training or national standards that promote best practice in oversight. The organization and practice of CRBs is wildly diverse—once again mirroring the police they oversee (Alpert et al. 2016). Third, Skolnick and Fyfe (1993) echo Reiner's observation about oversight appearing to be more independent and legitimate, but ultimately facing the same issues as juries—CRBs can also be partial, and they can be bamboozled—there is no guarantee they will ultimately be fairer, or neutral, or more critical of police than internal investigations—as was indeed the case in Kayla Moore's death. But they do appear to provide a cloak of respectability to the PD they notionally oversee. Finally, they are typically reactive rather than proactive—they depend on complaints being made, rather than actively investigating and overseeing police policies and practice (De Angelis et al. 2016a, Prenzler 2016a).

Alpert et al. (2016) note that CRBs are effectively a work in progress, and while they have manifold drawbacks, on balance they are an improvement on what came before them, i.e., nothing. This is not quite the view taken in Britain where a succession of police regulators over the previous forty years have been given more resources, more legal powers, and also gained more experience of their role, yet are still roundly criticised for the same issues they were in the 1980s (Baker 2016). The general consensus appears to be that it's better to have some oversight than none, and that this improves the societal perception of legitimacy in policing. Hardly a ringing endorsement, but such are the entrenched structures and systemic cultures manifest in policing. All of this has led to the outgrowth of other regulatory branches that attempt to pursue justice and accountability in cases where police use lethal force.

FEDERAL INTERVENTIONS

The persistent failure of so many PDs to reform despite obvious scandals from the 1980s onwards saw federal intervention become a reality with the 1994 Violent Crime Control and Law Enforcement Act (Vitale 2017). This act granted the DOJ powers to investigate systemic patterns and practices of policing within PDs (Jiao 2020, Taylor Ross 2016). Federal intervention provides one way to regulate the autonomy exercised by PDs (see Vitale 2017, Rushin 2017a). Rushin (2017a: 68) sums up this process as giving federal authorities the power to 'define what constitutes legitimate policing.' These interventions are termed 'consent decrees.' They mirror the principles of financial settlements considered earlier in this chapter. Federal authorities seek a negotiated solution with local authorities regarding the unconstitutional practices of the PD. It's notable, then, that these are not processes of enforcement. Law enforcement doesn't like having things enforced on it, it expects to be able to exercise a monopoly of enforcement over its sovereign domain.

The DOJ has a broad degree of discretion to intervene in specific PDs based on a wide range of criteria. That could include complaints from organizations such as the ACLU (as happened in Seattle after the killing of John T. Williams); a history of media headlines regarding specific PD activity; major scandals such as Rampart that initiated the LA consent decree; or whistle-blowers from inside the criminal justice system. It is unsurprising that a number of consent decrees have been instigated in the aftermath of high-profile PRDs, for example in New York (post Eric Garner), Baltimore (post Freddie Gray), and Ferguson (post Mike Brown) (Jiao 2020). Rushin (2017a) notes that it is not clear exactly which criteria are used in deciding how to intervene—ironic, given that wide ranging discretion without oversight also determines police power to intervene in citizens' lives. Less (or more) ironic are the complaints from PDs about supposedly devious federal practices and hidden biases when they are subject to these investigations—another example of enforcers resenting enforcement. Typically, the reasons for intervention appear to be based on reports of police brutality and discriminatory practices against minority populations (Vitale 2017). Federal interventions aim to produce long-term changes that reform the PD and reflect best practice in policing in the US (Jiao 2020).

The DOJ enters into a dialogue with the local government and PD. It negotiates a process of investigation that aims to discover what policies and practices the PD pursue with a view to assessing how they meet best practice in terms of policing, civil rights and legality. In this sense, one might argue that when acting in this capacity, the DOJ is the only agency capable of defining, evaluating and enforcing what is considered to be legitimate, consensual, best practice policing in the US. Once the PD's practice is assessed, the DOJ appointed monitor (usually a judge) sets out what police are expected to change, how they will go about doing that, over what period, and how the change will be measured in terms of its capacity to meet the DOJ's expectations (Rushin 2017a). This is the consent decree, which is usually fiercely negotiated over by both sides before it is signed. In New Orleans, even after it was signed, the chief of police tried to renege on it and appealed its implementation only to be overruled by a federal judge (Greene 2015). Once it is signed, the process of reform is monitored over a number of years before the settlement is determined to be complete and terminated. Rushin (2017a: 134) terms this a process of 'negotiated reform.' There are occasions when PDs have avoided consent decrees being imposed by preemptively adopting measures to correct their practices (Jiao 2020), inevitably leading one to ponder why those measures weren't simply introduced without the threat of federal intervention hovering over the PD.

Federal interventions are typically time consuming and costly (Butler 2017). It is not unusual for them to last five years, and in the case of Los Angeles and Detroit in excess of ten. The annual costs of pursuing consent decrees in LA and New Orleans ran to more than $2M, with the total cost for the former estimated to exceed $100M (Rushin 2017a: 53–55). The discretionary nature of consent decrees also mean that they are used with indeterminate frequency. In the 20 years following the first consent decree, the DOJ conducted 67 investigations into PDs across the US (Marcus, N. 2016). In the period between 2009 and 2016, there were fifteen consent decrees, but in the five years prior to 2009 there were none (Jiao 2020). Under President Trump, no consent decrees have been issued, with Attorney General Sessions overtly stating in November 2018 that it was not the responsibility of the federal government to manage nonfederal law enforcement agencies. Vitale (2017) notes that the apparently arbitrary nature of consent decrees means that the great majority of PDs need not worry about them. Even a successful intervention in the PD that borders yours does not mean it will have any effect on your PD.

There is little evaluation of the effectiveness of consent decrees, which seems remarkable given their cost and also the scope of the interventions. The limited evaluation that has occurred seems to suggest that they reduce instances of both police misconduct and the use of force (Jiao 2020). One obvious question is to consider how effective long-term change is after the decree is terminated. It might be the case that PDs revert to their old ways once oversight is removed, or that they change once the chief of police is replaced further down the line, as the turnover of chief officers in larger PDs tends to be relatively frequent. Consent decrees are coercive, and that often leads them to be viewed negatively by officers and unions as something that is imposed on them against their will (Jiao 2020). Not unlike police using their powers on citizens. Consent decrees can therefore be seen as a federal version of 'come along.'

EVALUATING THE BRICOLAGE OF REGULATORY MEASURES

Ultimately, we return to the running theme about lack of data. We just don't know enough about whether the measures surveyed in this chapter do or do not work. Skolnick and Fyfe (1993) point out that governmental research priorities have splashed cash on a variety of issues related to law enforcement and criminal justice but none, for example, on how effective CRBs are. This observation could be applied to any of the regulatory measures in the bricolage, once again underlining the low-level of importance ascribed to regulating police conduct. Whilst on one level settlements clearly seem abhorrent—the idea of calculating and budgeting for next year's police-related deaths appears obscene—they may have had unintendedly positive side effects. Once the public purse begins to hurt, politicians who are not necessarily predisposed to be concerned about minorities and rights can, on the other hand, get quite exercised about the fiscal implications of police brutality (Rappaport 2016). Skolnick and Fyfe (1993) believed that settlements drove a trend to the growing spread of PD use of force policies. They note such policies were often not adopted previously because they *were* a way of holding PDs to account, which is exactly *why* they were avoided—these policies are discussed in more detail in the following chapter.

There are some obvious issues that could be addressed in relation to the manifold failings in investigatory and accountability structures identified in this chapter. Because they're obvious, does not mean they will happen. Having an accurate count of the number of citizens killed by police each year is obvious, but it has not yet happened. The 'system' of death investigation requires better regulation and more uniform standards—both go hand in hand. That a significant number of deaths are classified incorrectly each year is a national scandal and should bring shame on the world's number one economic power. That PDs still largely investigate their own officers is an affront to modern conceptions of independence and accountability in the criminal justice system, and demonstrates a flagrant disregard for local communities who expect officers to be held accountable to the same laws as citizens. There should be an independent agency within each state that investigates PRDs and it should be headed by an independent prosecutor who is not entwined with local law enforcement officers, prosecutors and politicians.

In order to address the evident inability of bringing officers to justice in criminal courts, laws could be altered—or created—that specifically address officers' use of lethal force and establish measurable standards, such as not shooting citizens in the back, or if they are unarmed. The evidentiary bar could also be lowered in PRD cases. There is certainly an argument to be made that officers should be held to a higher standard than citizens, because they're trained professionals, but also because of the awesome powers they possess. The issue of civil solutions needs to be addressed because the use of financial settlements to sweep police brutality under the carpet is a stain on the national conscience. In order to have any degree of impact, financial settlements should be deducted from the PD's budget for the coming year. But there is also a case for spreading the cost directly across all officers in the PD so they each bear the financial impact when one of their brethren injudiciously exerts lethal force on a citizen. That might do something to loosen the 'blue code of silence.' Consideration should also be given to whether settlements being made against PDs could lead to further punishment from local governmental authorities in the form of fines for poor performance or malfeasance.

CRBs need more power and resources from local government and also need to be more standardized in terms of panel composition, policies and best practice. If the DOJ can enforce policy and best practice in policing via consent decrees, then it could also be encouraged to promote these across CRBs. The number of CRBs should also be increased. In an era where there is focus on defunding police, one obvious beneficiary could be organizations that oversee PDs. The criteria that initiate federal interventions need to be clarified and made more transparent—there should be a process that citizens or organizations can instigate if they want the DOJ to investigate their local PD. Likewise, PDs should be fully cognizant of the circumstances under which they might be subject to investigation to ensure that they are able to remain compliant with expected standards.

At their core, all of these suggestions have one thing in common: they aim to deter and prevent officers from using their weapon. Just as Fyfe wanted with his split second-syndrome, officers need to think a version of 'what would happen if I did nothing here?' Or 'what could happen to me if I fire my gun here?' It is not one, two or three things that need to change—a whole slew of change is required across a number of fronts. As has been demonstrated in this chapter, efforts at regulation have been piecemeal, and at best produced some sort of incremental changes in some PDs. Because of the lack of evaluation of the measures surveyed here, we don't really know the extent of any changes. If there was a more concerted attempt at evaluation, then the more useful and workable aspects of each mechanism could be adopted to build a more coherent and organized system of accountability that could then be monitored and evaluated moving forward. This chapter has largely considered retrospective attempts to produce justice and accountability in the aftermath of PRDs, the following chapter examines ways in which police might be better regulated to prevent these deaths occurring in the first place.

Chapter 5

Blue Codes and Bad Apples

Jonathen Santellana

Jonathen Santellana was a regular 17-year-old from a Hispanic background and was in his second year of high school in Houston. His dad, Joseph, says his son always had a 'big Kool-Aid smile' and was passionate about skateboarding from a young age. He was determined to be the best skater he could be, staying at the park from when it opened to when it closed. On 13th November 2013 he'd been into the Copperfield apartment block in Northwest Harris County to meet up with a friend, Steven Yarbrough, who lived in the building. He'd driven there with another friend, Kalee Marsteller, and she waited in the car for Jonathen to return. As Jonathen left the building, he caught the attention of Rey Garza, an off-duty cop working as a security guard in the apartment complex in which he lived. Within moments of Jonathen returning to his car he was shot dead by Garza.

According to Joseph, Garza's initial report stated that he'd seen Jonathen carrying something 'suspicious' to his car, possibly 'illegal drugs.' Garza went to his apartment and grabbed his personal handgun. He says he approached the vehicle displaying his badge, with his gun holstered, telling the occupants he was a police officer. He stated that Jonathen went to start his car at which point the off-duty officer opened the car door and reached in to the vehicle to confiscate the keys. Garza alleges that at this stage Jonathen reversed and pinned him against another vehicle. An expert reconstruction of the scene commissioned by the Santellana family demonstrated that this version of the event was 'not consistent with any factual evidence.'

Garza was a large, heavily built man. When he approached Jonathen's car, he was wearing grey shorts, sandals, and a sleeveless hooded tee-shirt, displaying his tattoos. Eyewitnesses say he brandished his gun and banged on Jonathen's window. At that moment, understandably, Kalee and Jonathen (both aged 17) were most likely fearful, believing he might have aggressive intentions. Kalee says he didn't tell them he was a police officer, and his appearance certainly didn't suggest it. The car engine had been running before Garza approached, so believing themselves to be in possible danger, Jonathen reversed. Garza immediately opened fire and shot Jonathen in the back and back of his head as he shielded Kalee from the gunfire.

At this point Jonathen lost control of the car and crashed into another vehicle, somehow ending up dead on the ground underneath that vehicle. It is not known whether he was thrown from the vehicle or left the car himself, badly injured. Seven shots were fired in total, with Kalee miraculously escaping unharmed. Steven Yarbrough attempted to film the scene in the immediate aftermath, but Garza approached and demanded he delete the footage. Kalee and another eye witness, Sheila Moreno, claimed that Garza neither displayed his badge nor explained that he was a cop as he approached Jonathen's car.

Garza testified that Jonathen did not threaten him, nor did he believe that he was a dangerous person, but that when he suddenly reversed the car he feared for his life, causing him to open fire for his own self-protection. A small amount of cannabis was recovered from Jonathen's car but neither he nor Kalee were armed. Jonathen's dad only found out about the incident from his daughter who had a connection with someone in the same building and called her. Joseph went straight to the building, understanding that Jonathen's car had been in an accident, but waited for three hours before receiving any information from the police in attendance. An initial investigation was conducted locally by the Navasota PD that employed Garza as an officer and called only Kalee as witness. Not only was Garza off-duty, he was outside his jurisdiction as he lived in Harris County.

The DA took Jonathen's case to a grand jury on three occasions but each time they declined to indict the officer. The grand jury proceedings were heard in private without the family present and on each occasion lasted just a few hours. The family's lawyer noted that in the history of Harris County it was unheard of for a grand jury to indict an officer. This was likely because judges legally used a partisan selection method for grand jurors that was different to juror appointments in civil and criminal cases. Jonathen's parents raised a civil case against Garza in 2015 on the basis that the Navasota PD failed to train officers in the 'appropriate use of force.'

In 2017 Garza appealed against being sued personally, claiming that he was discharging his duty as a police officer even though off-duty. The court found against Garza, stating that by acting outside his jurisdiction, and being employed on different contractual terms as a courtesy officer he was not acting as a police officer. The terms of employment for the job of courtesy officer at the apartment complex specifically prohibited the carrying and use of deadly weapons, and stated that he should 'act at the company's authority in the capacity of courtesy officer and not as an active/off-duty police officer.'

An appeal in 2019 at the Texas Supreme Court, in which Garza sought to overturn the 2017 case essentially aimed to ascertain whether a public servant such as a police officer is fulfilling their duty in that role, whenever and however those duties are carried out. Part of the case revolved around the distinction between being *allowed* to discharge duties when off duty and in an extraterritorial jurisdiction, and whether one *should* discharge duties in that situation. The judges apparently concluded that a licensed officer employed by a PD is working under a valid grant of authority irrelevant of where they are, what they are wearing and whether they show their ID badge. Or indeed whether they discharge those duties correctly or not. The law erred on the side of the officer despite apparently overwhelming evidence pointing to the extralegal use of lethal force.

Ultimately, after six years and multiple hearings, Garza walked free after fatally shooting an unarmed 17-year-old boy in the back whilst off duty and out of jurisdiction. He had been a police officer for only two years at the time of the killing and resigned from the police in September 2015. For Jonathen's mom, Roxana Harrison, her son's death is still very raw, and difficult to talk about. He was her baby, and she loved him dearly. His dad wonders what Jonathen would have done with his life. He wonders how good a skateboarder Jonathen could have become when his life was needlessly cut short. Joseph was emphatic in stating that he was 'not antipolice'—that one of his brothers is an officer, as are several friends. But he believes police shouldn't investigate themselves, and that officers are often too aggressive and should therefore be held to account for their actions if they use excessive force. And Garza? Joseph told me he joined another PD and is currently an officer in the Greater Houston area.

HISPANIC EXPERIENCES: 'JUAN CROW' AND 'DRIVING WHILE BROWN'

By this point in the book we've established that being part of a minority in the US makes you more likely to be the focus of police attention. Earlier chapters have covered the experiences of Native Americans and Black Americans in terms of how socioeconomic and sociopolitical structural factors affect their experiences of everything from housing, to health, education and jobs. That minority groups are also subject to disproportionate focus from police and criminal justice agencies is merely another manifestation of the structural inequalities that affect minorities in the US. Hispanic citizens represent the largest minority in the US, numbering about 57 million people, or 18% of the overall population (US Census Bureau 2020).

The experiences of Hispanic citizens are comparable to those of other minorities. Indeed, similar terms are used to describe those experiences. 'Juan Crow' is considered to be a set of principles akin to Jim Crow, whereby immigration statutes effectively circumscribe individuals' rights to live meaningful lives in US society. Vitale (2017) traces this back to the colonial policing tactics of Texas Rangers, echoing the historical antecedents of policing Black and Native American populations. The phrase 'Driving While Brown' refers to racial profiling that leads police to disproportionately target Hispanic drivers (Urbina and Alvarez 2018). Research on drivers in Iowa found police were four times more likely to stop Hispanic drivers than White (Muchetti 2005).

It is estimated that Hispanic males born in 2001 have a one in six likelihood of being incarcerated, compared to a one in seventeen chance for White males (Urbina and Alvarez 2017). Hispanic citizens are also significantly less likely to dial 911 than White citizens, partly because of fears of deportation, but also because of poor experiences based on previous contacts with officers (Gaines and Kappeler 2014). Skolnick's (1967) concept of the 'symbolic assailant' is also relevant, with a wide range of research and governmental reports noting the tendency of police to stereotype Hispanic males as problematic and potentially criminogenic (see, for example Urbina and Alvarez 2018, Vitale 2017, Gaines and Kappeler 2014, Rampart Independent Review Panel 2000, Christopher Commission 1991). Consequently, it's no surprise to learn that police are twice as likely to use force on Hispanic citizens than on White Americans (Gaines and Kappeler 2014).

The structural factors that affect minority outcomes mean that Native Americans, Black Americans and Hispanic Americans are disproportionately more likely to die after contact with the police than White Americans. We do not know to what extent Jonathen's race affected Garza's actions. But we do know that attempts to get justice for his death repeatedly ran into a brick wall, and that Jonathen's death is one among scores of Hispanic males killed by police in the US each year.

DISCRIMINATORY AND INDISCRIMINATE?

Most people reading this book will have seen video clips of officers shooting citizens dead in circumstances that appear to be disproportionate and unnecessary. Many will have read or heard of incidents where multiple police officers have fired scores of bullets at unarmed citizens, killing them outright. The fact that I don't need to even mention names and dates speaks to the ubiquity of these deaths. The lists go on. Once all of the lists start being compiled and analysed, one thing becomes clear—anyone at all can be killed by police in the US, irrespective of what their background or identity is. People of Color are undoubtedly disproportionately more likely to be killed by police than White people. Hundreds of White citizens are also killed by police every year at a less proportionate rate, but that makes little difference to them or the families and friends they leave behind. Young, old, able-bodied or not, mentally sound or mentally unwell, gay, straight, bisexual, male, female, trans, wealthy or not, homed or homeless—people from all of these groups are killed by police in the US every year. Police are both discriminatory and indiscriminate in deciding whose lives get terminated in America.

This book walks the line between showing these deaths as being part of systems and structures in the US and illustrating how those systems and patterns result in individual deaths. As a consequence, it considers what effects these deaths have on wider issues in the US in addition to considering the effects they have on the families and communities left behind in the aftermath of these deaths. It would be unfortunate, but understandable to think the events at Ferguson encapsulated all of the aspects related to deaths after police contact; or to believe that it represented a sea change in how this issue is perceived. One event, no matter how significant, cannot overturn decades of ingrained practices, cultures and systems that are embedded in the United States. The President's Task Force (2015) clearly set out its aspirations for a more guardian focused police service in the US, and had a clear wish list of how those aspirations might be realised. But, as we've seen throughout the previous five chapters, because it is a *wish* list—it cannot be applied in practice. So this chapter considers what sort of regulatory mechanisms are—and could be—applied in practice.

REGULATING DISCRETION: LOOKING FORWARD, LOOKING BACK

The measures discussed in the previous chapter typically focused on retrospective attempts to get justice after a PRD. Such actions function on a case-by-case basis in an attempt to hold individual officers to account. This is one of the reasons why they are largely ineffective, because they fail to consider the wider systems and practices that lead to more than a thousand citizens being killed every year by police. But also because trying to hold individual officers to account in legal settings is—as we saw in the previous chapter, and in Jonathen and Daniel's cases—fraught with complications. One argument says that if more officers were held to account in legal settings, this could act as a deterrent on the wider body of policing. That such actions might move from being purely retrospective interventions, to being a future oriented way of managing other officers' actions. The obvious outlier being the consent decree which considers both systemic patterns and processes in PDs but also looks at past events as a way of learning and informing future policies.

Police scholars have long identified two broad approaches determining how we can attempt to manage police activities. Accountability looks back at past events—it is retrospective; regulation looks forward in attempting to better manage future events—it is prospective. As methods of accountability generally fail in these cases (as indeed, they do in the rest of the English-speaking world of policing) the focus has shifted onto regulation. In particular, the regulation of discretion. The argument for regulation goes that rather than trying to hold officers to account for what they've done, it would be better to deter them from making poor decisions and thus prevent errors from occurring in the first place. Two initial policy reactions to the uprisings at Ferguson focused on the need for officers to wear body-worn cameras (BWCs) and the need for PDs to have clear use of force policies in place.

BODY-WORN CAMERAS

BWCs and use of force policies both attempt to provide transparency about officers' actions. They are both prospective measures, and one could be seen to complement the other. The real time use of BWCs aims to remind officers that whatever they do is being recorded and could potentially be used as evidence against them, and consequently aims to regulate their behavior. The principles of procedural justice come into play here as a way of minimising officer discretion and promoting what researchers term the 'civilizing effect' (see Gonzales and Cochran 2017: 309). If officers know they're being observed, they are more likely to overtly act in the role of a guardian, and some research suggests that citizens might also act with more civility knowing that they're on camera (Campeau 2015). BWCs are intended to produce greater accountability as a result of police practice being seen to be more transparent, which in turn promotes increased legitimacy (Gonzales and Cochran 2017, Nowacki and Willits 2018, President's Task Force 2015). Chan (1999) believed that accountability in policing was more a case of being able to *provide* an account of actions, than actually being held to account for them, and it seems likely that this applies to BWCs (Ariel et al. 2015). Cameras can only be as effective as the accountability mechanisms already in place. If they record malfeasance, it doesn't necessarily mean the PD will investigate it, or discipline/prosecute the officer (Vitale 2017, Pagliarella 2016). Laws, policies and tools that promote transparency and accountability can all be overcome or subverted by police cultural practices.

The case of Laquan McDonald in Chicago perfectly illustrates these observations in microcosm. Mr. McDonald was shot dead by Officer Jason Van

Dyke in 2014. The entire incident was recorded by dash mounted cameras and showed him firing 16 shots at Mr. McDonald within 6 seconds of leaving his cruiser. The local prosecutor initially found this to be a justified homicide as all the officers present corroborated Van Dyke's fabricated version of events. The city attempted to conceal the video footage by negotiating a $5M settlement with Mr. McDonald's family—making it a condition of the settlement that the footage could not be released. It was eventually released after 13 months when a judge overruled the terms of the settlement. During this time, it emerged that Van Dyke had previously been the subject of 20 complaints from citizens, one of which led to a settlement of $350,000 being awarded to a complainant (Zimring 2017). In 2019 he was convicted of second-degree murder and sent to prison for 6 years, 9 months.

In this one case we have many of the salient issues regarding transparency, accountability and justice in PRDs. There is damning evidence, but the police attempt to hide it, using the tried and trusted method of paying off the family. The settlement is subjected to legal challenge, and *five years later* the officer finally faces justice. The same evidence that produced a justified homicide verdict also led to a conviction for second-degree murder. As long as police own the video evidence, they can restrict access to it. And we have seen plenty of cases where evidence has disappeared, or officers have turned off their cameras prior to opening fire on citizens (Zamoff 2019). In New Orleans, DOJ analysis of the PD's use of BWCs found that 60% of the time no video was recorded or preserved (Greene 2015: 190). The aftermath of the Laquan McDonald case is also salutary. Once the film entered the public domain, the DA knew the public would be able to make their own evaluation of the evidence, and promptly decided to indict the officer. The mayor fired the chief of police and announced the need for major reforms, conveniently overlooking the scores of other police-related deaths in the city (Zimring 2017). These are the retrospective actions of political actors *providing* an account of themselves, but not necessarily being *held* to account. If one cop can be scapegoated, then action will be seen to have been taken, and that enables the system to then go on functioning more or less as it always has done.

When BWCs were first mooted as a solution to police malfeasance, they were viewed as a technological panacea. But that first flush of enthusiasm swiftly abated when it became clear that letting the sunshine of transparency flood in was more about the perception of accountability than necessarily the reality of it. Not only are there issues with video being preserved or recorded, but there are cases where not enough of the incident has been captured to be usable in the disciplining or prosecution of an officer (Zamoff 2019). Similar to consent decrees, there is limited evidence of widespread evaluation of the efficacy of BWCs, or of how widely they have been adopted by PDs (Nowacki and Willits 2018), although some studies have suggested they reduce the number of citizen complaints and officer use of force (Ariel et al. 2015). By 2016, it was estimated that about one-third of US PDs were using BWCs, but those that were using them were not necessarily using them for all officers, or all of the time (Zamoff 2019). Whilst it's uncertain what the long-term effect of BWCs will be, it seems they do add an extra piece of the jigsaw in regulating officers and making policing more transparent in some places, some of the time. Another example of incremental change that is partial, but better than nothing. The likelihood is that they also do something to improve the public's perception of policing. Would a body worn camera have been of use in promoting more professional conduct, or enabling accountability in Jonathen's case? I think the answer to that is: 'doubtful.'

Use of force policies represent another way of regulating officer behavior through training and measurement. If an officer is recorded using force on their BWC, they may claim that using force was justified if there was no PD policy regulating it, or if they hadn't been properly trained in what the policy was. If there is a clear policy, and they have been trained appropriately, then their actions can be evaluated and there is a visual record of what those actions were. Simply put, there has to be something that the officer can be held accountable *for*, which means something they can be measured *against*. It is not just a matter of evidence, because we've seen so many cases where the court of public opinion widely believes the officer to have acted injudiciously only for a DA not to indict, or a court not to convict. This is the sort of 'bottom-up' regulation that is quite different from attempts to get 'top-down' justice from legal or governmental institutions. It might be the case that both use of force policy and BWC footage could form the basis of a legal trial, but their intention is to better regulate all officers' actions on a daily basis and consequently reduce the instances in which force is used.

USE OF FORCE POLICIES

Use of force policies can be used in tandem with monitoring processes that evaluate how often specific officers use force. A common finding is that if these processes exist in meaningful ways in PDs then the use of force is not only reduced, but officers that use it are more likely to be held to account (Zimring 2017, Vitale 2017, Terrill and Paoline 2017, Simmons 2012). The finding that a small number of officers cause the great majority of use of force incidents is consistent in academic research into US policing (Hickman and Poore 2016, Zimring 2017, Skolnick and Fyfe 1993, Butler 2017). In LA, the Christopher Commission estimated that the core group of officers using excessive force could be zeroed down to 44 individuals (Terrill and Paoline 2015). We saw in chapter one that the federal investigation of Seattle

PD after the killing of John T. Williams discovered that 1% of officers were responsible for 18% of instances where force was used. Policies and data can provide opportunities for measurement and monitoring.

Senior officers in various PDs have campaigned for some time to develop systems that monitored the excessive use of police force. Even prior to the Rodney King beating, Skolnick and Fyfe (1993) noted that the then head of the IACP in association with a dozen other chiefs of police were calling for such a program. The President's Task Force (2015) makes clear that use of force policies should be mandatory for PDs; be an integral part of officer training; and used as an assessment tool to evaluate officer performance. At the same time, it also notes that not all PDs *do* have use of force policies, and that the requirement for all PDs to report the use of force since 1994 has never been met—just like the inability to record fatal incident data. PDs that require officers to notify them every time they draw their weapon (even if they don't fire it) have significantly lower numbers of PRDs, but Jennings and Rubado's (2017) research calculated only about half of PDs actually had this requirement. Once again, all of these issues reflect PDs capacity to voluntarily pick and mix which policies they adopt. Not only is the application of accountability patchy, so is the adoption of regulatory measures.

We don't know for sure how many forces do and don't have use of force policies; we don't know how often they use force; we don't know how many citizens they kill. We are continually reduced to best guesses. Gaines and Kappeler (2014) estimated that 48% of PDs had a definition of less than lethal force, 51% had a definition of how to avoid using excessive force, and 73% had a requirement to report the use of force by officers. We cannot be sure what those numbers are now, but it seems likely that larger PDs *have* adopted use of force policies (Terrill and Paoline 2017). One might imagine that use of force policies would be a priority for PDs. Every day they send officers out in the knowledge that force might be used, that they might draw their weapon, and sometimes use it. Formalising a clear policy on how and in what circumstances officers are mandated to use force limits their discretion and exerts 'organizational control' over officers (Willits and Nowacki 2014: 67). The fact that some PDs don't casts significant questions over what their priorities are in terms of serving and protecting citizens. This raises questions about how such policies might be formulated, but also why they have *not* been adopted.

One problem with formulating use of force policies is the subjective interpretation of what force is, and in what circumstances it might be used. As different PDs apply different classifications to the use of force continuum, it's not a surprise that this affects how their use of force policy is formulated. Terrill and Paoline's (2017 and 2012) research uncovered a bewildering variety of use of force policies employed by PDs. Due to the organizational fragmentation of forces across the country, overlapping PDs can have quite significant variances in how and in what circumstances they use force, and whether they even have a policy (Shane et al. 2017, Terrill and Paoline 2017, Wolf et al. 2009). Once again, we return to zip-code lottery. Officers' propensity to use force can be significantly affected by where they work, and this may or may not lead to citizens dying—it really can be that simple. Nor should we overlook the fact that officers are policing areas that have very different types of legislation regarding gun ownership and access, underlining the fragmented nature of legislation more generally in the US (Shane et al. 2017). There are, though, dissenting voices in the literature on use of force policies. Van Craen and Skogan (2017) argue that officers still have a good deal of discretion to use force even when the PD has a clear policy on how it should be used, and that police culture usually overrides policies and laws.

Much of this discussion is characterized by data and evidence. Officers can only be regulated based on what is known. If there are clear use of force policies that should be followed, they can (in principle, at least) be regulated and monitored. If it's known that specific officers are more likely to use force, they could be subject to more rigorous training and monitoring, be disciplined, and/or deployed in other roles. If it's known that certain types of citizens are more likely to have officers pull guns on them, then training and supervision could be designed to address that. If specific areas are hot spots in which police draw their weapons, those can be identified and police practice in those areas could be amended and daily briefings could reinforce that message to those shifts. There are a lot of 'ifs' and 'coulds' here, but none of this is rocket science. One might argue that the principles of zero-tolerance could apply to police in most of these scenarios—zero-tolerance of problem officers; of demographic and geographic bias; of using force where deescalation is preferable. But that's not the construct we abide by: a zero-tolerance approach applies to members of society, not, apparently, to members of the law enforcement fraternity.

POLICE CULTURE

Chapter one demonstrated how police culture functions in relation to the use of force and how it effectively subverts laws and policies, often by invoking officer discretion. Police culture also affects how officers may or may not be held to account, and how regulation may or may not function. Many family members in my research made explicit reference to the 'blue code of silence,' and the way in which officers—including those investigating the case—colluded with other officers and fixed their stories into a single narrative of the event that led to their loved one's death. A wide range of academic scholars have focused on police cultures over the last five decades, and their findings have remained relatively consistent. Police culture is seen as being *apart* from other cultures, including other first-responders (Crank 2016, Young 1991). The apparently unique nature of the role—being part of the community, but also apart from it—appears to be the main driver of this. One of the first things officers are typically told after completing their training is: 'forget what they taught you at training school, in this PD we do it like this.' Most of us have worked in a job where we can identify with that mentality, but most of us don't do a job that requires us to have a gun, or gives us a mandate to use it.

Officers quickly learn that to be part of the policing family, loyalty and obedience are key (Crank 2016, Manning 2010). Although, as we saw in chapter one, the danger of the role is overstated, it is a potentially dangerous job. Therefore, knowing you have backup you can rely on is vital to being confident in fulfilling your role (Bittner 1975, Punch 1985). If officers are perceived to be 'snitches,' such back-up might not appear. Stories about this are legion, as are those about officers being frozen out socially, ignored for promotion, and being given the least desirable jobs as part of their daily rota (Crank 2016, Manning 2010, Punch 2009). Officers tend to possess a sense of mission, which means they have a strong sense of morality and also of control. In combination, these factors mean that your co-workers are not just co-workers, they are fellow souls engaged in that mission and protectors of the moral good (Crank 2016, Reiner 2010). One by-product of this is that it largely excludes pretty much everyone else. Police culture can be reduced to an us/them dualism. Officers tend to socialise only with other officers, and this can obviously lead to a good deal of group think and a lack of acceptance of diversity, particularly if it challenges the morals of the dominant culture.

For this reason, policing culture is also seen to be essentially conservative, and consequently it attracts those types of individuals as recruits (Bieler 2016, Balko 2014, McCulloch 2001). Corollaries of conservatism are macho-ism and the belief in adhering to codes of behavior. It's estimated that 85% of police officers in America are male, so clearly it's a disproportionately male profession (Data USA 2020). But the machoism goes beyond being merely male. It can attract recruits who have aggressive tendencies, and these can be manifest in both physical and sexual violence. The two most common complaints Black women make against police are about violence and sexual assault (Butler 2017). A predominantly male and macho workforce does not properly represent 21st century America, which is increasingly plural and diverse. People who challenge the prevailing norms or have radical or progressive ideas are not typically attracted to policing as a vocation for obvious reasons, and we should bear this in mind when we call for the police to radically rethink their practices and orientation towards specific groups in society.

It's like asking confirmed meat eaters to go vegan overnight without any sort of transitional plan or without any sort of consultation about why it would be a good idea for them to do so.

Adhering to cultural codes is a common finding in policing research (Reiner 2010, Gaines and Kappeler 2014, Kraska 2007). One key question asked by many academics is how active officers are in following these codes. A useful example of this is in instances where police have used brutal physical force rather than using their guns. In the Rodney King beating, and the deaths of Eric Garner and George Floyd, there were several other officers present who did nothing to intervene to stop the violence, and also apparently did nothing to report the officer/s who used force. Those officers did not actively participate, but they enabled those acts to occur by their passivity. The codes of loyalty and adherence to the culture of policing overrode any beliefs they may have had about human rights or the sanctity of life. For many writers, this is the nub of culture—it's not the officers that commit egregiously malfeasant actions that exemplify police culture, it's the officers that do nothing to stop it (Punch 2009 and 1985, Phillips 2010).

OBSTACLES TO EFFECTIVE REGULATION

The 'blue code of silence' is highlighted by numerous authors in explaining how this works (Klockars 1985, Skolnick and Fyfe 1993, Vitale 2017, Phillips 2010). As officers belong to the same 'family of policing' they believe that airing problems in public is unacceptable. Hence there is no desire to speak out against poor practice, and even if Internal Affairs (IA) units examine these cases, they typically can't get other officers to give evidence against officers who illegitimately use lethal force. This is supported by Schaeffer and Tewksbury's (2018) research into police canteen culture—as the Baltimore PD officer who blew the whistle on how Freddie Gray was treated prior to his death was criticized by officers in the canteen for talking out of line and bringing shame on their colleagues.

Several research participants told me that in the months after the death of their loved one, other officers came forward in confidence and told them they knew that the death should have been avoided, or that the particular officer was known as a 'problem officer.' If all of this sounds remarkably similar to the concept of 'omerta' used by organised crime groups, that's because it is (see, for example Fassin 2013, Punch 1985). As a university lecturer, I often have students from large cities in my classes who say a version of 'everyone knows the 5-0 (police) are the biggest gang there is.' This is what happens when there is a mentality of 'us and them'; when the moral codes of the police are at odds with society's; and when officers have a sense of mission rather than codes of professional conduct. They close ranks, they stick together and exclude others, blocking out the world.

For these reasons, we should be wary when senior officers play the 'bad apple' card in police-related deaths. As was previously established, whilst it's undoubtedly the case that a minority of officers cause the majority of problems relating to extralegal violence and malfeasance, that does not mean the root cause is located in individual failure. Punch (2009) notes that this argument is as old as policing itself, and that policing is in and of itself a culture that produces problem officers. Of course not all, or even a majority are problem officers, but as we've seen above, this isn't about the majority of officers. Punch says combine this with an occupation that has a low level of supervision, a high degree of discretion, enables force to be used, and brings you into daily access with criminals who have ready access to cash, narcotics and other valuables, and you have a toxic mix that invites a number of officers to engage in corrupt practices. Various authors have noted that the use of extralegal force and corruption go hand in hand, and that the former tends to be a gateway to the latter (Skolnick 1967, Bittner 1975, Punch 1985, Crank 2016). For these reasons, Punch (2009) says that problem officers are not bad apples, they are the result of a culture that enables such a crop to come to fruition. They're not even the result of a diseased tree, he says, they're the product of a 'rotten orchard.' His use of metaphor is powerful in illustrating that anything involving police malfeasance is a result of culture that enables it to happen. That includes doing nothing and turning a blind eye.

Plenty of research has focused on how police exclude recruits from diverse backgrounds in terms of race, gender and sexuality. Similarly, other research has focused on recruits who enter the police with positive and progressive attitudes, convinced they're going to make a difference, only to find out that after a few years on the job those attitudes have altered as they have become effectively institutionalised into police culture (Crank 2016, Reiner 2010, Punch 1985). A common finding is that culture trumps law, policy and protocol. Officers are experts at deflecting, obstructing, withholding, dissembling, managing perception and manipulating systems (Manning 2010, Punch 2009). Those are not necessarily negative attributes for an officer to have, but they can become negative if they're used to cover up the abuse of citizens' rights, or commit morally dubious or outright criminal acts. Having discussed regulation, accountability and culture throughout the book and established that achieving the former two concepts appear to be more aspirational than reachable, this is the point at which it is worth examining what we mean by accountability. If we want more of it, we need to be sure what we mean by 'it.'

WHAT IS ACCOUNTABILITY?

Accountability is a nebulous concept, and this is perhaps at the heart of why it is difficult to achieve in practice (Bovens 2007). It's a word that's easy to use, and easy to get behind—who on earth would vote for something to be unaccountable, or run an organization that pledged to be less accountable? One of the reasons for this ambiguity is that it dovetails with other words that are also difficult to define—we think of accountability as being linked to justice, and democracy. But what are they? To hold someone to account is an obvious starting point—what most families of the deceased want is to know that the officer that used lethal force has had to properly account for their actions. By extension, it might also be the case that the PD could also be held to account if they failed in their duty to properly train and oversee the officer, for example if they let the officer carry on with patrol duty despite knowing them to be mentally unwell. One can think of plenty of examples where people or organizations are held to account, but where the outcomes produced are considered to be unsatisfactory. So it's not just about being able to hold someone or something to account, it is *how* they are held to account and what the *outcome* of that process is. With regard to PRDs in the US it is evident that police and justice organizations are typically not held to account in respect of either of these criteria.

In principle, accountability should be built into policing. Police rely on societal consent and legitimacy, which is granted on the basis that police perform a legitimate and useful function for society. If they err or stray from that, then society has a legitimate right to ask them to account for how and why that happened, and how they intend to correct it. If that explanation is neither forthcoming nor persuasive, then society, or groups within it, has a right to withdraw consent. In short form, this is what happened at Minneapolis in 2020, Ferguson in 2014, LA in 1991, Detroit in 1967, and on, and on.

Mirroring the discussion in this chapter, and wider in the book, accountability is about perception and reality. Police are aware of this, and for all of the PDs that react with force and aggression, there are plenty that do engage with challenges and attempt to find resolutions that assuage community concerns. The PDs that react to protests and uprisings with paramilitary force make an unequivocal statement about how they see their role—we can leave them to one side. We wouldn't have BWCs, CITs, a focus on procedural justice, implicit bias training, and use of force policies without a large number of PDs wanting to engage with communities. But we should question their motivation for doing so: are PDs adopting these measures because they think they'll be perceived as being more accountable, or because they believe they will actually *be* more accountable? If these attempts are performative, then they are likely to fail because in the long run they will be revealed for what they really are when crises occur. So far, the book has demonstrated the scale and extent of change required in order to address the issues that characterize police-related deaths in the US. The only way progress can be achieved is to have police buy-in to the fundamental principle that things have to change, that new approaches are required. Police culture needs to shift to embrace a new form of policing, because as we've seen, it pushes back against attempts to have change imposed on it by laws, policies or protocols.

To underscore the eternally intractable nature of these issues, I want to highlight an article written at the turn of this century by Katheryn Russell (2000), which talks about the 'dance' that happens when police brutality occurs. Firstly, expressions of outrage by local communities are met with calls for calm by voices in authority. Second, authorities publicly classify the incident as an aberration and reinforce the message that the vast majority of officers do a good job. Third, there are persistent attempts to smear the victim of the incident. Fourth, protests from the local community are met with more calls for calm, sometimes from voices within the community. Finally, after there has been enough time for everyone to cool off, a grand jury declines an indictment and no officers are held accountable. These principles still hold broadly true to the vast majority of PRDs today, underlining the normality and persistence of these deaths (see, for example Lowery 2017). Russell's paper is taken from a book responding to the fatal shooting of Amadou Diallo in New York in 1999, another name to add to a list, in case we've forgotten.

CAN THE PATTERN BE BROKEN?

Given the repeated failures of mechanisms designed to either hold police to account or regulate their activities, and the persistence of 'the dance' highlighted by Russell, one is bound to ask an uncomfortable question: is a criminal court the right forum to pursue these cases? Undoubtedly there are obvious examples where officers appear to have summarily executed citizens, and in these cases they should be tried for homicide or manslaughter. It seems unlikely that the majority of cases would fall into this category, however, so in light of the signal failure of criminal justice to achieve resolution in these cases, one is bound to ask two further questions: Firstly, should laws be altered to enable criminal prosecutions to occur? Second, should an alternate forum be introduced to adjudicate in police-related deaths? Skolnick and Fyfe (1993) point to the fact that criminal courts are notoriously limited in their effectiveness, even in relatively straightforward cases that deal with typical offenses to the criminal code. Throw in expert defendants who know how to play the criminal justice system, and all of the other impediments set out during this and the previous chapter and it seems clear that the die are loaded in favour of the police in this scenario. There is also an issue of principle to consider. Reiner (2010) notes that commentators on the criminal justice system who usually advocate leniency in order to reduce prison numbers and minimize the effects of criminalization on citizens often become enthusiastic advocates of this approach when the accused happen to be police officers. A number of authors believe that if a principal outcome of the investigatory process is to better learn lessons that prevent future deaths and thus cut the overall number of deaths, then attaining this via our existing criminal justice system is unlikely (Zimring 2017, Shane 2013, Doyle 2010, Skolnick and Fyfe 1993).

From this perspective, Doyle (2010) argues that the main focus of policing should be to promote a culture of safety. There are a number of implications that flow from this. One is that it clearly endorses the idea of officers as guardians, with all of the concurrent principles of communication and deescalation one would expect. A second is that it attempts to solve the problem of police-related deaths from the bottom up by creating a culture which seeks to learn lessons from errors. This is, in effect, a program that seeks to refashion the profession of policing in the image of aviation or medicine (see, for example Reason 1997). Key to this approach is creating an environment where honest reviews of errors can be undertaken without blame being ascribed, and technical experts deliver findings that senior professionals can both accept and acknowledge the need to learn from. In short, a nonadversarial forum driven by best practice and compliance. This approach focuses on situational learning, much as air crash investigators forensically examine why actions were taken in specific situations, and how we can learn not to make the same mistakes given the same circumstances and situations (Shane 2013). From this perspective, Zimring (2017) makes valuable points about officers being discouraged from firing multiple shots and also not firing at citizens with knives. From his analysis of The Counted database, he estimates that potentially hundreds of lives could be saved each year if these two practices were taught and adopted.

Doyle (2010: 135) notes that near misses in aviation and medicine are seen as opportunities for lessons to be learned that could prevent future critical incidents, whereas in the criminal justice system they're viewed with relief—almost as success stories. We don't know how many near misses there are each year in America—another example of data failure—but an educated estimate must put the number in the hundreds. A systematic review of these might yield important lessons that could reduce future deaths. The nearest we have to this is the use of consent decrees to review and evaluate police practice, but outside of the PD under investigation there's no sign that these lessons are disseminated further. Whilst Doyle's (2010) ideas appear laudable, it's not at all clear that they would be palatable either to PDs, or to campaigners who typically focus on holding police to account rather than demanding lessons be learned. It's also worth noting that a version of this approach has purportedly been attempted for some years in Britain, with police regulators following similar principles, only for the number of PRDs to rise inexorably (Baker and Pillinger 2020).

The opening four chapters of this book examined how, why and in what circumstances police used lethal force on citizens in the US. The previous two chapters discuss the types of mechanisms and processes that currently exist, and could potentially exist in order to regulate police practice and hold them to account when lethal force is used in an unnecessary, unreasonable or disproportionate way. What has been missing in the discussion thus far is a consideration of how this epidemic of avoidable killing affects the citizens left behind in the aftermath of these deaths, how it affects communities across the US, and how it undermines beliefs, norms and value systems that underpin the very foundations of democracy, justice and liberty in America. The following chapter examines the human and societal costs of police-related deaths.

Chapter 6

Walk in My Shoes

James Paschal Jr.

James Paschal Jr. arrived too early in this world. At birth he weighed 3lb and 13oz—not many people gave him a chance of survival. He was the sixth grandchild in the family, but always used to joke with his cousins that he was the first. As he grew older, he became very protective of his little sister, who was one year younger—seeing her upset made him upset too. James was four years old when he saw a police officer shoot his dad dead in Greensboro NC in 1990. James Paschal Sr. was a Black male aged 30. He was undergoing a mental health crisis, mistakenly believing that his wife—JoAlice Doggett-Smith—was trying to take their kids away from him. James Sr. had initially threatened his wife and her parents with two fishing knives, but his mother-in-law had managed to calm him and he'd put the knives down. Eyewitnesses said the family members had hugged and appeared to have made up. But neighbors had already called 911 and police attended the family home. When the officers arrived, they walked towards James Sr., who was holding both knives. Officer Earl Locklear called on him to drop the knives, which James Sr. allegedly failed to do. JoAlice told me Officer Locklear initially sprayed James Sr with mace before stepping back and firing four shots into his chest, killing him outright. Onlooking neighbors wondered why it was necessary to fire four shots, with one stating: 'Why'd they have to shoot him four times? To me, that's police brutality.' Neighbors described James Sr. as a quiet, friendly man who was probably undergoing some sort of crisis at the time he was killed, one eyewitness said: 'It was like he was out of it, in another world or something.'

Eighteen years later, aged 22, James Jr. was himself shot dead by police in Greensboro. Like his dad, James Jr. left behind a four-year-old son made fatherless by the police use of lethal force. He was unarmed and shot ten times by Officer Schultheis of Greensboro PD. James Jr had allegedly been involved in an altercation with his girlfriend. The police statement after his shooting claimed that he was wanted for alleged assault on a female, injury to personal property, and unauthorized use of a car. Officers were consequently searching for him and stopped his car in the early morning of April 19, 2008. There were no eyewitnesses to what unfolded, but according to the DA's report, he was shot after walking towards Officer Schultheis, who was working patrol duty alone. There was a significant inconsistency in the police version of events and forensic photography undertaken by the ME. The officer claimed that James Jr had advanced on him with his hand in the waist band of his pants, and feared he was reaching for a weapon. JoAlice told me that in the autopsy photographs, it seemed clear that his left shoulder had been largely blown off by gunfire and his arm rearranged to be stuck in his waistband. In my research, I saw two other cases that were very similar to this, where limbs had been more or less severed and then rearranged in order to fit with the police narrative of what had allegedly occurred.

James Jr. had been convicted of robbery and obtaining property under false pretences in 2003. He was released from prison 8 months before he was killed—he was still on probation at the time of his death. His mom told me that he'd battled with anger his whole life in the aftermath of seeing his dad killed in 1990. She doesn't make any attempt to minimize what her son did that led to him being incarcerated. But she does make it emphatically clear that he had no history of violence, and was unarmed when he was fatally shot. She feels that the police and media constructed a narrative that: 'used his past, not his present.' There was no mention of the fact that he'd gone through school whilst incarcerated, or that he was training to be a chef after having worked in the prison kitchen. In both cases, the DA found the killings to be justified, leaving JoAlice and her family to try and piece their lives together and move on from the aftermath of two fatal incidents as a result of contact with the police.

JoAlice told me that these incidents were the 'thorns in her flesh.' After her husband was shot dead, James Jr. and his younger sister became introverts overnight, and wouldn't go out to play with other kids anymore. She had to potty train both of them again, and they had persistent nightmares. Even now her daughter remains an introvert and doesn't like to be left alone in her own home. JoAlice found her faith to be a major comfort in helping her come to terms with the trauma that has occurred in her life. She talked at length about the harassment and intimidation she'd been subject to in the aftermath of James Jr's death. The police were obviously aware that she was the former wife of James Sr., and that appears to have affected how they dealt with JoAlice. I think it's noteworthy that JoAlice refused to talk with the media after both shootings, so what follows should be read in that context. She was not publicly outspoken, she did not lead a campaign or protests, like we've seen in some of the previous cases in this book. She tried to move on quietly with her life and keep her family together.

Days after James Jr. was buried, she noticed that a police cruiser often tailed her for a while before eventually drifting away from her car. JoAlice worked at a car dealership at that time and used to start work at 5.30am, her job was to get the cars lined up for the day. One winter morning after James Jr.'s death she found herself face down in the snow having been wrestled to the ground by officers who claimed she was trying to break in. She was wearing a coat with the company logo on it and had keys to the building in her hand. Officers still took her to the station and she had to be freed by her boss. She told me police have followed her to her house, to restaurants, and to her college. They have harassed her in McDonalds, and pulled her over whilst driving and cuffed her because she allegedly failed to put on a signal when turning right, only to then let her go.

At James Jr.'s funeral, the officer involved in the fatal incident appeared among the congregation. The night before his burial, some of James Jr.'s friends were so concerned that his body might be removed by officers they slept overnight in the graveyard. You might think this is excessive, but by the time you get to the end of this chapter your views might be challenged. Either way, their concerns were real to them, and come from a deep-seated generational distrust and fear of police and the criminal justice system.

JoAlice says she lost people she considered friends, people shunned her in the community, and she had church engagements cancelled. She says the generational trauma in her community is like a 'ticking time-bomb.' She has learned to forgive the police and not to hate them, largely because of the strength of her faith. But she wants to see officers better educated, better trained, and more aware of local community issues. She firmly believes that: 'firing a weapon is easier than dealing with people—take off the badge, be human.'

Having survived premature birth, James Jr. was taken from this world prematurely in what the criminal justice system termed a 'justified shooting.' We have come full circle in a number of ways. James's father was shot by police in front of him, and eighteen years later, he himself was shot dead by police, leaving a son behind. Ta Nehisi-Coates (2015a) says that Black Americans have now arrived at the point where they realise what their perceived worth is to society: nothing. But life forces us all to go on. Hope is (hopefully) the last thing to die. JoAlice was the penultimate participant in the research project, our interview was a few weeks before I flew home. It felt to me like the project had itself come full circle. I came away from meeting her thinking—how do humans move on from these appallingly traumatic events? What does it do to our worldview, how does all of this affect wider society?

Danielle Willard, John T. Williams, Nate H. Pickett II, Kayla Moore, Jonathen Santellana, Daniel Ficker, James Paschal Jr. Another list of avoidable deaths to add to the pantheon in the United States. But there are no memorials for this group of fallen citizens. Nowhere public that families can go and mourn their loved ones. Nowhere visitors can pay their respects. The first four chapters of this book examined how police-related deaths occur, and the previous two chapters considered how police might or might not be held accountable for them. This chapter surveys the human cost of these deaths, not only for the families left behind, but the effects on wider communities and populations across America. It argues that these deaths have toxic effects that go far beyond merely policing and criminal justice, and corrode the basis of society, government and democracy itself.

EXPERIENCES OF BEREAVEMENT

When someone close to you dies unexpectedly, you feel a bewildering number of emotions: disbelief, shock, and anger being the most obvious. It's commonly said that losing a child is one of the most traumatic things that can happen to parents, because it upsets the natural order of things (Raphael 1995). We expect to die before our children. We hope to have had a good life and enabled them to thrive and build their own lives. We certainly don't expect them to die before they've been able to live full adult lives, or reach for some of their hopes and dreams. Nor do we expect to have to look back on their lives wondering 'what if?' All of this, I think, is a given for any sort of unexpected death in one's family.

But what happens when that unexpected death occurs because a police officer killed your loved one? How do you process that? How do you move on from it—*can* you move on from it? What does it do to your view of the world given that the public servants you thought were there to serve and protect us were the very same people who killed a member of your family? Who then smeared them, and tried to cover up the death. Then colluded with the justice system to ensure that you could neither get to the truth of how your loved one died, nor get justice for their death? How do you feel when you see the officer who fired those shots walking around the supermarket shopping with their family while you're at the checkout?

There is a hierarchy of who is deemed worthy of grief. A spectrum exists on which the deceased are placed based on how society viewed them when they were alive. This gets reinforced if they die after contact with police. Families in my research project routinely talked about how their experiences 'didn't fit' with other types of bereavement, and there were multiple variations on this. Going to a counselling group which contained parents whose children were killed in homicides was to realise that your relative's death was further down the spectrum of allowable grief. Because a police shooting always contained a tinge from other bereaved parents of 'well, there must have been some reason for it.' One of the mothers in the project told me: 'They sent me an invite for a homicide meeting. When I get there, there's a panel of police officers, there are other people who haven't been killed by police, just regular people whose kids who have been killed by other individuals. So when they ask me to introduce myself I stood up and I told them what happened and they all turned peak red and I was never invited back again.'

IMPACT ON HEALTH AND WELLBEING

Little has been said about the physical effects on the relatives in the aftermath of police-related deaths, but it made a major impact on my understanding of this issue from early on in the research process. Participants commonly talked about being unable to eat or sleep properly for years after the killing, and in some there was a tendency to overrely on alcohol or prescription medication. Several participants talked about being unable to function at all in the weeks after their loved one's death—that they needed to be washed, dressed and fed by friends or family members. I noticed that it was typical for families to talk about the deceased in the present tense, as though they were still alive (see, for example Ford 2004). I was also struck by what I came to term the '4am syndrome.' This seemed to be the point at which people finally gave up trying to sleep and got up. Variously, they would look through old photographs, or letters connected to their relative; or they would just sit and be lost in thought. But most often they would wade through documents relating to the death, convinced that they had overlooked key details that could get to the truth of what had happened, despite being aware that they'd looked at those documents hundreds of times before. The desolation of grief was felt differently by individual family members, and they knew there were times when it was better to leave certain family members alone because trying to comfort them might make things worse. Several people talked about waking to hear another family member crying in another part of the home and realising they were best left with their own thoughts. Anger often emerges from grief and trauma (Kübler-Ross 1984). In Greene's (2015) research into the Danziger bridge killings in New Orleans in 2006, a mother talks about how her son is regularly so furious about his dad being killed that he wants to provoke a confrontation with officers so he can also be killed. A sobering reminder that JoAlice's story is not unique.

Aside from the physical health aspects, these deaths unsurprisingly affected the mental wellbeing of families. There were numerous instances of participants being hypervigilant due to overtly intrusive attention from local law enforcement, as was the case in JoAlice's experience. One example that typified this was a wife whose husband was shot dead by police. She told me that a police cruiser was routinely parked outside her house after she had secured a financial settlement for his death. Because she lived in a cul-de-sac, the only reason that car was there was because officers deliberately drove there. She got to the point where she took a coffee pot and two cups out to the officers—they looked at her through the window, and slowly drove off—this occurred on a daily basis for weeks. A significant number of participants said they'd been routinely tailed by police cruisers on and off for months after the death. Another common comment was that social media and/or email accounts had been hacked to remove information or post offensive messages. Rick Williams told me that SPD officers routinely called him 'John' for years after his brother's death, in his opinion deliberately trying to provoke him into reacting.

DIGNITY AND RESPECT

In the first couple of months of the research I thought 'well, if I were in their shoes I might also be hyper-vigilant.' By the time I got to the end of the project it was much clearer to me that there is a form of psychological warfare that some officers in some PDs regularly practice to terrorise families. When I asked family members why they thought that was, they invariably replied with a version of 'because they hate us, they hate the fact that we persisted in trying to get justice for our loved one.' Essentially, this was seen as another form of resistance. As we saw in chapter one , police particularly dislike people who don't comply. It appears that not only were the citizens who died perceived as 'assholes,' but their families were too. This seemed even more so if they'd received financial settlements, as these payments were apparently viewed as a mark of disrespect against the officers and PD. Given that a significant number of relatives secure financial settlements as a result of police-related deaths, one might think that officers would connect this to settlements being common and reflect on what that says about their practice and role in society. Or not, perhaps.

In the immediate aftermath of the death, families were routinely obstructed in their attempts to view the body of their relatives, with coroners or MEs denying them access, usually for at least one week after the death. In two instances, families discovered that their loved one was registered by morticians under a different name, presumably to prevent families trying to visit them. When families were able to see the body of their relative, in two cases the body was still handcuffed. In two other examples, the entirety of the deceased's internal organs were removed, put into garbage sacks and then stuffed back into the body cavity before being released to the funeral parlor. In three cases, bodies were buried without all of their organs, with either their heart, or brain (or both) missing. Those organs have never been located, and it's not at all clear why they were retained. Not much dignity in the termination of life, or in death. A corporeal reminder of the relative value assigned to the deceased.

Time and again I was struck by the dignity and fortitude with which families bore their burdens and how they were able to continue with a different version of their lives. Undoubtedly they had been deeply affected by their bereavement, but they were able to make adjustments about how they dealt with the world. Some believed that they had remade themselves as different, better people as a result of the life lessons they'd learned. Others found meaning and comfort in religion; some in activism. The apparent monolithic indifference of police and criminal justice agencies, who seemed to carry on as though nothing out of the ordinary had happened, seemed to be in stark contrast to the way in which families processed these deaths. What might this indifference be able to tell us about police-related deaths?

INDIFFERENCE IN THE FACE OF AN EPIDEMIC

What are the longer-term effects of this fatal epidemic of avoidable deaths? A key finding up until this point in the book has been that the apathy, pragmatic legitimacy, indifference—call it what you will—of the dominant majority in some ways enables these deaths to occur, to persist, and to leave the essential machinery of policing intact. Evidently this suggests a high degree of tolerance for violence in US society. To enable this to occur is one thing, but what about the aftermath of the occurrence, is there apathy and indifference there too? I think this is an important question to ask: do the relatives left behind also not count?

The scale of killing by guns in the US is difficult to overstate. In 2017, the FBI (2018) recorded the homicides or nonnegligent manslaughter of 16,617 citizens—that's 45 per day. In 2018, more than 24,000 people took their own lives with a gun—65 per day. Combine the number of homicides and suicides—it gives a figure of in excess of 40,000 deaths in a year. Is this what President Trump was referring to with the phrase 'American carnage'? Take a moment to consider your own circle of family and friends, and you'll appreciate how many people might be affected by a single death. It's by no means a stretch to say that these deaths could affect the lives of in excess of 250,000 citizens in a single year. A national prevalence study in the 1990s found that 9% of those surveyed had close friends or family members murdered—a group termed 'co-victims of homicide' (Peterson Armour 2002). With this scale of bereavement, one might imagine that services exist to support the bereaved, at least in terms of counselling—not least because many covictims are likely present at the time of their loved one's death. In fact, there is little federal or state interest in covictims of homicide, and consequently limited academic interest as well. Spungen (1998, xi) notes they are: 'Subjected not simply to a conspiracy of silence but to a state of invisibility.' Evidently there are direct parallels here with the relatives of people who die after contact with police.

In addition to overlooking police-related deaths, we apparently overlook the people left behind in the aftermath of them. If we can get some idea about why this is, it might tell us why there is so little interest in such deaths. Generating interest in an issue is a precondition to effecting change on it. Until it becomes a focus of attention for a majority of people in society there is little hope of altering the way this issue is perceived. In my research, a common response amongst participants was to say that few people were interested in hearing their story, or of empathising with their grief. This led to further pain and trauma on their behalf, a form of secondary victimization that Spungen (1998: 10) terms the 'second wound.' One mother told me: 'I feel like I made [my son] a promise that I would never stop telling his story where I believed anybody gave a shit. It's just that people don't, they really don't, it's uncomfortable.' If the people who died are considered to be of little consequence, are their relatives and friends 'allowed' to grieve for them? Is this why the bereaved families in my research ran into a quagmire of apathy from their fellow citizens, and were shunned by people who'd previously been friends, work colleagues and neighbors?

DISENFRANCHISED GRIEF

Kenneth Doka's (1989) work on AIDS related deaths in the 1980s found that loved ones left behind in the aftermath of these deaths were not granted the status of 'normal grievers.' There were a variety of reasons for this: firstly, the person who died was seen to have brought the death on themselves. Second, the bereaved family was seen to be tainted by association with the deceased. Third, there were a complex mix of factors that led to the death which most people in society would rather not examine and consequently found easier to ignore.

Doka called the inability for grieving to be recognised as 'disenfranchised grief.' Society constructs who can be mourned and grieved. For a long time—certainly up until the Ferguson uprising—this didn't typically apply to citizens who died after police contact, because 'they musta done somethin.'

Disenfranchised grief reflects societal hierarchies already surveyed in this book. At the bottom of this hierarchy of allowable grief are the usual suspects: People of Color, the mentally unwell, homeless, and those dependent on substances (Baker et al. 2019).

The use of the word 'disenfranchised' tells us that being enfranchised is a social process determined by societal values, and here again, we return to the dominant majority. Culture is a significant determinant in defining how grief is regulated (Hochschild 2003, Peterson Armour 2002). Essentially, we learn how to grieve in a socially acceptable way through conditioning—by observing and processing other examples of how bereaved families grieve. But the great majority of bereaved families grieve a death caused by socially explicable causes—illness, old age, or in an accident, for example. Most of us have experienced this process, or know someone who has—it's an integral aspect of the human condition. In these instances, we don't need to be *actively* 'enfranchised' to grieve—we just do.

When a death is not socially recognisable it becomes clear that nothing just 'is' when it comes to grieving for a loved one—grieving is a construct. There is a wide variety of literature on disenfranchised grief as it applies to various atypical examples where someone you were close to dies. A few examples illustrate the complexities of this issue. With perinatal deaths (see, for example Lang et al. 2011), the parents and families-to-be grieve someone that was living, but not born. Most people outside of the family struggle to conceive of how to approach this subject, so it's commonly ignored for the sake of their own feelings, not for the sake of the feelings of the bereaved. And the bereaved relatives know this, they know it's not socially acceptable to grieve in public for the death of their unborn child. If your ex-partner, who you lived with for twelve years and with whom you had a good relationship after breaking up dies, and you currently live with a new partner and your two children, are you properly able to grieve for your ex? Wouldn't your friends find that a bit odd, wouldn't your own family find it odd—and wouldn't that affect how you showed your grief, and who you showed it to? If your pet dies (see, for example Cordaro 2012), and you are heartbroken, most people would understand that, but what if you were still heartbroken and mourning that loss nine months later? Most people would consider that excessive and not necessarily be sympathetic to the way you really felt. One unifying element in these three disparate examples is that society determines what sort of grief is allowable, and by extension, what isn't. A second unifying feature emerges from this—the requirement to grieve in private.

IF YOU CUT US, DO WE NOT BLEED?

One factor that determines whether grief can be validated is the perceived moral worth of the deceased. If they are perceived to have somehow caused the events that led to their death, this can be seen to devalue any sense of loss that might be felt in relation to their death (Bell et al. 2012). Similarly, if the deceased is perceived to come from a marginalised group, this can also minimise any sympathy the dominant societal majority might feel (Grant and Green 2008; Fowlkes 1990). These factors are compounded by the lack of sympathy or compassion shown by the media or criminal justice system to the deceased and their relatives (Jones and Beck 2007). It seems clear that the process of police rapidly ensuring that the narrative of these deaths focuses on what the deceased was alleged to have done, and what sort of character they were, is a way of diminishing any sympathy the dominant majority might feel for them by effectively stigmatizing them (Baker 2019a, Baker et al. 2019).

The knock-on effect of all of this is that families become isolated, unable to grieve in a way that is socially normal, and consequently are unable to achieve closure. This can be compounded by the inability to apprehend the killer of their relative, and by often having to endure lengthy court processes which effectively puts their grief on hold (Peterson Armour 2002). The intrusion of law enforcement and the media into their lives are seen to be examples of secondary victimization which reinforce those feelings (Jones and Beck 2007). Unsurprisingly, these experiences deepen and strengthen the feelings of hopelessness, despair, anguish and trauma that families experiencing disenfranchised grief can feel (Spungen 1998). White participants typically believed that their loved one was smeared in terms of their supposed mental ill health, or as being dependent on substances. People of Color felt that the initial focus on their loved one was on their skin color, and how by implication this marked them out as suspect before any further labels could be attached to them, denigrating their character or behavior (Baker et al. 2019).

Participants of Color felt that these experiences were explained by, and reflective of, the racism they experienced as a result of structural practices. Coming from communities already marked by historical oppression and inequality, their perception was that neither they nor their loved one would be considered a loss to society, and that somehow their relative's death would be constructed as either inevitable, or necessary, or both. One Black mother told me: "I didn't get the chance to have a judge, a court date. I didn't get to see the officer stand up and say anything—I haven't [even] seen him. The justice system just said 'you know what, that's another one gone'; that's how I feel 'just another one gone.' It was like—we killed your son, move on."

Black families whose children died commonly said they tended to be given sympathy within their communities, but only for a certain period of time, after which there was an expectation that they should 'get on with it, and move on.' To which one father said: "They are like 'you should be over that by now,' and I am like 'are you out of your mind, it isn't ever going away'—it is 24/7, it is." Or a mother's view: "A lot of people will tell you 'you need to get past that,' but you can't tell me how to feel or how I should feel, you haven't walked in my shoes." White families tended to talk about how they were shunned and largely disbelieved when they campaigned for justice for their relative, because they didn't fit the stereotype of who died in police-related deaths.

To some degree, Black participants were unsurprised by their experiences because they saw them as reflecting previous instances of structural and systemic racism they'd experienced. A number of Black participants from southern states made direct reference to generational experiences of plantation slavery and Jim Crow practices, and how that related to their understanding of what had happened to their loved one. This chimes with literature that identifies the intergenerational nature of trauma that builds over time and passes down through generations (see, for example Bryant et al. 2017). It can be seen in higher levels of mental illness in children of Color, but also in behaviour modification as was seen in chapter three (see also Bryant et al. 2017). People of Color can thus be said to be multiply marginalised and subject to multiple levels of victimization when a relative is killed after contact with police. The lack of societal compassion and empathy can be further understood and explained by examining the concept of 'belief in a just world.'

BELIEF IN A JUST WORLD

The concept of 'belief in a just world' was first proposed by Lerner (1980: 11) who saw it as a 'fundamental delusion' that people invested in to make sense of their life experiences. It provides a framework that enables us to navigate and rationalize adverse experiences by perceiving the world as being a broadly just and fair place. In this sense, the concept acts as a buffer that enables us to explain any disappointments and perceived injustices we feel as being blips in the general scheme of things. In this version of a just world, people get what they deserve. If we work hard, follow the rules and generally stick to the status quo, good things will typically happen in our lives. If you apply for a promotion at work and don't get it, you tell yourself that the successful applicant had better qualifications, or more experience, or a better skill set than you did. You might feel that they really got the job because they're a White male and you're a Black female, and/or that they knew the head of the promotion panel. But if you invest in that worldview, then you may begin to view the world as unjust. If you do that, then your place in it becomes uncertain—what's the point in applying for the next promotion? There's no point in applying for a different job, because you probably won't get that either. We make sense of setbacks by rationalising them in a way that enables us to bounce back and overcome negative feelings by explaining them as short-term misfortunes. Because of this, believing in a just world neces- sarily means one carries a built in degree of denial that enables us to reframe incidents as a technique of self-protection (Bastounis and Minibas-Poussard 2012, Gruman and Sloan 1983).

Believing in a just world is intimately bound up with notions of what is just and unjust, but also with one's sense of identity. To feel part of a just world, one feels included and valued—a productive and useful citizen within wider systems of meaning. People who have a high level belief in a just world are usually able to adapt to adverse events because of these views, but they typi- cally also possess conservative values (Lerner 1980, Beierlein et al. 2011). To believe in a just world, one must not just abide by the status quo, but actively buy into it. That means buying into many of the constructs that have been dismantled in this book. Getting on means accepting that bad things happen, but on the whole, the world is a fair and just place.

Implicit in this worldview is the belief that people get what they deserve. So if they consistently have bad outcomes, it must be because they've done bad things, or been bad people, or both. For this reason, people with a high level of belief in a just world are typically identified as being victim blam- ers, and also possessing harsher views towards citizens from minority com- munities or marginalised groups (Adolfson and Strömwall 2017, Bastounis and Minibas-Poussard 2012). One example of this is Johnson et al.'s (2019) research demonstrating that the race of citizens shot dead by police in spe- cific areas correlated to violent crime rates in those areas. People with a high belief in a just world would view this as people 'getting what they deserve.' In this world-view, identity, values and relative worth are tightly bound up with perceptions of justice and injustice and seen to be broadly similar with the processes that define the enfranchisement of grieving.

RACIAL DIMENSIONS

During my research it became obvious that prior to the death of their loved one, People of Color had little trust in the criminal justice system—they had a low level of belief in a just world. Consequently, although they were furious, distraught and traumatised by the killing, they were relatively unsurprised at how the criminal justice system responded to them in the aftermath of their relative's death. One Black mother summed up a commonly held view: 'The role of the police is not to protect and serve the people, it's to protect and serve the system. To preserve the status quo: who gets what, who lives where, who gets to say what—that's what the system is supposed to do.' We can see here that 'the system' in this sense goes beyond the criminal justice system to encompass societal structures. The criminal justice system is seen as only one part of a wider system of oppression and inequality.

There was a general lack of trust in politics, government, democracy, fairness, equality and legal processes. Participants of Color frequently gave examples of everyday harassment and prejudice that they felt exemplified their experiences of life. This reflects Hagiwara et al.'s (2015) research into Black citizens' experience of healthcare in the US, that they had very low expectations of receiving good quality healthcare, so they believed they 'got what they deserved.' Clearly there are major social problems if a large group of citizens have so little faith in fundamental structures that are intended to provide services and support to them. This gives us a clear sign that the effects of police-related deaths go far beyond the police and criminal justice system in America.

On the other hand, White participants largely had a more positive belief in a just world prior to their relative being killed, and a higher level of expectation that the death would be properly investigated, leading to some sort of accountability in the aftermath of the death. This was not the case in their experiences and consequently their belief systems were fundamentally challenged. They commonly talked about how their previously held beliefs were mistaken, and that this had been learned from bitter experience. One aspect of this was a capacity to reflect on their previously high level of belief in a just world. They acknowledged how difficult it would be to convince others of their experiences, because they knew they themselves would be sceptical of them had they not had first-hand experience of a police-related death. They recognised the reactions of wider society to their loss in terms of victim blaming because they'd also previously held similar views.

One White father summed up a common sentiment: 'I didn't even realise till my daughter was killed that this system existed, and I don't think most people do . . . because all the preconceived bias they may have, and you know it creates cognitive dissonance from what they believe is the truth.' Cognitive dissonance occurs when the belief that police exist to serve and protect is overturned by the reality of an officer killing your loved one and not being held to account for their actions. Cognitive dissonance taps into the fundamental principles of denial and avoidance on which belief in a just world is founded. Most people believe they inhabit a just world, and perceive the other world to be a 'world of victims' (Lerner 1980: 23–26). Therefore, until an issue of injustice directly affects you, your belief in a just world is unlikely to alter. It's clear that this links to Terpstra and Trommel's (2009) concept of pragmatic legitimacy.

We should remember that although these beliefs appear heartless, they are largely related to personal self-preservation and wellbeing, something we can all recognize. Making sense of the world is a way to ensure normality and be a functional human. We might make a decision to *act* as though the world is just and fair rather than actually believing it *is* just and fair (see Bastounis and Minibas-Poussard 2012, Faccenda and Pantaléon 2011). Another way of explaining this mindset is to consider how much effect humans can actually have on unjust situations produced by sociopolitical and sociolegal structures. Most of us have felt powerless before institutions at some point in our lives, and uncertain of how to deal with their decisions or behaviors. If we maintain a belief in a just world, it can help us cope with that. If we don't do that, we risk becoming engulfed by feelings of powerlessness and overcome by helplessness—that route could lead to mental ill health. In short: if we can't change things, why challenge them, because it will only lead to pain and disappointment. So it's more useful for our wellbeing to invest in a comforting construct.

CONSTRUCTING OUTLOOKS ON LIFE AND DEATH

Belief in a just world, disenfranchised grief and procedural justice bring together a variety of issues that influence our outlook on life. They all relate directly to our sense of self-identity and self-worth. If we believe we're being listened to, and being taken account of, we feel that we are a part of wider society. That positively affects our health, and the relationships we have with our families, friends and wider communities. It makes us more likely to trust people and organizations, and believe in the structures and processes that underpin our societies. This in turn makes us more likely to participate in those structures and processes, and be positively engaged in our social worlds. These are basic principles informing how we live in democracies. That we count, that things are fair, that the truth will come out, and there will be justice that overturns incidents of injustice.

If this is not the case, that we feel we're not listened to, and not taken account of, then clearly this will negatively affect our identities and sense of self-worth. If you have a low belief in a just world, feel that the justice system is a producer of unjust outcomes, and are prevented from grieving in the same way as your neighbor, then clearly this will have deleterious effects on your health and engagement with the world. One aspect of this can be seen in Desmond et al.'s (2016) research into Black communities in the US that found they were significantly less likely to call 911 than White communities in the same city. As was previously noted in this chapter, we're not talking about a few thousand people, we're talking about millions of people cut adrift from mainstream society because of their experiences. If one maintains a belief in a just world because the alternative is too awful to contemplate, then we should acknowledge that the alternative is the actual lived experience of millions of one's fellow citizens. Ignorance may be bliss for some people, but denial and avoidance is not always possible, or preferable in life, as most of us know from other forms of life experience. The limited research on police-related deaths only serves to underline the perceived relative lack of value of those who die and the loved ones they leave behind. Lives that could have been lived, stories that will never be told. Children who will never become parents, or go on to be grandparents. Ronnie Greene (2015: 208) closes his book on police killings in New Orleans by quoting Sherrel Johnson talking about her son James Brisette who was shot dead by police aged 17: "I wonder what he would be. I wonder 'what if.' My whole life . . . is spent wondering."

Another often overlooked issue is how officers are affected by PRDs. I don't necessarily mean the officer/s who fired their weapons, but also officers that witnessed the death, or were affected by the aftermath of such deaths. The health of officers, particularly in terms of mental health, and susceptibility to alcohol or drug dependency, has been highlighted as a point of concern by a number of writers (see Bishopp and Paquette Boots 2014, Crank 2016). It seems likely that officers could be adversely affected by PRDs, whether they're able to admit it or not. Reducing the number of PRDs and instances where force is used is likely to benefit officers as well as the communities they're sworn to serve and protect. Sugimoto and Oltjenbrun's (2001) research on police officers working in fatal incidents found that police culture disenfranchises officers and survivors from grief as it prevents the recognition of any relationship between officers and the deceased. It also fails to recognise either party as grievers; and regards the death as relatively inconsequential. It seems unlikely that all officers feel this way in the aftermath of fatal incidents, but their occupational culture forces them to block any feelings of grief they might have. This could have consequences on their wellbeing, but also their future performance.

A consistent finding on police culture is that officers tend to become cynical and disaffected in their jobs (see, for example Reiner 2010, Punch 2009). Crank (2016), as an ex-officer, reflectively ponders the issue of officer suicide. He says that if Van Maanen (1978) was right about officers viewing a group of citizens as assholes, and if they then become imbued with a deep cynicism about their role, it's inevitable some of them will come to the conclusion that they, too, are assholes for doing a job that regularly deals with assholes, and turn the gun on themselves. Just as the huge suicide count of citizens in the US doesn't generate much discussion, nor do the reasons for officer suicide or mental ill health. There is a lack of honest dialogue about this whole issue. It might be that death itself is considered to be a contentious subject to discuss in the US, as has been noted by a variety of authors (Gorer 1995, Gawande 2015)

STRUCTURAL VIOLENCE

I have focused on structural issues as being key to understanding how and why people die after contact with police. As we move towards a conclusion, it is necessary to consider other ways in which we might make sense of how the structures and systems examined in these seven chapters prove to be so resistant to change, and how we seem to be stuck in a repetitive cycle of death and trauma. One potential approach comes from the field of peace studies. The concept of structural violence was first proposed by Johan Galtung (1969). He argued that violence is not only something manifest as a direct, physical action, it can also affect individuals in indirect and invisible ways. Using this lens, violence is seen to restrict a person's ability to achieve their goals by blocking them via unseen structural restraints. Examples of this are poor quality education, housing, and employment—any or all of which could prevent individuals reaching their potential. If someone living in a society which has a modern healthcare system dies from TB, then clearly that is avoidable and for Galtung (1969: 168–171) 'violence is present'; similarly, 'if people are starving when this is objectively avoidable, then violence is committed.'

As such, structural violence focuses on inequality in specific groups in society in seeking to explain how disproportionate outcomes persistently occur with minority groups in society. Societal power bases enable such structures to operate because it is in their interests to do so. It is not necessarily a deliberate intention to withhold resources, or inflict violence. In this way, structural violence can be both indirect and invisible. From this perspective, violence can also be latent—the threat of it occurring is enough for it to create an atmosphere of malevolence and affect peoples' behavior and outlook on society. The latency means that there can be a deep undercurrent of potential violence that would only require a minor incident to spark it, like a trap waiting to be sprung (Galtung 1969: 172). It's difficult to read this and not think of the uprisings that can occur after police-related deaths.

In the 21st century, these ideas have been extended by Jamil Salmi (2004). For him, violence by omission is a form of indirect violence that can be represented as types of 'social violence.' One example Salmi gives is the tens of thousands of deaths each year due to the absence of gun control laws in the US. Omission is seen as leading to avoidable deaths. He adds a further category of 'alienating violence,' defined as 'denying a person the right to psychological, emotional, cultural or intellectual integrity' (Salmi 2004: 59). This can be seen to directly apply to many of the principles identified in the discussion of disenfranchised grief and the belief in a just world, in addition to applying to the disproportionate police focus on minorities.

Both Galtung and Salmi make clear that violence can also be physical and direct, but for both of them violence exists on a continuum—one might argue a continuum of visibility. Explicit violence can be captured on film, but structural, indirect or alienating violence cannot. For both authors, any harm that can be reasonably avoided can be considered to be a form of violence, and clearly police-related deaths can fall into this category. Thinking about these issues differently and reframing them is one way in which we might break the cycle on police-related deaths. The concept of structural violence also goes some way to explaining the rise and growth of campaign groups like BLM in trying to draw attention to acts of daily, ritual aggression which have apparently been invisible for so long. It was notable, for example, that in the aftermath of George Floyd's death in 2020, a number of media commentators focused on damage to buildings in the subsequent uprisings, rather than on damage inflicted on humans.

Pre-Ferguson there was limited interest and focus on police killings, so much so that they are still not counted in a way that can be considered to be accurate. Suicides go similarly uncounted by federal and state agencies. The same applies to those people who are left behind in the aftermath of homicides. It's probably a conservative estimate to say that since the turn of the century these issues combined have directly led to approximately 850,000 deaths, and gone on to affect the lives of a further six to ten million people. This is not a particularly edifying picture, even less so when one considers the lack of attention given to these life and death issues by mainstream society. Who counts? Maybe the question should be: who cares? All of this matters because it poisons the well that society drinks from. It corrodes the structures of society, damaging belief in justice, law, democracy, participation and ultimately the whole idea of public services. It degrades our sense of meaning and fairness, of rightness and equality. Be in no doubt that these deaths have effects that go far beyond merely policing and criminal justice. All of this affects our identity because it affects how we value human life. We are social animals, not individuals that live in silos. If the Covid-19 pandemic has taught us anything, it taught us that.

Chapter 7

Business as Usual?

This book argues that police-related deaths are the result of systemic and structural issues that exist in the US. These deaths should not be considered as individual 'tragedies' in terms of police/citizen interactions. Three deaths per day suggest they are normal. As the book represents the conclusion of a five year research project, it seems appropriate to reflect on aspects of it at the beginning of this final chapter. It was a difficult task to select the individual case studies for this book. In reality, I could have picked any of the deaths that I investigated during the research. What quickly struck me was the similarity of stories I heard from families who'd had loved ones killed by police in the US. Given that I conducted interviews in 16 different states, and that the deaths represented a fairly broad demographic in terms of race, gender, and age, this similarity seemed particularly significant. Because of this representative spread, some basic but original findings leapt out, and can be seen in aspects of this book. Of the seven deaths considered in the previous chapters, only two occurred in large cities—John T. Williams in Seattle, and Jonathen Santellana in Houston. PRDs are not just a 'big city' issue. Data from The Counted in 2016 ranked PRDs per capita by state; rated from one to ten the states where citizens were most likely to be killed by officers were: Alaska, New Mexico, Oklahoma, DC, Arkansas, Arizona, West Virginia, South Dakota, Colorado and Alabama. With the possible exception of DC these states are not what one might consider to be the 'usual suspects.' Of the cases examined in this book, three were shot by either off-duty cops or undercover officers. PRDs are not just about uniformed patrol officers. The age of those who die is another area where presumptions are challenged. Zimring (2017: 48) notes that one third of those who die in PRDs are over 40: 'Crime is a young man's game in the United States but being killed by a police officer is not.' To understand more about police-related deaths, we need to know more about them. We can't expect to effect change if we don't know what it is we're trying to change from.

RETHINKING POLICE-RELATED DEATHS

In the fall of 2016, I was invited to participate in a panel discussion at a college about police-related deaths. At that time, the two PRDs causing national outrage were Keith Lamont Scott in Charlotte (NC), and Terence Crutcher in Tulsa (OK). Both men were Black, in their 40s, unarmed and shot dead within a few days of each other. These deaths were the catalyst for the panel discussion, and several hundred people attended. I was conscious of being the only non-American on the panel, but also that I was apparently the only academic expert on police-related deaths too. I was curious about how the debate would turn out, and what the tone of it would be. Nearly everyone present was a student, or worked in some capacity or other for the college. From the outset, I was startled at the lack of knowledge in the room on the issue, and about policing more generally. It became obvious that most people saw these deaths as tragic or egregious one-offs. A majority of people didn't seem to really know what stop and frisk was, how traffic stops worked, or how police routinely targeted minority populations. If you're from a major city in the US you might be rolling your eyes reading this—and I understand that—but a significant proportion of Americans don't live in large cities, and we need to remember that, too. A theme of this book is that more people need to ask more questions. Those questions need to come from a knowledge based on understanding some of the key issues related to police practice in the United States.

Towards the end of the meeting each panel member was asked to give a view on 'what would happen next in the aftermath of the deaths of Keith Lamont Scott and Terence Crutcher?' The gist of each participant's response was, more or less—things had to change to ensure justice, liberty and equality for all. But whilst this aspiration for change was certainly earnest and well-intentioned, how such change was to come about was (to me, at least) uncertain. Each speaker was clapped enthusiastically after their piece. I spoke last, and bluntly said that nothing would happen in the aftermath of these deaths. Police would carry on killing citizens as usual, because such deaths were structural—not at all one-offs—in fact they were probably doing so somewhere in the US right now as we sat in the hall. That didn't go down terribly well with the audience. I wasn't booed or barracked, but what I said was largely received in silence. I concluded by suggesting that police-related deaths should be reframed as preventable deaths and addressed as a healthcare crisis in order to reduce the number of deaths—that got a more positive response. I've kept this discussion in mind as I have written this book. It seems likely that in the four years since then, more people in the US know more about policing, justice and PRDs than was previously the case—I hope so. I hope this book can add to the canon of knowledge on these issues and enable readers to better understand how this complex jigsaw fits together. In this conclusion I want to look hard, carefully, and straight ahead at this problem and how it might be addressed in a variety of practical and realistic ways. I hope you'll forgive me if I'm a little aspirational as well.

CONTINUITY AND CHANGE

Activist groups who have been working in this sphere for decades know from bitter experience not to be overly encouraged by the huge uprising that followed George Floyd's death. At the time of writing, it remains uncertain what sort of changes might be wrought. All of the evidence, though, suggests that there will likely be both continuity and change in relation to police-related deaths. Incremental change will occur in PDs across the US. It's likely that more officers will be prosecuted for PRDs, and reasonably likely that more will also serve time as a result. The reduction of police budgets and reallocation of funds to service providers in the community is likely to become more commonplace. The general trend that had already begun to proscribe police use of force by having more specific policies in place will probably continue. Similarly, parts of the US are likely to curtail or completely ban police from using weapons such as flash-grenades and tear gas. It is possible that the use of SWAT teams will be reduced, and that the number of SWAT teams in smaller PDs will diminish. These are all real changes, it would be churlish to suggest otherwise. And they may lead to a reduction in the number of PRDs.

If we look at each of those issues in turn, we're less likely to feel optimistic. Prosecutions are likely to occur in high profile cases only when there is plenty of evidence that officers used lethal force (Jones-Brown and Blount Hill 2020). With more than a thousand police-related deaths a year, it seems unlikely that there will be a prosecution rate of more than 2%, or a conviction rate of more than 1% in the foreseeable future. Cutting $150M from the LAPD budget sounds like a major step forward, until one acknowledges that their total budget is $1.7Bn—representing a cut of about 9%. Another note of caution can be struck in relation to the city of Minneapolis. In June 2020, the city council attempted to progress legislation aiming to defund the PD and introduce a more holistic approach to promoting community safety. Five months later, it granted the Minneapolis PD an extra $500,000 due to a surge in the rate of violent crime (Washington Post 2020). The trend towards clearer use of force policies, using less paramilitary style ordnance and SWAT deployment was already in train. If that has been speeded up, so much the better. But it doesn't represent 'new change,' even if it has been repackaged and sold in that way.

Other initiatives that attempt to address issues related to PRDs have been examined in more detail in previous chapters. Whilst BWCs, implicit bias training, CITs and procedural justice can be seen as positive signs of change from within the criminal justice system, they should also be viewed with caution. BWCs are meant to enable a more transparent style of policing, but policing isn't in essence a transparent practice, nor is it driven by transparent policies or regulated by transparent governance. In this sense, we can see a bolt-on idea, leaving the underlying principles and practice of policing largely unchanged. Implicit bias training and procedural justice are both grounded in the principle of training officers to better understand the communities they police, and thus practice in a more respectful and consensual manner.

So whereas BWCs are meant to address issues in the here and now with real time recording, the training of officers aims to produce long-term cultural change in police practice by encouraging officers to be more reflective and thoughtful about their craft. It's also intended to improve perceptions about how they are seen to be doing their job, thus enhancing police legitimacy. But once again we return to the lack of data. We don't know how many PDs use BWCs or how often; we don't know how many PDs use the principles of procedural justice or awareness of implicit bias in their training; nor do we know the form such training might take. We don't know how any of these measures are being evaluated, in fact we don't even know *if* they are being evaluated. Like so many other issues related to police-related deaths, we just don't know.

INSTITUTIONAL REACTIONS TO CRITICISMS AND CRISES

James Gilsinan (2012) uses the biological term 'isomorphism' to characterize policing. This means that the outward appearance of it may change dependent on environmental conditions, but the root of it remains the same. We can see this with BWCs, implicit bias training and procedural justice, all of which are reactions to societal demands for change. They may be entirely well-meaning and well-intentioned reactions, but that doesn't alter the fact that they also enable the root to remain unchanged. A corollary of this is that once environmental conditions change again, the root can produce a different outgrowth—or go back to how it appeared in a previous iteration. One further consideration is that these changes come about as a result of being under pressure. Like all other organizations (and people, usually) policing only accedes to change in times of crises. Times of crises do not represent ideal opportunities for organizations to reflect on the nature of things, about what could be done differently, or how roles could be reimagined. Instead they produce relatively direct solutions that can be implemented rapidly in order to address the current crisis.

Implicit bias training and procedural justice rely on officers putting training into practice. In order for them to do that, buy-in is required, and this runs into the rock of police culture. If policing largely focuses disproportionately on suspect populations, then implicit bias training won't change that. Having a better sense of who one is dealing with is signally different to asking why police are focusing so much of their time on those communities in the first place. The principles underpinning procedural justice are largely antithetical to the valorization of force and authority in US policing. They also run contrary to the trend towards paramilitarism and using force to suppress legitimate protests about the very force that provoked protests in the first place. Both implicit bias training and procedural justice are at best attempts to ameliorate some of the very deep-seated principles that underpin the structures and systems of policing in the US. At worst they are merely distractions—something to provide an attractive façade to cloak the unpleasant realities felt by many minorities during interactions with officers.

Police and governmental authorities are experts at deflection, obfuscation, and obstruction. They're also adept at stating they hear the voice of the people and will change. They know they have to maintain enough legitimacy to satisfy most of the population, most of the time, on most issues, and go about their business with that in mind. Put bluntly: they're good at hunching their shoulders, bulling their way through the storm and waiting for it to pass. These concessions—which is what they surely are—are minimal. They're merely crumbs from the high table. The fact that these issues are beginning to be discussed in wider circles of society is heartening. The more people know about an issue based on evidence, the more they understand it. Once more people know about the reality of policing, they might become more aware of how it has affected so many others for so long. But it's striking that we still lack so much evidence on the specific issue of PRDs, and this is a real cause for concern.

The lack of knowledge inevitably hinders efforts to effect changes in the number of deaths, police practice, and all the rest of it. One obvious approach to take towards reducing the number of deaths is to adopt a situationally based approach to analysing patterns, trends and causes in relation to these deaths, much as the police do when attempting to minimise crime and regulate order. But there is no Compstat for PRDs, it goes without saying. At PD level, this would involve monitoring and evaluating a range of patterns. Tightening up use of force policies, gathering accurate data on when force is used, and identifying the officers that are most likely to use it, where and in what circumstances. By focusing on practice, the practice can be regulated. There could be increased focus on why and in what circumstances officers fire multiple shots, and an analysis of why shots are fired at fleeing suspects, for example.

SITUATIONAL AND INCREMENTAL CHANGE

Throughout the book it's been very clear that the hugely fragmented nature of policing in the US represents significant challenges to applying best practice, promoting accountability, learning lessons and implementing change. Perhaps the only holistic and concerted attempts at this are via consent decrees, but these are time and resource intensive interventions that can neither be widely nor frequently used. It seems likely that a form of state-based intervention might be more realistic and more effective. Each state should have an independent agency that collates all of the available data from PDs in their jurisdiction on a mandatory basis and uses it not only to promote better practice but also to intervene and enforce more consistent standards of policing where applicable.

Such an agency could focus on problem PDs, and on problem officers within those PDs. There could be a focus on whether shots should be fired at citizens wielding knives, or being more specific about what sort of knife might merit an officer using their weapon. The recruitment of officers could be made more thorough with a focus on identifying officers who move PDs in an attempt to leave their poor records behind (Goldman 2016). Such officers are often referred to as 'gypsy cops' (see CBS 2016); an obvious example in this book being the officer who shot Jonathen Santellana dead. Investigative reporters in California discovered that in the decade prior to 2019, one in five officers in McFarland PD had been previously fired, sued for misconduct, or convicted of criminal offenses (Sacramento Bee 2019). Nor is this issue limited to the US. In London in 2009, Ian Tomlinson was found to have been unlawfully killed by PC Simon Harwood after being hit with a baton and pushed to the ground. In the investigations that unfolded after the death, it emerged that PC Harwood had a long list of disciplinary transgressions and had left one police force prior to a disciplinary hearing, only to rejoin a different force at a later stage (Baker 2016).

The composition of officers within PDs was something many families in my research commented on. Typically, participants focused on young and/or inexperienced officers, and their unsuitability to work in complex environments. It's notable that of the cases considered in this book, John T. Williams, Nate H. Pickett II and Jonathen Santellana were all shot dead by officers with fewer than two-years' service. Similarly, a number of families commented on the use of ex-military personnel and how that affected their outlook as police officers. These concerns are not unfounded. A number of researchers have found that younger and less experienced officers, and those who previously served in the military are more likely to use force (McElvain and Kposowa 2004, Terrill and Paoline 2015, Nix et al. 2017).

There could be a focus on not preferring ex-military personnel and instead focusing on recruiting more women and People of Color, in addition to raising the bar in terms of the educational standard required to be an officer. State oversight agencies could also promote an improved quality of training that places increased emphasis on the needs of citizens who are mentally impaired and/or homeless. Those agencies could enhance focus on how People of Color are policed and encourage the formalization of police-community relationships. One further obvious strategy that could be adopted would be to facilitate multiagency working between police and healthcare agencies, social and youth work provision, charities and activist groups. Underpinning all of this is one fundamental proposition: if there were fewer contacts between police and citizens, period, then there would be fewer police-related deaths.

These issues all represent incremental changes. If—and it's a very big if—they could be adopted and applied across the nation, it would reduce the number of people's lives terminated by police each year in the US. It would reduce the number of times that force is used by police, and reduce the severity of that force when it is used. The changes would almost certainly improve police legitimacy and begin to foster better relationships with communities. The fact that these changes haven't occurred yet tells us a lot about the current state of affairs, for these changes aren't exactly rocket science—they would be relatively easy to adopt, in principle.

CULTURAL CHANGE

I've presented a long list of reasonably achievable measures above that might produce relatively meaningful change. Academic literature on policing tells us that this is what police and regulators usually aim at first when it comes to attempting to change policing practice, and it can certainly be seen in the approach adopted by consent decrees. However, the literature also tells us that to effect more widespread and long-lasting change, the culture of policing needs to shift. A key reason why incremental change is focused upon, is that it's much easier to impose and measure than changes to police culture. The President's Task Force (2015) was correct to propose that officers should be guardians, not warriors. If that mindset were adopted by PDs across the land, we'd start to look at policing as a different sort of occupation than we do at present. The recruitment and training of officers would change to emphasise communication skills, deescalation and conflict resolution. SWAT teams would pretty much disappear, and those that remained would be there for the original reasons for which they were conceived: hostage situations and sieges (Kraska 2007).

The number one goal of police officers should be to preserve life, as is the case in the UK. If that is the ultimate goal of each officer, then the last thing they should be thinking about is using their weapon. Another black hole of knowledge is the absence of literature on police training or knowledge of first-aid in the US. I'm uncertain as to whether that is because such training isn't common, or whether it's just not researched. Undoubtedly, there will be cases where officers have to shoot citizens to protect their own lives or the lives of others. But what we don't know, because of the lack of data, is how many could be shot and still live if officers were trained and regulated in a different way; or how many lives would be saved because officers didn't fire at all. If life is to be preserved, PDs could be encouraged to work with other organizations to learn lessons about how to deal with vulnerable groups. We know from CITs that there is some evidence they appear to work, so it could also work in other situations such as with younger people, homeless people, or people who are dependent on substances.

If these practices could be adopted, we'd move closer to what the original idea of policing was in the US—the 'peace officer.' We would not be far away from Shane (2013) and Doyle's (2010) vision of police as 'safety officers.' If a culture of safety could begin to grow in policing, the organic effects of that might produce results that are currently not even being conceived of— it's a world we can only imagine. We need to remember that SWAT teams, paramilitarization and the police pursuing Wars on Terror and Drugs are relatively new developments in the history of policing the US. If policing can be reformulated to adopt those approaches, we might just as well imagine a completely different type of approach and provision.

Police culture is seen as being the most influential factor affecting how officers undertake their work. The fact that so much academic research has been conducted on police culture over such a long period of time is testament to its enduring grip. A wide range of literature on policing from the previous fifty years has been surveyed in this book, and perhaps the most consistent observation one can make is that the principles underpinning police culture have remained relatively unchanged during this period. The writings of Egon Bittner from the 1960s remain unerringly relevant despite the huge changes to society, governance, law, civil rights, technology and the media. His observations that policing focuses disproportionately on minorities; relies on the capacity to use force; and is rarely held accountable for these issues remain as accurate today as when he originally wrote them. Therefore it behoves us to consider possible solutions that transcend policing entirely, particularly given the isomorphic tendencies of policing already identified.

POLICE-RELATED DEATHS AS
HEALTHCARE EMERGENCIES

It might be necessary to reimagine police-related deaths in order to reframe them and make progress, something the book has aimed to do by demonstrating how the jigsaw fits together and how it won't be easy to take it apart and rebuild it in a different way. PRDs are *avoidable deaths*. They are *preventable*. We know (roughly) how many there are; we know where they are; we know who is predominantly affected by them; we increasingly know more about the circumstances that lead to citizens' deaths.

If these deaths resulted from a disease, and we had knowledge of all the issues above, we'd do something about it to reduce the number of preventable deaths. Reimagining this as a healthcare issue rather than a law enforcement issue could be one way of trying to break the cycle on how we view such deaths. Gary Slutkin's (2013) studies begin from the hypothesis that violence is a virus—it can be studied, measured and reduced by applying epidemiological principles. Slutkin's work reframed the approach to gun violence and deaths in parts of the US as a healthcare issue. In this view, violence is contagious, and the way to reduce it is threefold. First, transmission needs to be interrupted—trained professionals need to ensure that the potential for violence to be used is disrupted. Second, there needs to be an attempt to prevent the spread of violence by outreach workers checking in on those who have used it previously to monitor their behaviour and outlook. Third, these two steps can lead to new norms being established around what is considered acceptable and desirable. Slutkin (2013) is emphatic in believing that the use of violence is not an issue determined by 'bad guys' and so should not therefore be exclusively dealt with by the criminal justice system.

We could apply the first and second principles to PDs and use of force policies being used in conjunction with training and monitoring processes. These could lead to the third principle being engaged, whereby a critical mass of police officers buy into these principles and collectively shift policing culture to a point where using violence is no longer valorized, but problematized. This could represent the beginnings of a culture of safety, as distinct to a culture of enforcement. Notably, this change would be generated within the profession of policing and promote buy-in over enforcement through regulation. The Covid-19 pandemic might have shifted the terrain a little on this issue, with an increasing number of commentators pointing out that police killing is a deadly virus, as is racism.

Then again, there are plenty of other healthcare issues relating to preventable deaths that remain unaddressed despite us knowing about them for decades. Most of which result in a much more significant death toll than the number of citizens who die after police contact. As I write this, the Covid-19 pandemic is killing more than a thousand people a day in the US, and it is widely predicted that the final death toll will exceed some half a million souls. The number of deaths by guns in the US stands at about 110 per day, or 40,000 per year. This seems to go largely unremarked, yet these deaths are also clearly preventable. It seems that after every mass shooting people say 'this time it's going to be different,' before the issue once again fades away or is kicked into the long grass.

Deaths in healthcare, largely as a result of societal inequalities and a dysfunctional healthcare system, remain stubbornly unaddressed despite various commissions and attempts to reform healthcare provision in the US. There appears to be a broad coalition of politicians, activists and academics in agreement that prisons don't work if their purpose is to rehabilitate offenders. But we still use them to incarcerate more than two million humans with a further four million souls still on probation or parole (Vitale 2017). All of these issues are deeply embedded in the fabric of society. How much does society *want* change? Because that is a fundamental question that could enable change in the arena of police-related deaths. When we consider the issue of preventable deaths from the perspectives set out above, suddenly PRDs don't look so exceptional. They appear remarkably quotidian, an entirely normal, everyday way to die in America. Presenting them as unusual or exceptional is part of the construct we buy into that blinds us to the dismal reality of violent and preventable death in the United States. The supposedly atypical nature of these deaths presents them as being difficult to address. But in reality, on the continuum of preventable deaths in the US, they're entirely predictable. Another construct shatters on contact with reality.

RECOGNIZING PROBLEMS AND SOLUTIONS: RECONCILIATION

The apparently intractable nature of this problem has historical precedents elsewhere on our planet. In South Africa, the brutal apartheid regime was dismantled from within, a new constitution was written, and the police force was reimagined (Spies 2002). In Northern Ireland, long-term violence and killing was halted by both sides agreeing a ceasefire based on establishing a new form of democratic rule, by agreeing to renounce violence and by also reimagining the role of the police (Landon 2005). Common to both countries' processes were some fundamental points. One was a recognition that in order to break the deadlock, save lives, and reduce harm, suffering and trauma, both sides had to accept that they were fundamentally part of the problem, and were therefore also fundamentally part of the solution (Maylor and Spivak 2018, Fitz-Gibbon 2016).

From that point there could be an acceptance that their future positions had to alter, and had to better take into account the other's views, not just oppose them (Spies 2002). How are we to deal with centuries of historical oppression? The pain, the deaths, the suffering? By having an honest conversation about it, by acknowledging and accepting that wrongs were done and errors were made. Writing about the peace process in South Africa, Maylor and Spivak (2018) cite Archbishop Desmond Tutu: 'We needed to acknowledge that we had a horrendous past. We needed to look the beast in the eye, so that the past wouldn't hold us hostage anymore.' The nature of racialized violence and intergenerational trauma in South Africa would appear to have parallels with police-related deaths in the US. These are no small issues, certainly not. But the way to break out of stasis isn't incrementally, it has to be radical. Incremental approaches at reform have failed, time and time again. In South Africa and Northern Ireland there was a political will to change, to break the deadlock. This did not only come from formally elected politicians or leaders, but was subject to a myriad of other influences within their societies. Ultimately, it took the courage and fortitude of political leaders to significantly alter their previously entrenched positions in order to reshape a national dialogue of change (Landon 2005, Fitz-Gibbon 2016).

There are plenty of grassroots organizations in the US urging and supporting change. It remains to be seen whether there are a sufficient number of political figures with hearts and souls strong enough to be able to formalize such changes. One outcome of this might be to have a commission on truth and justice that examines historic cases and aims to formally acknowledge historic wrongs, whether at an institutional or individual level. South Africa and Northern Ireland, to some extent, put the need for truth and reconciliation above the need for accountability in order to be able to move forward with their peace processes (Maylor and Spivak 2018, Landon 2005). The overarching principles that change is a *process* founded on *dialogue* between all sides is key to both countries' experiences in transitioning to peaceful democracies (Powell 2009, Spies 2002). I am not suggesting that either South Africa or Northern Ireland represent some sort of utopian ideal. Both societies are still beset by all manner of serious challenges as a result of their respective historical legacies, but the principle stands that they were able to break out of a deeply harmful and apparently insoluble stalemate (Spies 2002, Nyuykonge and Zondi 2017, Landon 2005, Fitz-Gibbon 2016).

A running theme in this book is that there are different constructions of America, and that they are understood and experienced in different ways. The outcome of the 2020 election underlined this point, with the electorate split into two divergent camps, each with an apparently quite different view of what the United States is, and what it should be. We should therefore strike a note of caution in relation to the discussion above, particularly in the aftermath of the storming of the Capitol in DC in January 2021. Dialogue requires the various actors and camps involved in communities, policing, governmental and criminal justice organisations to *want to talk*. Can this happen in America, where the country is perhaps characterized more by division than union? Writing about how the South African peace process unfolded, Spies (2002) cites a key stakeholder stating: 'Over time we learned to turn away from our habit of fearing one another and instead begin to face our common problems and jointly find solutions. . . . As former adversaries found one another's humanity throughout the country, so the foundation began to be built for a place where we could one day all be human beings together.' Ceasefires in both countries were key to establishing a path towards nonviolent transitions, and to also demilitarizing police and security forces (Maylor and Spivak 2018, Landon 2005). One might argue that the term 'ceasefire' could be useful in rethinking and reformulating what policing could be in the US. In South Africa and Northern Ireland, the peace process was marked by police gradually becoming less prominent in everyday life due to the increasing pacification of society. As one participant of Landon's (2005: 70) research in Northern Ireland put it: 'We have a somewhat imperfect peace . . . [but] there's a lot of people alive today who would probably otherwise be dead, had the ceasefires not been in place.'

NOT KNOWN, WHO WANTS TO KNOW?

In 2002, James Fyfe wrote an article called 'Too Many Missing Cases: Holes in Our Knowledge About Police Use of Force' in which he was critical of the lack of official data on the use of force, noting that the great majority of what we knew came from journalists. He went on to be critical of academic researchers for not pursuing this subject, believing that to some extent it reflected a sort of elephant in the room of policing and justice research. When I read that article, I can't help but feel Fyfe was issuing a clarion call for academic researchers to seize the torch he and Jerome Skolnick set down in their 1993 book 'Above the Law,' written in the aftermath of the Rodney King beating. Arguably, Franklin Zimring (2017) wrote the first definitive evidence-based book on PRDs in the US. He made good use of data from The Counted, but also noted the paucity of academic research on this issue, reflecting Fyfe's observations 15 years previous. This situation began to change from about 2016 onwards as more academics began to write about PRDs, perhaps unsurprisingly in the aftermath of Ferguson. What is notable, though, is how many of these articles are critical of the lack of available data, but then go on to use it anyway, or to use datasets from PDs about the use of force or other related issues. There is little in the way of empirical field research on this issue. This not only says something about the issue itself, but also about academia. One might imagine that researchers could have examined media reports, or analysed the secondary data generated by crowd-sourced databases—and this has happened to a limited extent (see respectively, the former: Hirschfield and Simon 2010, Schroedel and Chin 2020; and the latter: Feldman et al. 2017).

Other approaches could consider either coroners or MEs involved in such deaths and what their work and/or perspectives on this issue might tell us; or evaluate the work of local prosecutors or attorneys employed by families of loved ones in relation to these deaths. A further possibility would be to conduct research on officer perceptions of this issue, or how they believe change might be effected that reduces the number of deaths. The growing use of CRBs points to another prospective avenue to research—examine the work of the very people tasked with overseeing the police in their locality. Another fruitful approach would be to consider the role of activist groups in seeking changes to police practice and regulation. There are a wide variety of these groups across the US, and they have made interventions on this issue in a number of ways. *If* there is empirical academic field-based research into coroners/MEs; local prosecutors and attorneys; members of CRBs; police officers' perceptions; or the views of activist groups then I am not aware of it, albeit it could be in progress at the time of writing.

But it tells us some uncomfortable truths about PRDs—not only do we lack data, we're not that interested in generating it. Most academic articles tend to cleave to the available secondary data generated by official authorities. At what point did academics decide to be so uncritical about an issue that is so evidently critical? Malcolm Young (1991: 48) was a senior officer in the British police, and his comments on police culture and practices strike a sobering note here. He says police are uninterested in social scientific research into their role—because they're fully aware of what they do and how it works: 'Who inside the system needs to be told what is well understood? Silence continues to maintain the hegemony, and social change only occurs when irresistible and more powerful forces are brought to bear from the outside.' As well as reflecting poorly on police, criminal justice and society, PRDs show academia in an unflattering light.

CHANGING THE PARAMETERS OF THE
DISCUSSION ON POLICE-RELATED DEATHS

In the face of the apparent inability of policing and the criminal justice system to reform, it's not surprising that campaigners have abandoned calls for reform and switched tack in attempting to force change. One strand of this approach is to hit police where it hurts—in their funding stream. As policing and politics in the US is inextricably linked, pressure on politicians can produce budgetary change that redefines issues in terms of how they should be addressed. Throughout the book we've examined a variety of issues that police are expected to deal with where many people would seriously question their professional competency to do so: mental ill-health, homelessness, alcoholism, drug dependency, and young people. In so many ways, police are square pegs hammered into round holes. And we know the type of damage well-intentioned but ill-advised hammering can cause. Funding bespoke agencies to address these problems could produce better outcomes for people that require help and support. It would also reduce the number of citizens criminalized as a result of who they are rather than what they've done; reduce demands on police resources; and ultimately be less expensive than current approaches (Vitale 2017).

Beyond defunding, the abolitionist argument emerges from the movement to abolish prisons (McLeod 2019). This is a reflection on societal evolution that believes if we could do without the police for the majority of human history, we can just as easily do without them now, and find a different way to promote safety and order in our communities. Vitale (2017) states that society requires safety and security, but they should not necessarily be provided by police, who have a historically poor record in doing so. The abolitionist movement seeks to transform society by focusing on harm reduction and a more equitable distribution of resources (McLeod 2019, Siegel 2017). As such, it is umbilically linked to Galtung (1969) and Salmi's (2004) conceptions of structural violence examined in the previous chapter. It proposes dismantling our current system of criminal justice and democracy and building new systems that place human development and safety at the centre of public service provision. Siegel (2017) argues that the only way to address the disproportionate focus of policing on People of Color is to remove police from the equation. Because they are so inextricably bound up with the oppression of People of Color, any attempt to reform them is essentially a fantasy. Police are well versed in shaping the agenda of discussions and framing issues from their perspective. In effect, managing the construction of reality in a way that suits their agenda. As Young (1991: 52) pointedly notes: 'Institutions have the pathetic megalomania of the computer whose whole vision of the world is its own program.' So deleting the program and reprogramming the system is considered to be the most effective way to move forward. Collectively, these arguments represent the ultimate response to the structural and systemic issues highlighted in this book, by aiming to do away with the structures and systems entirely (McLeod 2019).

The emergence of 'safety zones' in various cities in the aftermath of police-related deaths suggest that the abolitionist argument is gaining traction in a way that would have been unthinkable pre-Ferguson. This indicates that the work of BLM and so many other activist groups in the US is shifting the terrain of the debate on police-related deaths. The demographic shift of the US population gives us another pointer for how societal views on police-related deaths might change. In a 2017 Gallup survey, one of the groups that showed a decrease in confidence with the police was the 18–34 age group. Post-Ferguson, and now post–George Floyd, this seems likely to be of even more influence on how the debate on policing might play out in the US. Similarly, the increasing number of People of Color could add weight to this shift. White Americans are projected to be a minority by 2042, and in the under-18 age bracket by 2023 (PEW 2016). Demographic changes may produce demands for changes in police culture and practice.

Another way of reimagining police-related deaths is to reconsider what we mean by *rights*. The US has clung to the principle of civil rights rather than human rights in a way that reminds us of its tendency towards exceptionalism as distinct from universalism (see, for example Alexander 2012, Katz 2015). In June 2020, the UN Human Rights Committee issued a resolution mandating the preparation of a comprehensive report into 'systemic racism [and] violations of international human rights law against Africans and people of African descent by law enforcement agencies.' It stated that this was intended 'to contribute to accountability and redress for victims' (UN 2020). Various activist groups I worked with believed that a key way to drive change on these issues was to involve global organizations like the UN to intervene on the basis of human rights violations. A study by Amnesty International, for example, found that no state in the US complied with international law and standards on officer use of lethal force (Price and Payton 2017). In Europe, most countries are signatories of the European Convention on Human Rights (ECHR). This guarantees a number of human rights that override national laws. If a citizen feels their rights have been contravened, in principle they can appeal beyond the supreme court of their country and have their case heard by the European Court of Human Rights. This has consequently wrought changes to national laws based on verdicts it has delivered, which have impacted on how, for example, police-related deaths are investigated in terms of independence and rigor (Baker 2016). As a starting point, every PD in the US should clearly acknowledge the sanctity of human life. That would make a clear statement about the fundamental rights of humans in the US. This could be followed by a pledge to preserve lives using the principles of deescalation and medical intervention when required.

This book demonstrates that PRDs in the United States are innately bound up with the social, political, legal and cultural structures of the country. That is why this is a structural issue and that's why it's systemic. Any attempt to reduce the number of citizens killed means there will need to be an acknowledgment that structural and systemic change is required. That means not just on the part of police or other criminal justice agencies. They are one, albeit important, part of the jigsaw that represents the structural composition of the US. If police are a reflection of the society they serve, then it follows that society will need to change too. In the 1930s, George Orwell noted that there was persistent and widespread criticism of the British Empire from a broad group of liberal and left-wing groups within Britain. But what was its aim? It's one thing to be critical, another to propose solutions. Orwell proposed framing the question differently. Rather than ask 'what are the problems with the British Empire?'; the question should really be 'are you prepared to dismantle the British Empire?' This, he said, might elicit quite a different response from the critics, because the consequences of such actions would impact all societal groups. There would be implications for everyone, one wouldn't just be making criticisms of structures and systems safe in the knowledge that you would personally remain unaffected by any such changes.

We can sit back and say these issues are structural and systemic and thus keep them at arm's length. But this conveniently overlooks the fact that structures are made and maintained by humans, and that systems are too. Change must come from within society, which is to say, from the citizens. If you are committed to ending inequalities based on race, does that mean you're also committed to actions that enable more People of Color to have a better education, better housing, better jobs, and better healthcare? Even if that means your own standard of living, your own quality of life, or the standard of your family's access to these basic requirements for life might dip while a new equilibrium is established? In essence, that was Orwell's point.

Structures and systems are made and maintained by humans, so we can reimagine and remake them. If we can declare Wars on Drugs and Terrorism, then we can also stop them and start Wars on Poverty, Poor Quality Education and Unaffordable Healthcare. Why not talk about love, respecting every human as one's equal, the abolition of poverty, and making good quality education and proper healthcare accessible to all? Perhaps it could be a 21st century version of the American dream.

Bibliography

Adeshina, E (2014). Indictments, Convictions of Police Officers in Civilian Deaths Rare. Available at: http://www.chicagoreporter.com/indictments-convictions-police-officers-civilian-deaths-rare/ Accessed November 18th, 2018.

Adolfsson, K, and Strömwall, LA (2017). 'Situational Variables or Beliefs? A Multifaceted Approach to Understanding Blame Attributions'. *Psychology, Crime and Law*. 23 (6). 527–552.

Albalate, D (2013). 'The institutional, economic and social determinants of local government transparency'. *Journal of Economic Policy Reform*. 16. 90–107.

Alexander, M (2012). *The New Jim Crow: Mass Incarceration in the Age of Colorblindness*. New York. The New Press.

Alpert, GP, Cawthrway, T, Rojek, J, and Ferdik, K (2016). 'Citizen Oversight in the United States and Canada: Applying Outcome Measures and Evidence-Based Concepts'. In Prenzler, T, and den Heyer G (eds). *Civilian Oversight of Police: Advancing Accountability in Law Enforcement*. Boca-Raton. Taylor and Francis. 179–204.

Anaïs, S (2014). 'Making Up Excited Delirium'. *Canadian Journal of Sociology*. 39 (1). 45–64.

Angiolini, E (2017). *Report of the Independent Review of Deaths and Serious Incidents in Police Custody.*

Ariel, B, Farrar, W, and Sutherland, A (2015). 'The Effect of Police Body-Worn Cameras on Use of Force and Citizens' Complaints Against Police: A Randomised Trial.' *Journal of Quantitative Criminology*. 31. 509–535.

Australian Institute of Criminology (2013). Police shootings of people with a mental illness. *Research in Practice* [online], 34. Available from: http://www.aic.gov.au/publications/current%20series/rip/21-40/rip34.html [Accessed 29 September 2013].

Bacevich, AJ (2005). *The New American Militarism: How Americans Are Seduced by War.* Oxford. Oxford University Press.

Baker, D, and Norris, D (2021). 'Policing societies with firearms: evaluating the US and England and Wales'. In Poole, H, and Sneddon, S (eds). *Firearms: Global perspectives on consequences, crime and control.* London. Taylor and Francis.

Baker, D, and Norris, D (2020). 'Families' experiences of deaths after police contact in the United States: Perceptions of justice and injustice'. *International Criminal Justice Review.*

Baker, D, and Fidalgo, M (2020). "It's not OK to shoot and kill Americans": Families' perceptions of police use of lethal force in the United States'. *Journal of Crime and Justice.*

Baker, D (2019a). 'Using narrative to construct accountability in cases of death after police contact'. *Australian and New Zealand Journal of Criminology.* 52 (1). 60–75.

Baker, D (2019b). 'Five years after Ferguson, has anything changed?' *New Statesman.* Available at: https://www.newstatesman.com/world/north-america/2019/08/five-years-after-ferguson-has-anything-changed

Baker, D, and Pillinger, C (2020). '"These people are vulnerable, they aren't criminals": Mental health issues and deaths after police contact in England'. *The Police Journal: Theory, Practice, Principles.* 93 (1). 65–81.

Baker, D, and Pillinger, C (2019). '"If you call 911 they're going to kill me": Mental health and deaths after police contact in the United States'. *Policing and Society.* https://doi.org/10.1080/10439463.2019.1581193

Baker, D, Cherneva, V, and Norris, D (2019). 'Disenfranchised grief: families' experiences of deaths after police contact in the United States'. *OMEGA: Journal of Death and Dying.* https://doi.org/10.1177/0030222819846420

Baker, D (2018). 'Making sense of "excited delirium" in cases of death after police contact'. *Policing: A Journal of Policy and Practice.* 12 (4). 361–371.

Baker, D (2016). *Deaths after police contact: constructing accountability in the 21st century.* London. Palgrave-Macmillan.

Balko, R (2014). *Rise of the Warrior Cop.* United States: Public Affairs.

Bastounis, M, and Minibas-Poussard, J (2012). 'Causal Attributions of Workplace Gender Equality, Just World Belief, and the Self/Other Distinction'. *Social Behavior and Personality.* 40 (3). 433–452.

Beierlein, C, Werner, CS, Preiser, S, and Wermuth, S (2011). 'Are Just-World Beliefs Compatible with Justifying Inequality? Collective Political Efficacy as a Moderator'. *Social Justice Research.* 24. 278–296.

Bell, J, Stanley, N, Mallon, S, and Manthorpe, J (2012). 'Life will never be the same again: Examining grief survivors bereaved by young suicide'. *Illness, Crisis and Loss.* 20 (1). 49–68.

Bertot, JC, Jaeger, PT, and Grimes, JM (2010). 'Using ICTs to create a culture of transparency: E-government and social media as openness and anti-corruption tools for societies'. *Government Information Quarterly.* 27. 264–271.

Bieler, S (2016). 'Police militarization in the USA: the state of the field'. *Policing: An International Journal of Police Strategies and Management.* 39 (4). 586–600.

Bishopp, SA, and Paquette Boots, D (2014). 'General strain theory, exposure to violence, and suicide ideation among police officers: A gendered approach'. *Journal of Criminal Justice*. 42. 538–548

Bittner, E (1975). *The Functions of the Police in Modern Society: A Review of Background Factors, Current Practices and Possible Role Models*. New York: Aronson.

Bittner, E (1967). 'Police discretion in the emergency apprehension of mentally ill persons'. *Social Problems*. 14. 278–292.

Borum, R, Deane, M, Steadman, H, and Morrissey, J (1998). 'Police perspectives on responding to mentally ill people in crisis: Perceptions of program effectiveness'. *Behavioral Sciences and the Law*. 16 (4). 393–405.

Bovens, M (2007). 'Analysing and assessing accountability: a conceptual framework'. *European Law Journal*. 13 (4). 447–468.

Bradford, B, Jackson, J, and Stanko, E. (2009). 'Contact and Confidence: Revisiting the Impact of Public Encounters with the Police'. *Policing and Society*. 19 (1). 20–46.

Brodeur, J-P (2010). *The Policing Web*. New York. Oxford University Press.

Brown, D (1991). *Bury My Heart at Wounded Knee: An Indian History of the American West*. London. Vintage.

Brown, MK, Carnoy, M, Currie, E, Duster, T, Oppenheimer, DB, Shultz, MM, and Wellman, D (2003). *Whitewashing Race: The Myth of a Color-Blind Society*. Berkeley. University of California Press.

Bryant-Davis, T, Adams, T, Alejandre, A, and Gray, AA (2017). 'The Trauma Lens of Police Violence against Racial and Ethnic Minorities'. *Journal of Social Issues*. 73 (4). 852–871.

Butler, P (2017). *Chokehold: Policing Black Men*. NYC. New Press.

Campbell, BA, Nix J, and Maguire, ER (2017). 'Is the number of citizens fatally shot by police increasing in the post-Ferguson era?' *Crime and Delinquency*. 1–23.

Campeau, H (2015). '"Police Culture" at Work: Making Sense of Police Oversight'. *British Journal of Criminology*. 55. 669–687.

Center for Constitutional Rights (2012). *Stop and Frisk: The Human Impact*. Available at: https://ccrjustice.org/stop-and-frisk-human-impact

Center for Law and Social Policy (2015). College Preparation for African American Students:

Centers for Disease Control and Prevention (2019). Infant mortality. Available at: https://www.cdc.gov/reproductivehealth/maternalinfanthealth/infantmortality.htm

Gaps in the High School Educational Experience. Available at: https://cdn.uncf.org/wp-content/uploads/PDFs/College-readiness2-2.pdf?_ga=2.170012512.1305630060.1592931293-1178179463.1592931293

Cesario, J, Johnson, DJ, and Terrill, W (2019). 'Is There Evidence of Racial Disparity in Police Use of Deadly Force? Analyses of Officer-Involved Fatal Shootings in 2015-2016'. *Social Psychological and Personality Science*. 10 (5). 586–595.

Chan, J (1999). 'Governing Police Practice: Limits of the new accountability'. *British Journal of Sociology*. 50 (2). 251–270.

Chemerinsky, E (2001). 'The Role of Prosecutors in Dealing with Police Abuse: The Lessons of Los Angeles'. *Virginia Journal of Social Policy and the Law*. 8 (2). 305–327.

Christopher Commission (1991). *Report of the Independent Commission on the LAPD*. Available at: http://www.parc.info/client_files/Special%20Reports/1%20-%20 Chistopher%20Commision.pdf Accessed 21/10/14

Coates, T-N (2015a). *Between the World and Me*. Melbourne. Text Publishing.

Coates, T-N (2015b). 'A Corruption Beyond Chicago's Top Cop'. *The Atlantic*. Available at: https://www.theatlantic.com/notes/2015/12/ corruption-beyond-chicago-top-cop/418215/

Coglianese, C (2009). 'The transparency president? The Obama administration and open government'. *Governance*. 22. 529–544.

CBS (2016). 'Push to keep "gypsy cops" with questionable pasts off the streets'. Available at: https://www.cbsnews.com/news/gypsy-cops-with-questionable-pasts-hired-by-different-departments-lack-of-oversight-police/. Accessed 22/9/20.

Conti, N (2011). 'Weak Links and Warrior Hearts: A Framework For Judging Self And Others In Police Training'. Police Practice and Research 12 (5). 410–423.

Contradie, P, and Choenni, S (2014). 'On the Barriers for Local Government Releasing Open Data'. *Government Information Quarterly*. 31 (1). 10–17.

Cordaro, M (2012). 'Pet loss and disenfranchised grief: Implications for mental health counselling practice'. *Journal of Mental Health Counseling*. 34 (4). 283–294.

Crank, JP (2016). *Understanding Police Culture*. 2nd edn. New York. Routledge.

Crawford-Roberts, A, Shadravan, S, Tsai, J, Barceló, NE, Gips, A, Mensah, M, Roxas, N, Kung, A, Darby, A, Misa, N, Morton, I, and Shen, A (2020). 'George Floyd's Autopsy and the Structural Gaslighting of America'. *Scientific American*. Available at: https://blogs.scientificamerican.com/voices/ george-floyds-autopsy-and-the-structural-gaslighting-of-america/

Currie, E (2020). *A Peculiar Indifference: The Neglected Toll of Violence on Black America*. New York. Metropolitan.

Dai, M, Frank, J, and Sun, I (2011). 'Procedural justice during police-citizen encounters: The effects of process-based policing on citizen compliance and demeanor'. *Journal of Criminal Justice*. 39. 159–168

Data USA (2020). *Police Officers*. Available at: https://datausa.io/profile/soc/333050/

De Angelis, J (2016). 'What Do Citizens Think About Police Accountability Measures? Lessons From Community Attitudinal Surveys'. *Criminal Justice Policy Review*. 27 (5). 520–536.

De Angelis, J, Rosenthal, R, and Buchner, B (2016a). *Civilian Oversight of Law Enforcement: A Review of the Strengths and Weaknesses of the Various Models*. Available at: https://d3n8a8pro7vhmx.cloudfront.net/nacole/pages/161/ attachments/original/1481727977/NACOLE_short_doc_FINAL.pdf?1481727977

De Angelis, J, Rosenthal, R, and Buchner, B (2016b). *Civilian Oversight of Law Enforcement: Assessing the Evidence*. Available at: https://d3n8a8pro7vhmx. cloudfront.net/nacole/pages/161/attachments/original/1481727974/NACOLE_ AccessingtheEvidence_Final.pdf?1481727974 den Boer, M (1998). 'Steamy Windows: Transparency and Openness in Justice and Home Affairs'. In Deckmyn, V, and Thomson, I (eds). *Openness and Transparency in the European Union.* Maastricht. European Institute of Public Administration.

DOJ (2011). Investigation of the Seattle Police Department. Available at: https://www.justice.gov/sites/default/files/crt/legacy/2011/12/16/spd_findletter_12-16-11.pdf. Accessed 16th July, 2020.

Desmond, M, Papachristos, AV, and Kirk, DS (2016). 'Police violence and citizen crime reporting in the black community'. *American Sociological Review.* 81 (5). 857–876.

Doka, KJ (ed) (1989). *Disenfranchised grief: Recognising hidden sorrow.* New York: Lexington.

Doyle, J (2010). 'Learning from Error in American Criminal Justice'. *Journal of Criminal Law and Criminology.* 100 (1). 109–149.

Dunham, RG, and Petersen, N (2017). 'Making Black Lives Matter: Evidence-Based Policies for Reducing Police Bias in the Use of Deadly Force'. *Criminology and Public Policy.* 16 (1). 341–348.

Dworkin, R (1978). *Taking Rights Seriously.* Cambridge. Harvard University Press.

Dyson, S, and Boswell, G (2006). 'Sickle Cell Anaemia and Deaths in Custody in the UK and the USA'. *The Howard Journal.* 45 (1). 14–28

Emsley, C (2010). *The Great British Bobby: A History of British Policing from the Eighteenth Century to the Present.* London. Quercus.

Epp, CR, Maynard-Moody, S, and Haider-Markel, D (2014). *Pulled Over: How Police Stops Define Race and Citizenship.* Chicago. University of Chicago Press.

Eterno, J, and Silverman, E (2010). 'The NYPD's Compstat: compare statistics or compose statistics?' *International Journal of Police Science and Management.* 12 (3). 426–449.

Faccenda, L, and Pantaléon, N (2011). 'Analysis of the Relationships between Sensitivity to Injustice, Principles of Justice and Belief in a Just World'. *Journal of Moral Education.* 40 (4). 491–511.

Fairfax, RA (2017). 'The Grand Jury's Role in the Prosecution of Unjustified Killings – Challenges and Solutions'. *Harvard Civil Rights-Civil Liberties Law Review.* 397. 1–19.

Fassin, D (2013). *Enforcing Order: An Ethnography of Urban Policing.* Cambridge. Polity.

FBI (2018). 2017 Crime in the United States. Retrieved from https://ucr.fbi.gov/crime-in-the-u.s/2017/crime-in-the-u.s.-2017/tables/table-12.

FBI (2020). Law Enforcement Officers Killed and Assaulted (LEOKA). Program. Available at: https://www.fbi.gov/services/cjis/ucr/leoka. Accessed 16/9/20.

Feldman, JM, Gruskin, S, Coult, BA, and Krieger, N (2017). 'Quantifying under-reporting of law enforcement-related deaths in United States vital statistics and news-media-based data sources: A capture-recapture analysis. *PLoS Medicine.* 14 (10).

Finch, BK, Beck, A, Burghart, DB, Johnson, R, Klinger, D, and Thomas, K (2019). 'Using Crowd-Sourced Data to Explore Police-Related-Deaths in the United States (2000-2017): The Case of Fatal Encounters'. *Open Health Data.* 6. 1.

Fitz-Gibbon, A (2016). *Talking to Terrorists, Non-Violence, and Counter-Terrorism.* London. Palgrave-Macmillan.

Ford, C (2004). 'Understanding Our Pain: The Experiences of African American Women Through the Death and Dying Process'. In Fagan, A (ed) (2004). *Making Sense of Dying and Death.* Amsterdam. Rodopi. 51–66.

Fowlkes, MR (1990). 'The social regulation of grief'. *Sociological Forum.* 5 (4). 635–652.

Franz, S, and Borum, R (2011). 'Crisis Intervention Teams may prevent arrests of people with mental illness'. *Police Practice and Research.* 12 (3). 265–272.

Fridell, L (2017). 'Explaining the disparity in results across studies: Assessing disparity in police use of force'. *American Journal of Criminal Justice.* 42. 502–513.

Fridell, L, and Lim, H (2016). 'Assessing the racial aspects of police force using the implicit and counter-bias perspectives'. *Journal of Criminal Justice.* 44. 36–48.

Fyfe, J (1986). 'The Split-Second Syndrome and Other Determinants of Police Violence'. In Campbell, C, and Gibbs, J (eds). *Violent Transactions.* Oxford. Blackwell.

Fyfe, J (2002). 'Too many missing cases: Holes in our knowledge about police use of force'. *Justice* Research and Policy. 4. 87–102.

Fryer, RG (2016). 'An Empirical Analysis of Racial Differences in Police Use of Force'. *National Bureau of Economic Research.* Working Paper 22399.

Gaines, L, and Kappeler, V (2014). *Policing in America.* 8th edition. London. Anderson.

Galtung, J (1969). 'Violence, peace and peace research'. *Journal of Peace Research.* 6 (3). 167–191

Gascón, LD, and Roussell, A (2019). *The Limits of Community Policing: Civilian Power and Police Accountability in Black and Brown Los Angeles.* New York. NYU Press.

Gau, JM, Corsaro, N, Stewart, EA, and Brunson, RK (2012). 'Examining macro-level impacts on procedural justice and police legitimacy'. *Journal of Criminal Justice* 40. 333–343

Gawande, A (2015). *Being Mortal: Illness, Medicine, and What Matters in the End.* London: Profile.

Gilsinan, J (2012). 'The Numbers Dilemma: The Chimera of Modern Police Accountability Systems'. *Saint Louis University Public Law Review.* 32. 93–108.

Gonzales, AR, and Cochran, DQ (2017). 'Police-Worn Body Cameras: An Antidote to the "Ferguson Effect"?' *Missouri Law Review.* 82 (2). 299–337.

Gorer, G (1995). 'The Pornography of Death'. In Williamson, JB, and Shneidman, ES (eds). *Death: Current Perspectives.* 4th edn. London. Mayfield. 18–22.

Gov. UK (2020). Stop and search. Available at: Stop and search - GOV.UK Ethnicity facts and figures (ethnicity-facts-figures.service.gov.uk). Accessed 29/11/20.

Grant, V, and Green, L (2008). 'Gagged grief and beleaguered bereavements? An analysis of multidisciplinary theory and research relating to same sex partnership bereavement'. *Sexualities.* 11 (3). 275–300.

Green, B, and Roiphe, R (2017). 'Rethinking Prosecutors' Conflicts of Interest'. *Boston College Law Review.* 58 (2). 463–538.

Greene, R (2015). *Shots on the Bridge: Police Violence and Cover-up in the Wake of Katrina*. Boston. Beacon.

Gross, JP (2016). 'Judge, Jury and Executioner: The Excessive Use of Deadly Force by Police Officers'. *Texas Journal of Civil Liberties and Civil Rights*. 21 (2). 155–181.

Gruman, J, and Sloan, R (1983). 'Disease as Justice: Perceptions of the Victims of Physical Illness'. *Basic and Applied Social Psychology*. 4 (1). 39–46.

Hagiwara, N, Alderson, C., and McCauley, J (2015). '"We Get What We Deserve": The Belief in a Just World and its Health Consequences for Blacks'. *Journal of Behavioural Medicine*. 38 (6). 912–921.

Hails, J, and Borum, R (2003). 'Police training and specialized approaches to respond to people with mental illnesses'. *Crime and Delinquency*. 49 (1). 52–61.

Hall, A, and Coyne, C (2013). 'The Militarization of U.S. Domestic Policing'. *The Independent Review*. 17 (4). 485–504.

Hall, AV, Hall, EV, and Perry, JL (2016). 'Black and Blue: Exploring Racial Bias and Law Enforcement in the Killings of Unarmed Black Male Civilians'. *American Psychologist*. 71 (3). 175–186.

Hall, CA, Kader, AS, McHale, AMD, Stewart, L, Fick, GH, and Vilke, GM (2013). 'Frequency of signs of excited delirium syndrome in subjects undergoing police use of force: Descriptive evaluation of a prospective, consecutive cohort'. *Journal of Forensic and Legal Medicine*. 20. 102–107.

Hancock, L (2005). 'Significant Events in the Northern Ireland Peace Process: Impact and Implementation'. In Noel, S (ed). *From Power Sharing to Democracy*. Montreal. McGill-Queens Press. 67–84.

Hickman, M, and Poore, J (2016). 'National Data on Citizen Complaints About Police Use of Force: Data Quality Concerns and the Potential (Mis)Use of Statistical Evidence to Address Police Agency Contact'. *Criminal Justice Policy Review*. 27 (5). 455–479.

Hirschfield, P, and Simon, D (2010). 'Legitimating police violence – newspaper narratives of deadly force'. *Theoretical Criminology*. 14 (2). 155–182.

Hochschild, AR (2003). *The managed heart. Commercialization of human feelings*. Berkley, CA: University of California Press.

Hogg, R (2016). 'Left Realism and Social Democratic Renewal'. *International Journal for Crime, Justice and Social Democracy*. 5 (3). 66–79.

Holmes, MD, and Smith, BW (2012). 'Intergroup dynamics of extra-legal police aggression: An integrated theory of race and place'. *Aggression and Violent Behaviour*. 17. 344–353.

Jackson, J, and Bradford, B (2010). 'What is Trust and Confidence in the Police?'. *A Journal of Policy and Practice*. 4 (3). 241 248.

Jackson, J, Bradford, B, Hough, M, Myhill, A, Quinton, P, and Tyler, TR (2012). 'Why do People Comply with the Law?: Legitimacy and the Influence of Legal Institutions'. *The British Journal of Criminology*. 52 (6). 1051–1071

Jackson, R (2016). 'If they Gunned Me Down and Criming While White: An Examination of Twitter Campaigns Through the Lens of Citizens' Media'. *Cultural Studies: Critical Methodologies.* 16 (3). 313–319.

Jacobi, JV (2000). 'Prosecuting Police Misconduct'. *Wisconsin Law Review.* 789. 781–853.

James, L (2018). 'The Stability of Implicit Racial Bias in Police Officers'. *Police Quarterly.* 21 (1). 30–52.

Jennings, JT, and Rubado, ME (2017). 'Preventing the Use of Deadly Force: The Relationship between Police Agency Policies and Rates of Officer-Involved Gun Deaths'. *Public Administration Review.* 77 (2). 217–226

Jentzen, J (2009). *Death Investigation in America: Coroners, Medical Examiners, and the Pursuit of Medical Certainty.* Cambridge. Harvard University Press.

Jiao, AY (2020). 'Federal consent decrees: a review of policies, processes, and outcomes'. *Police Practice and Research.*

Johnson, DJ, Tress, T, Burkel, N, Taylor, C, and Cesario, J (2019). 'Officer characteristics and racial disparities in fatal officer-involved shootings'. *PNAS.* 116 (32). 15877–15882

Jones-Brown, D, and Blount-Hill, K-L (2020). 'Convicted: Do Recent Cases Represent a Shift in Police Accountability? A Research Note'. *Criminal Law Bulletin.* 56 (2). 270–299.

Jones, S, and Beck, E (2007). 'Disenfranchised grief and nonfinite loss as experienced by the families of death row inmates'. *OMEGA.* 54 (4). 281–299.

Kahn, KB, Steele, JS, McMahon, JM, and Stewart, G (2017). 'How Suspect Race Affects Police Use of Force in an Interaction Over Time'. *Law and Human Behaviour.* 41 (2). 117–126.

Kappeler, V, and Kraska, P (2015). 'Normalising Police Militarization, Living in Denial'. *Policing and Society.* 25 (3). 268–275.

Katz, W (2015). 'Enhancing Accountability and Trust with Independent Investigations of Police Lethal Force'. *Harvard Law Review Forum.* 128 (6), 235–245.

Kelling, G, and Wilson, J (1982). 'Broken windows: the police and neighborhood safety'. *Atlantic Monthly.* 249 (3): 29–38.

Kerr, AN, Morabito, M, and Watson, AC (2010). 'Police encounters, mental illness, and injury: An exploratory investigation'. *Journal of Police Crisis Negotiations.* 10. 116–132.

Kleinig, J (2014). 'Legitimate and Illegitimate Uses of Police Force'. *Criminal Justice Ethics.* 33 (2). 83–103.

Klinger, D, Rosenfeld, R, Isom, D, and Deckard, M (2015). 'Race, Crime, and the Micro-Ecology of Deadly Force'. *Criminology and Public Policy.* 15 (1). 193–222.

Klockars, C (1985). *The idea of the police.* Beverly Hills. Sage.

Kraska, P (2007). 'Militarization and Policing – Its Relevance to 21st Century Police'. *Policing: A Journal of Policy and Practice.* 1 (4): 501–513.

Kübler-Ross, E (1984). *On Death and Dying.* London. Tavistock.

Lamont Hill, M (2016). *Nobody: Casualties of America's War on the Vulnerable, from Ferguson to Flint and Beyond.* New York. Atria.

Landon, H (2005). 'Significant Events in the Northern Ireland Peace Process: Impact and Implementation.' In Noel, S (ed). *From Power Sharing to Democracy: Post-Conflict Institutions in Ethnically Divided Societies*. Montreal. McGill-Queen's University Press. 67–84.

Lang, A, Fleiszer, A, Duhamel, F, Sword, W, Gilbert, K, and Corsini-Munt, S (2011). 'Perinatal loss and parental grief: The challenge of ambiguity and disenfranchised grief'. *OMEGA*. 63(2), 183–196.

Lange, JE, Johnson, MB, and Voas, RB (2005). 'Testing the Racial Profiling Hypothesis for Seemingly Disparate Traffic Stops on the New Jersey Turnpike'. *Justice Quarterly*. 22 (2). 193–223.

Lara, I (2017). 'Shielded from Justice: How State Attorneys General Can Provide Structural Remedies to the Criminal Prosecutions of Police Officers'. *Columbia Journal of Law and Social Problems* 50 (4), 551–582.

Lavizzo-Mourey, R, and Williams, D (2016). 'Being Black is Bad for Your Health'. US News. April 14th, 2016. Available at: https://www.usnews.com/opinion/blogs/policy-dose/articles/2016-04-14/theres-a-huge-health-equity-gap-between-whites-and-minorities

Lerner, MJ (1980). *The Belief in a Just World: A Fundamental Delusion.* New York. Plenum.

Letitia, J (2014). Prosecutors and Police: the Inherent Conflict in our Courts. Available at: http://www.msnbc.com/msnbc/prosecutors-police-inherent-conflict-our-courts. Accessed November 7th, 2018.

Lowery, W (2017). *They Can't Kill Us All: The Story of Black Lives Matter.* London. Penguin.

Mak, G (2014). *In America: Travels with John Steinbeck.* London. Harvill Secker

Malmin, M (2013). 'Warrior Culture, Spirituality, and Prayer'. *Journal of Religion and Health 52. 740–758.*

Manning, P (2010). *Democratic Policing in a Changing World*. Boulder: Paradigm.

Marcus, J (2016). 'Bringing Native American Stories to a National Audience'. Neiman Reports. Available at: https://niemanreports.org/articles/bringing-native-american-stories-to-a-national-audience/

Marcus, N (2016). 'From Edward Garner to Eric Garner and Beyond: The Importance of Constitutional Limitations on Lethal Use of Force in Police Reform'. *Duke Journal of Constitutional Law and Public Policy.* 12 (1). 53–106.

Marenin, O (2016). 'Cheapening Death: Danger, Police Street Culture, and the Use of Deadly Force'. *Police Quarterly*. 19 (4). 461–487.

Mawby, R (2002). *Policing Images: Policing, Communication and Legitimacy.* Cullompton. Willan.

Maylor, N, and Spivak, R (2018). *Truth and Reconciliation: The South African Model.* OEF Research. Available at: https://oefresearch.org/think-peace/truth-and-reconciliation-south-african-model

McCormick, ML (2015). 'Our Uneasiness with Police Unions: Power and Voice for the Powerful?' *Saint Louis University Public Law Review.* 35 (47). 47–65.

McCulloch, J (2001). *Blue Army: Paramilitary Policing in Australia.* Melbourne. Melbourne University Press.

McDonald Henning, K (2016). '"Reasonable" Police Mistakes: Fourth Amendment Claims and the "Good Faith" Exception After *Heien*'. *St John's Law Review*. 90. 271–327.

McElvain, JP, and Kposowa, AJ (2004). 'Police officer characteristics and internal affairs investigations for use of force allegations'. *Journal of Criminal Justice*. 32. 265–279.

McLaughlin, E (1994). *Community, Policing and Accountability*. Aldershot. Avebury Press.

McLeod, AM (2019). 'Envisioning Abolition Democracy'. *Harvard Law Review*. 132. 1613–1649.

Meade, B, Steiner, B, and Klahm, CF (2017). 'The effect of police use of force on mental health problems of prisoners'. *Policing and Society*. 27 (2). 229–244.

Miller, W (1976). *Cops and Bobbies: Police Authority in New York and London, 1830-1870*. Chicago: University of Chicago Press.

Moore, S, Robinson, M, Adedoyin, A, Brooks, M, Harmon, D, and Boamah, D (2016). 'Hands up – Don't shoot: Police shooting of young black makes: Implications for social work and human services'. *Journal of Human Behaviour in the Social Environment*. 26 (3–4). 254–266.

Morabito, M (2007). 'Horizons of Context: Understanding the Police Decision to Arrest People with Mental Illness'. *Psychiatric Services*. 58 (12). 1582–1587.

Morabito MS, Kerr, AN, Watson, AC, Draine, J, and Angell, B (2012). 'Crisis Intervention Teams and people with mental illness: Exploring the factors that influence the use of force'. *Crime and Delinquency*. 58 (1). 57–77.

Muchetti, A (2005). 'Driving While Brown: A proposal for Ending Racial Profiling in Emerging Latino Communities'. *Harvard Latino Law Review*. 8 (1). 1–32.

Mulvey, P, and White, M (2014). 'The potential for violence in arrests of persons with mental illness'. *Policing: An International Journal of Police Strategies and Management*. 37 (2). 404–419.

Murphy, P., Eckersley, P, and Ferry, L. (2017). 'Accountability and transparency: Police forces in England and Wales'. *Public Policy and Administration*. 32 (3). 197–213.

National Institute of Medicine (2003). *Medicolegal Death Investigation System*. Washington, D.C. National Academies Press.

Nelson, J (ed). (2000). *Police Brutality*. New York. W.W. Norton & Co.

NYPD (2017). *NYPD response to OIG Report: Putting Training into Practice: A Review of NYPD's Approach to Handling Interactions with People in Mental Crisis*. Available at: https://www1.nyc.gov/assets/nypd/downloads/pdf/oig-report-responses/nypd-response-oig-cit-041817.pdf (Accessed 12 October 2018)

Nix, J, Campbell, BA, Byers, EH, and Alpert, GP (2017). 'A Bird's Eye View of Civilians Killed by Police in 2015: Further Evidence of Implicit Bias'. *Criminology and Public Policy*. 16 (1). 309–340.

North, D (2018). 'The Mystery of Hanoi Hannah'. *New York Times*. 2/8/18.

Nowacki, JS, and Willits, D (2018). 'Adoption of body cameras by United States police agencies: an organisational analysis'. *Policing and Society*. 28 (7). 841–853.

Nyuykonge, C, and Zondi, S (2017). 'South African Peacebuilding Approaches: Evolution and Lessons'. In Call and de Coning (eds). *Rising Powers and Peacebuilding: Breaking the Mold?* London. Palgrave-Macmillan. 107–125.

Otu, N (2006). 'The Police Service and Liability Insurance: Responsible Policing'. *International Journal of Police Science and Management* 8 (4), 294–315

Pagliarella, C (2016). 'Police Body-Worn Camera Footage: A Question of Access'. *Yale Law and Policy Review.* 34. 533–543

Perry, AL, Rothwell, J, and Harshbarger, D (2018). 'The devaluation of assets in black neighborhoods'. Available at: https://www.brookings.edu/research/devaluation-of-assets-in-black-neighborhoods/

Peterson Armour, MP (2002). 'Journey of family members of homicide victims: A qualitative study of their posthomicide experience'. *American Journal of Orthopsychiatry.* 72 (3). 372–382.

Phillips, S (2010). 'Police officers' opinions of the use of unnecessary force by other officers'. *Police Practice and Research.* 11 (3). 197–210.

Piquero, AR, Gomez-Smith, Z, and Langton, L (2004). 'Discerning fairness where others may not: Low self-control and unfair sanction perceptions'. *Criminology.* 42 (3). 699–733

Pollack, HA, and Humphreys, K (2020). 'Reducing Violent Incidents between Police Officers and People with Psychiatric or Substance Use Disorders'. *The Annals of the American Academy.* 687. January.

Powell, J (2009). *Great Hatred, Little Room: Making Peace in Northern Ireland.* London. Vintage.

PEW Trusts (2019). 'A Pileup of Inequities: Why People of Color Are Hit Hardest by Homelessness'. Available at: https://www.pewtrusts.org/en/research-and-analysis/blogs/stateline/2019/03/29/a-pileup-of-inequities-why-people-of-color-are-hit-hardest-by-homelessness

PEW Research Centres (2016). '10 demographic trends shaping the US and the world'. Available at: https://www.pewresearch.org/fact-tank/2016/03/31/10-demographic-trends-that-are-shaping-the-u-s-and-the-world/

Prenzler, T (2016a). 'Scandal, Inquiry, and Reform: The Evolving Locus of Responsibility for Police Integrity'. In Prenzler, T, and den Heyer G (eds). *Civilian Oversight of Police: Advancing Accountability in Law Enforcement.* Boca-Raton. Taylor and Francis. 3–28.

Prenzler, T (2016b). Police Views on Processing Complaints against Police'. In Prenzler, T, and den Heyer G (eds). *Civilian Oversight of Police: Advancing Accountability in Law Enforcement.* Boca-Raton. Taylor and Francis. 95–118.

President's Task Force on 21st Century Policing (2015). *Final Report of the President's Task Force on 21st Century Policing.* Washington, DC: Office of Community Oriented Policing Services.

Price, J, and Payton, E (2017). 'Implicit Racial Bias and Police Use of Lethal Force: Justifiable Homicide or Potential Discrimination'. *Journal of African American Studies.* 21. 674–683.

Prison Policy Initiative (2020). 'What data exists about Native American people in the criminal justice system?' Available at: https://www.prisonpolicy.org/blog/2020/04/22/native/

Punch, M (2009). *Police Corruption: Deviance, accountability and reform in policing*. Cullompton: Willan.

Punch, M (1985). *Conduct Unbecoming: The Social Construction of Police Deviance and Control*. London. Tavistock.

Punch, M (1979). 'The Secret Social Service'. In Holdaway, S (ed). *The British Police*. London. Sage.

Rampart Independent Review Panel (2000). *A report to the Los Angeles Board of Police Commissioners concerning the operations, policies, and procedures of the Los Angeles Police Department in the wake of the Rampart scandal.* Available at: https://www.law.berkeley.edu/php-programs/faculty/facultyPubsPDF.php?facID=4878&pubID=16

Raphael, B (1995). 'The Death of a Child'. In Williamson, JB, and Shneidman, ES (eds). *Death: Current Perspectives.* 4th edn. London. Mayfield. 261–275.

Rappaport, J (2016). 'How Private Insurers Regulate Public Police'. *Harvard Law Review*. 130. 1539–1614.

Ray, R, Brown, M, Fraistat, N, and Summers, E (2017). 'Ferguson and the death of Michael Brown on Twitter: #BlackLivesMatter, #TCOT, and the evolution of collective identities'. *Ethnic and Racial Studies*. 40 (11). 1797–1813.

Razack, S (2015). *Dying from Improvement: Inquests and Inquiries into Indigenous Deaths in Custody.* Toronto: University of Toronto Press.

Reason, J (1997). *Managing the Risks of Organizational Accidents*. Farnham. Ashgate.

Reaves, BA (2009). 'Bureau of Justice Statistics Special Report: State and Law Enforcement Training Academies, 2006'. U.S. Department of Justice, April 14. https://www.bjs.gov/content/pub/pdf/slleta06.pdf

Reiner, R (2013). 'Who governs? Democracy, plutocracy, science and prophecy in policing'. *Criminology and Criminal Justice.* 13 (2). 161–180.

Reiner, R (2010). *The Politics of the Police*. 4th edn. Oxford: Oxford University Press

Reiner, R (1991). 'Multiple Realities, Divided Worlds – Chief Constables Perspectives on the Police Complaints System'. In Goldsmith, AJ (ed). *Complaints Against the Police: The Trend to External Review.* Oxford. Clarendon Press. 211–231.

Rickford, R (2016). 'Black Lives Matter: Toward a Modern Practice of Mass Struggle'. *New Labor Forum.* 25 (1). 43–42.

Roiphe, R (2017). 'The Duty to Charge in Police Use of Excessive Force Cases'. *Cleveland State Law Review.* 65 (4). 503–517.

Rossler, M, and Terrill, W (2017). 'Mental Illness, Police Use of Force and Citizen Injury'. *Police Quarterly.* 20 (2). 189–212.

Rubin, LJ (2018). "A torrent of ghastly revelations": what military service taught me about America'. *The Guardian*. December 18th.

Ruiz, J, and Miller, C (2004). 'An exploratory study of Pennsylvania police officers' perceptions of dangerousness and their ability to manage persons with mental illness'. *Police Quarterly.* 7 (3). 359–371.

Rushin, S (2017a). *Federal Intervention in American Police Departments.* Cambridge. Cambridge University Press.

Rushin, S (2017b). 'Police Union Contracts'. *Duke Law Journal.* 6 (66). 1191–1284

Russell, KK (2000). '"What Did I Do to Be So Black and Blue?": Police Violence and the Black Community'. In Nelson, J (ed). *Police Brutality.* New York. W.W Norton & Co. 135–156.

Sacramento Bee (2019). '"Second chance PD". One California town's history of employing cops with troubling pasts'. Available at: https://www.sacbee.com/news/ investigations/article237090084.html. Accessed 2/2/20.

Salmi, J (2004). 'Violence in Democratic Societies: Towards an Analytic Framework', in Hillyard, P, Pantazis, C, Tombs, S and Gordon, D (eds). *Beyond Criminology: Taking Harm Seriously.* London. Pluto Press. 55–66

Samuel, E, Williams, R, and Ferrell, R (2009). 'Excited delirium: Consideration of selected medical and psychiatric issues'. *Neuropsychiatric Disease and Treatment.* 5. 61–66.

Sargeant, E, Murphy, K and Cherney, A (2014). 'Ethnicity, trust and cooperation with police: Testing the dominance of the process-based model'. *European Journal of Criminology.* 11 (4). 500–524.

Schaeffer, BP, and Tewksbury, R (2018). 'The Tellability of Police Use-of-Force: How Police Tell Stories of Critical Incidents in Different Contexts'. *British Journal of Criminology.* 58 (1). 37–53.

Schrader, S (2019). *Badges Without Borders: How Global Counterinsurgency Transformed American Policing.* Berkeley. University of California Press.

Schroedel, JR, and Chin, RJ (2020). 'Whose Lives Matter? The Media's Failure to Cover Police Use of Lethal Force Against Native Americans'. *Race and Justice.* 10 (2). 150–175.

Schulhofer, SJ, Tyler, TR, and Huq, AZ (2011). 'American policing at a crossroads: Unsustainable policies and the procedural justice alternative'. *The Journal of Criminal Law & Criminology.* 101. 335–374.

Shane, JM, Lawton, B, and Swenson, Z (2017). 'The prevalence of fatal police shootings by US police, 2015–2016: Patterns and answers from a new data set'. *Journal of Criminal Justice.* 52. 101–111.

Shane, J (2013). *Learning from Error in Policing: A Case Study in Organisational Accident Theory.* Heidelberg. Springer.

Sherman, LW (2018). 'Reducing Fatal Police Shootings as System Crashes: Research, Theory, and Practice'. *Annual Review of Criminology.* 1. 421–449.

Siegel, M (2017). 'The dilemma of "racial profiling": an abolitionist police history'. *Contemporary Justice Review.* 20 (4). 474–490.

Simmons, KC (2012). 'Stakeholder Participation in the Selection and Recruitment of Police: Democracy in Action'. *Saint Louis University Public Law Review.* 32 (7). 7–32.

Skolnick, J, and Fyfe, J (1993). *Above the Law: Police and the Excessive Use of Force.* New York. The Free Press.

Skolnick, J (1967). *Justice without Trial: Law Enforcement in a Democratic Society.* New York. Wiley.

Slutkin, G (2013). 'Violence is a contagious disease'. In Patel, DM, Simon, MA, and Taylor, RM (eds). *Forum on Global Violence Prevention Board on Global Health.* Washington, DC. National Academies Press. 94–111.

Spies, C (2002). *South Africa's National Peace Accord: Its structures and functions.* Conciliation Resources. Available at: https://www.c-r.org/accord/public-participation/south-africas-national-peace-accord-its-structures-and-functions

Spitzer, S (1975). 'Toward a Marxian Theory of Deviance'. *Social Problems.* 22 (5). 638–651.

Spungen, D (1998). *Homicide: The hidden victims.* London, UK: Sage.

Stinson, PM (2017a). "Charging A Police Officer in Fatal Shooting Case Is Rare, And A Conviction Is Even Rarer".*CriminalJusticeFacultyPublications,*May31.https://scholarworks.bgsu.edu/cgi/viewcontent.cgi?article=1079&context=crim_just_pub

Stinson, PM (2017b). "Police Shootings Data: What We Know and What We Don't Know." *Criminal Justice Faculty Publications,* April 20. https://scholarworks.bgsu.edu/cgi/viewcontent.cgi?article=1077&context=crim_just_pub

Stoughton, S (2015). "Law Enforcement's 'Warrior' Problem." *Harvard Law Review* 128 (6). 225–234.

Storey, M (2012). 'Explaining the Unexplainable: ED Syndrome and its Impact on the Objective Reasonableness Standard for Allegations of Excessive Force'. *Saint Louis University Law Journal.* 56. 633–663.

Stuntz, WJ (2011). *The Collapse of American Criminal Justice.* Boston. Harvard University Press.

Sugimoto, JD, and Oltjenbruns, KA (2001). 'The environment of death and its influence on police officers in the United States'. *OMEGA.* 43(2). 145–155.

Taylor Ross, C (2016). 'Policing Pontius Pilate: Police Violence, Local Prosecutors, and Legitimacy'. *Harvard Journal on Legislation.* 15 (8). 755–780.

Terpstra, J, and Trommel, W (2009). 'Police, managerialisation and presentational strategies'. *Policing: An International Journal of Police Strategies and Management.* 32 (1). 128–143.

Terrill, W, and Paoline, EA (2017). 'Police Use of Less Lethal Force: Does Administrative Policy Matter?' *Justice Quarterly.* 34 (2). 193–216.

Terrill, W, and Paoline, EA (2015). Citizen Complaints as Threats to Police Legitimacy: The Role of Officers' Occupational Attitudes'. *Journal of Contemporary Criminal Justice.* 31 (2). 192–211.

Terrill, W, and Paoline, EA (2012). 'Examining Less Lethal Force Policy and the Force Continuum: Results From a National Use-of-Force Study'. *Police Quarterly.* 16 (1). 38–65.

Terrill, W (2005). 'Police use of force: A transactional approach'. *Justice Quarterly.* 22 (1). 107–138.

Teplin, LA, and Pruett, NS (1992). 'Police as street corner psychiatrists: Managing the mentally ill'. *International Journal of Law and Psychiatry.* 15 (2). 139–156.

The Century Foundation (2019a). 'Attacking the Black–White Opportunity Gap That Comes from Residential Segregation'. Available at: https://tcf.org/content/report/attacking-black-white-opportunity-gap-comes-residential-segregation/

The Century Foundation (2019b). 'Racism, Inequality, and Healthcare for African-Americans'. Available at: https://tcf.org/content/report/racism-inequality-health-care-african-americans/

The Counted (2017). 'People Killed By Police In The US In 2016'. The Guardian. Accessed November 17 2017. https://www.theguardian.com/us-news/ng-interactive/2015/jun/01/the-counted-police-killings-us-database

Thomas, S, and Watson, A (2017). 'A focus for mental health training for police'. *Journal of Criminological Research, Policy and Practice.* 3 (2). 93–104.

Thompson, L, and Borum, R (2006). 'Crisis Intervention Teams (CIT): Considerations for knowledge transfer'. *Law Enforcement Executive Forum.* 6 (3). 25–36.

Thompson, M, and Kahn, KB (2016). 'Mental Health, Race and Police Contact: Intersections of Risk and Trust in the Police'. *Policing: An International Journal of Police Strategies and Management.* 39 (4). 807–819.

Tolliver, WF, Hadden, BR, Snowden, F, and Brown-Manning, R (2016). 'Police killings of unarmed Black people: Centering race and racism in human behaviour and the social environment context'. *Journal of Human Behavior in the Social Environment.* 26 (3). 279–286.

Tyler, TR (2004). 'Enhancing Police Legitimacy'. *The Annals of the American Academy of Political and Social Science.* 593 (1). 84–99.

Tyler, TR, and Huo, YJ (2002). *Trust in the law: Encouraging public cooperation with the police and courts.* New York: Russell Sage Foundation

Tyson, T (1999). *Radio Free Dixie: Robert F. Williams and the Roots of Black Power.* Chapel Hill. University of North Carolina Press.

United Nations (2020). *Implementation of Human Rights Council resolution 43/1.* Available at: OHCHR | Implementation of Human Rights Council resolution 43/1 Accessed 24/1/21

United States Bureau of Labor (2019). Labor force characteristics by race and ethnicity, 2018. Available at: https://www.bls.gov/opub/reports/race-and-ethnicity/2018/home.htm

United States Census Bureau (2020). Real Median Household Income by Race and Hispanic Origin: 1967 to 2019. Available at: https://www.census.gov/content/dam/Census/library/visualizations/2020/demo/p60-270/figure2.pdf

United States Census Bureau (2013). Poverty Rates for Selected Detailed Race and Hispanic Groups by State and Place: 2007-2011. Available at: https://www.census.gov/library/publications/2013/acs/acsbr11-17.html

Urbina, M, and Alvarez, S (2018). *Hispanics in the U.S. Criminal Justice System: Ethnicity, Ideology and Social Control.* Illinois. Charles C Thomas.

Urbina, M, and Alvarez, S (2017). *Ethnicity and Criminal Justice in the Era of Mass Incarceration: A Critical Reader on the Latino Experience.* Illinois. Charles C Thomas.

Van Craen, M, and Skogan, WG (2017). 'Officer Support For Use of Force Policy: The Role of Fair Supervision'. *Criminal Justice and Behaviour.* 44 (6). 843–861.

Van Maanen, J (1978). 'The Asshole'. In Manning, PK, and Van Maanen, J (eds). *Policing: A View From the Street.* Santa Monica. Goodyear Publishing. 221–237.

Vilke, G, Payne-James, J, and Karch, S (2012). 'Excited delirium syndrome (ExDS): Redefining an old diagnosis'. *Journal of Forensic and Legal Medicine.* 19 (1). 7–11.

Vitale, AS (2017). *The End of Policing.* London. Verso.

Waddington, PAJ (1999). *Policing Citizens.* London: UCL Press.

Walker, S (2006). *History of the Civilian Oversight Movement.* Chicago: American Bar Association Section of State and Local Government Law.

Washington Post (2020). 'Minneapolis violence surges as police officers leave department in droves'. Available at: Minneapolis violence surges after George Floyd's death as police officers leave the department in droves. Accessed 24/1/21.

Watson, A, and Fulambarker, A (2012). 'The Crisis Intervention Team Model of Police Response to Mental Health Crisis: A primer for Mental Health Practitioners'. *Best Practice Mental Health.* 8 (2). 1–8.

Watson, A, Swartz, J, Bohrman, C, Kriegal, L, and Draine, J (2014). 'Understanding how police officers think about mental/emotional disturbance calls'. *International Journal of Law and Psychiatry.* 37 (4). 351–358.

Wells, W, and Schafer, JA (2006). 'Officer perceptions of police responses to persons with a mental illness'. *Policing International Journal of Police Strategies and Management.* 29 (4). 578–601.

Weitzer, R (2017). 'Theorizing Racial Discord over Policing Before and After Ferguson'. *Justice Quarterly.* 34 (7). 1129–1153.

Wetli, C (2006). 'Excited Delirium'. In Ross, D, and Chan, T (eds). *Forensic Science and Medicine: Sudden Deaths in Custody.* Totowa. Humana Press. 99–112.

Whitaker, R (2002). *Mad in America: Bad science, bad medicine, and the enduring mistreatment of the mentally ill.* Cambridge: Basic Books.

Willis, J, and Mastrofksi, S (2012). 'Compstat and the New Penology: A Paradigm Shift in Policing?' *British Journal of Criminology.* 52 (1). 73–92.

Willits, D, and Nowacki, J (2014). 'Police organisation and deadly force: an examination of variation across large and small cities'. *Policing and Society.* 24 (1). 63–80.

Wolf, R, Mesoch, C, Henych, M, and Thompson, LF (2009). 'Police use of force and the cumulative force factor'. *Policing: An International Journal of Police Strategies and Management.* 32 (4). 739–757.

Wood, J, Swanson, J, Burris, S, and Gilbert, A (2011). *Police interventions with persons affected by mental illnesses: A critical review of global thinking and practice.* Centre for Behavioural Health Services and Criminal Justice Research: Rutgers University. Available at: http://develop.cla.temple.edu/cj/people/documents/Police_Interventions_Monograph_March_2011.pdf. Accessed 3/4/18.

Worden, RE, and McLean, S (2017). *Mirage of Police Reform: Procedural Justice and Police Legitimacy.* Oakland, CA: University of California Press.

Wozniak, J (2016). 'Missing the moral: Excited delirium as a negative case study of moral panic'. *Punishment and Society.* 18 (2). 198–219.

Yancy, G, and Jones, J (eds) (2013). *Pursuing Trayvon Martin: Historical Contexts and Contemporary Manifestations of Racial Dynamics.* Lexington Books. Lanham.

Younge, G (2020). 'We Can't Breathe'. *New Statesman.* June 3rd. Available at: https://www.newstatesman.com/politics/uk/2020/06/we-cant-breathe

Younge, G (2016). *Another Day in the Death of America*. London. Guardian Books.

Young, M (1991). *An Inside Job*. Oxford. Oxford University Press.

Zamoff, M (2019). 'Assessing the Impact of Police Body Camera Evidence on the Litigation of Excessive Force Cases. *Georgia Law Review*. 54 (1). 1–59.

Zimring, FE (2017). *When Police Kill.* London. Harvard University Press.

Zinn, H (2003). *A People's History of the US: 1492—Present*. 3rd edn. New York. Pearson Longman.

Index

Orwell, George, 126

Paoline, EA, 83
Paquette Boots, D, 11
paramilitarization of the police,
　12–14, 47, 55–56. *See also*
　warriors, police as
Paschal, James, Jr, 93–95
Paschal, James, Sr, 93–95
Patton, George, 13
PDRs. *See* police-related deaths (PRDs)
PDs (police departments). *See* police;
　specific police departments
peace officers, 118
peace process, 122
Peel's assessment of new police, 35
perception: of community engagement,
　88–89; measurement of crime and,
　35; order maintenance and, 30–31;
　use of lethal force and, 17–18
perinatal deaths, 101
Philadelphia PD, 13
Pickett, Nathaniel H (Nate): death of,
　19–21, 22; jury award, 68; officer's
　background, 35, 116–17; street
　justice and, 24, 30
pilot analogy, 6, 90–91
piss collars, 35
police: geographical organization,
　xxiv–xxv, 45; as guardians, xxv–
　xxviii, 33, 47, 90, 117–18; historical
　perspective, xxii–xxiv; inconsistency
　of narratives, 19–21, 94;
　inexperience of, 116–17; overlapping
　roles of, xxi–xxiv; public perceptions
　of, 29; recruitment of, 35, 117;
　relative danger compared to other
　jobs, viii, 11–12, 85; tolerance for
　mistakes by, 66; warriors as, xxv–
　xxviii, 3, 11, 47. *See also* community
　policing; paramilitarization of
　the police; regulation of policing;
　training of police; *specific police
　departments*

police-related deaths (PRDs):
　Black citizens more frequently
　targeted, xviii–xix, 22, 24–25, 34;
　demographics, 111; discriminatory
　and indiscriminate, 78–79; lack
　of data on, xvi–xvii, 72–73, 109,
　122–23; officers' reactions to, 48–49,
　60, 107; prosecutions, 60, 64–65,
　66–67; repercussions for officers,
　xix; similarity of stories, 111. *See
　also* accountability for police-related
　deaths; The Counted website; use of
　force; *specific deaths; specific police
　departments*
Police Review Commission
　(PRC), 40–41
policies, 83–84. *See also* accountability
　for police-related deaths; body-worn
　cameras (BWCs); President's Task
　Force on 21st Century Policing
　(PTF); use of force
policing culture: about, 16–18, 84–86;
　'blue code of silence,' 84, 86;
　changing, 61, 115, 117–18; cynicism,
　107; danger of job overstated, 11–12,
　85; influence of, 118; machoism,
　85; as obstacle to regulation, 86–88;
　passivity during PRDs, 86; us *vs.*
　them dualism, 85, 86. *See also*
　suspect population
politics: apartheid and Northern Ireland
　comparisons, 120–22; dialogue and
　change, 120–22; social problems
　and, 55. *See also* dominant majority
poverty, 22–23, 26–27
powerlessness, 106
power relationships, 41–42
pragmatic legitimacy, 49–50, 105
PRC. *See* Police Review Commission
President's Task Force on 21st Century
　Policing (PTF): best practices, 46,
　65; procedural justice, 54–55; use
　of force policies, 83; warrior or
　guardian question, xxvi–xxvii, 117–
　18; as wish list, 79

About the Author

David Baker, PhD, is lecturer in the Sociology, Social Policy, and Criminology Department at the University of Liverpool, UK. This is his second book on police-related deaths, the first focused on this issue in England and Wales. In addition, he has published numerous journal articles on this subject. *Police-Related Deaths in the United States* is the result of field-based research funded by a Fulbright scholarship.

www.ingramcontent.com/pod-product-compliance
Lightning Source LLC
Chambersburg PA
CBHW022319280326
41932CB00010B/1156